Regional Inequality in Transitional China

This book investigates uneven regional development in China – with particular focus on the cases of Guangdong and Zheijiang provinces – which have been at the forefront of debate since Chinese economic reform.

Rapid economic growth since the 'opening-up' of China has been accompanied by significant disparities in the regional distribution of income: this book represents one of the most recent studies to present a picture of this inequality. Built upon a multi-scale and multi-mechanism framework, it provides systematic examination of both the patterns and mechanisms of regional development and inequality in provincial China, emphasizing the effects of economic transition. Approaching from a geographical perspective, its authors consider the interplay between the local, the state, and the global forces in shaping the landscape of regional inequality in China. Extensive empirical findings will prove useful to those researching other developing countries within the frontier of globalization and economic transition.

Felix Haifeng Liao is an Associate Professor of Geography at the University of Idaho in the United States. His research interests are in the areas of economic and urban geographies, regional development, urban environmental planning, and geographic information systems (GIS) applications. He has used mixed-methods, GIS, spatial analysis and modeling, and spatial optimization to examine issues related to China's urban and regional development, transnational corporations, land and resource management, and other environmental and equity-related problems in China and the United States. He has published widely in geography journals and other interdisciplinary journals in the field of environmental science, urban studies, and sustainability science. His research has been funded by the NSF, the Natural Science Foundation of China (NSFC), United States Department of Agriculture (USDA), and Idaho NSF EPSCoR (Experimental Program to Stimulate Competitive Research).

Yehua Dennis Wei is a Professor in the Department of Geography at the University of Utah in the United States. He is an economic/urban geographer and development specialist, with research interests in globalization, urbanization, and regional development in China. Using recent developments in geographical information systems (GIS), Wei has investigated the effects of globalization and economic transition on cities, regions, and places with respect to regional inequality, urban transition, foreign investment, innovation, and sustainable development. Wei is the author of *Regional Development in China: States, Globalization, and Inequality* and more than 200 journal articles and book chapters. His research has been funded by the NSF, Ford Foundation, Lincoln Institute of Land Policy, National Geographic Society, and Natural Science Foundation of China (NSFC). He has received awards for research excellence from the NSFC (Outstanding Young Scientist Award), Association of American Geographers' (AAG) Regional Development and Planning Specialty Group, University of Wisconsin-Milwaukee, and the Chinese Academy of Sciences. His professional services include advisor/panelist for the NSF, consultant to the World Bank, overseas evaluation experts of the Chinese Academy of Sciences, Chair for AAG's China, Asian, and Regional Development and Planning specialty groups, Vice President of Chinese Professionals in GIS, etc.

Li Huang is a doctoral graduate in the Department of Geography, University of Idaho in the United States. His primary research interests are in economic geography, regional development and inequality, land and resource management, and GIScience. He obtained his bachelor of science degree in GIS and a master's degree of science in urban and regional planning from Peking University in China.

Routledge Contemporary China Series

For more information about this series, please visit: www.routledge.com/Routledge-Contemporary-China-Series/book-series/SE0768

Regional Inequality in Transitional China

Felix Haifeng Liao,
Yehua Dennis Wei,
and Li Huang

Routledge
Taylor & Francis Group

LONDON AND NEW YORK

First published 2021
by Routledge
2 Park Square, Milton Park, Abingdon, Oxon OX14 4RN

and by Routledge
52 Vanderbilt Avenue, New York, NY 10017

Routledge is an imprint of the Taylor & Francis Group, an informa business

British Library Cataloguing-in-Publication Data
A catalogue record for this book is available from the British Library

Library of Congress Cataloging-in-Publication Data
A catalog record has been requested for this book

ISBN: 978-1-138-06067-8 (hbk)
ISBN: 978-1-315-16296-6 (ebk)

Typeset in Times New Roman
by Wearset Ltd, Boldon, Tyne and Wear

Contents

Figures

Tables

Contributors

Felix Haifeng Liao is an Associate Professor of Geography at the University of Idaho in the United States. His research interests are in the areas of economic and urban geographies, regional development, urban environmental planning, and geographic information systems (GIS) applications. He has used mixed methods, GIS, spatial analysis and modeling, and spatial optimization to examine issues related to China's urban and regional development, transnational corporations, land and resource management, and other environmental and equity-related problems in China and the United States. He has published widely in geography journals and other interdisciplinary journals in the field of environmental science, urban studies, and sustainability science. His research has been funded by the NSF, the Natural Science Foundation of China (NSFC), United States Department of Agriculture (USDA), and Idaho NSF EPSCoR (Experimental Program to Stimulate Competitive Research).

Yehua Dennis Wei is a Professor in the Department of Geography at the University of Utah in the United States. He is an economic/urban geographer and development specialist, with research interests in globalization, urbanization, and regional development in China. Using recent developments in geographical information systems (GIS), Wei has investigated the effects of globalization and economic transition on cities, regions, and places with respect to regional inequality, urban transition, foreign investment, innovation, and sustainable development. Wei is the author of *Regional Development in China: States, Globalization, and Inequality* and more than 200 journal articles and book chapters. His research has been funded by the NSF, Ford Foundation, Lincoln Institute of Land Policy, National Geographic Society, and Natural Science Foundation of China (NSFC). He has received awards for research excellence from the NSFC (Outstanding Young Scientist Award), Association of American Geographers' (AAG) Regional Development and Planning Specialty Group, University of Wisconsin-Milwaukee, and the Chinese Academy of Sciences. His professional services include advisor/panelist for the NSF, consultant to the World Bank, overseas evaluation experts of the Chinese Academy of Sciences, Chair for AAG's China, Asian, and Regional Development and Planning specialty groups, Vice President of Chinese Professionals in GIS, etc.

Li Huang is a doctoral graduate in the Department of Geography, University of Idaho in the United States. His primary research interests are in economic geography, regional development and inequality, land and resource management, and GIScience. He obtained his bachelor of science degree in GIS and a master's degree of science in urban and regional planning from Peking University in China.

Acknowledgments

This book is mainly based on research that has been conducted since 2010. The Department of Geography, the University of Utah and the Department of Geography, the University of Idaho provided an excellent environment for this book project. We would also like to acknowledge the funding of the US National Science Foundation (1759746), the Ford Foundation (0155–0883), and the National Natural Science Foundation of China (41329001).

Earlier versions of some chapters were presented at the International Conference on Territorial Inequality and Development (Puebla, Mexico, January 25–27, 2016): Sections 3.1, 3.2 in Chapter 3 and Section 4.1 in Chapter 4, with materials, figures and tables updated, are based on Liao and Wei (2016) *Sixty Years of Regional Inequality in China: Trends, scales, and mechanisms*. Working Paper Series N° 202. Rimisp, Santiago, Chile. Sections 2.1, 3.3, 3.4, 4.2, and 4.3, and Chapter 7, with materials revised, are reprinted from Huang (2020) *Analyzing the Spatiality of China's Regional Inequality in a Geographic Information System (GIS) Environment*, doctoral dissertation, University of Idaho, copyright (2020). Section 2.2 and Chapter 8, with materials revised, are based on Liao and Wei (2018) Regional inequality in China: Scales, mechanisms, and beyond, in *The Sage Handbook of Contemporary China*. We would also like to thank Elsevier for granting permission to reproduce the journal articles published in *Applied Geography*: Chapter 5 and Section 6.3 in Chapter 6, with some figures and tables updated, are reprinted from Liao and Wei (2012) Dynamics, space, and regional inequality in provincial China: a case study of Guangdong province, and Liao and Wei (2015) Space, scale, and regional inequality in provincial China: a spatial filtering approach, and Liao (2014) *Geographic Information System Spatial Analysis of Urban and Regional Development in China: A case study of Guangdong province*, doctoral dissertation, University of Utah.

1   Introduction

On December 16, 2016, *The Economist*, a reputable magazine across the globe, highlighted in its Twitter account that "Regional inequality is proving too politically dangerous to ignore." Using the example of the United States, it is argued that the declining industrial heartland has pushed Donald Trump to victory in the presidential election. In many developing and transitional economies, the geographically uneven distribution of income, and more broadly, wealth, has become a major threat to national unity and societal stability.

Inequality has long been a subject of intense debates and has drawn renewed worldwide attention, due largely to the uneven consequences and recovery of the recent global financial crisis (Stiglitz 2012; Piketty 2014). Renewed attention has also been paid to spatial inequality or the spatial dimension of inequality. Geographers and planners are particularly interested in spatiality of inequality, with key terms such as space, place, location, scale, network, and mobility (Konsolas, Papadaskalopoulos, and Plaskovitis 2013; Wei 2015; Pike, Rodríguez-Pose, and Tomaney 2017; Diez-Minguela, Martinez-Galarraga, and Tirado-Fabregat 2018). Convergence often masks spatial concentration and polarization, and regional inequality may rise at one geographical scale but declines at another scale. While the United States concerns mainly urban inequality, regional inequality, such as the core–periphery divide and rural–urban gaps, remains an important dimension of inequality in many developing countries, including China.

China has recorded spectacular economic growth since the reform launched in the late 1970s. While millions of people have been lifted out of poverty, the fruits of economic development are still not fully shared by all people, and the gap between the rich and poor is argued to be widening (World Bank 2011). Income inequality in Chinese society is considered to be among the world's worst (Xie and Zhou 2014; Wildau and Mitchell 2016). According to the World Bank's estimation, the Gini coefficient of income inequality in China was as high as 0.42 in 2012, which was ranked the third-highest among the world's 25 largest countries by population. The coast–interior divide persists and even widened after the reform. Using the indicator of GDP per capita, the rich–poor ratio between the richest province and the poorest one peaked at 16 in 2002 (Tian *et al.* 2016; CSB 2018). The poorest provinces, such as Gansu, Yunnan,

Guizhou, and Guangxi, remain the poorest. The gap between rich and poor regions within provinces also remains large, and spatial polarization even intensified in many provinces. Geographic inequality is a major concern of the Chinese government since rising regional inequality threatens national unity and social stability and conflicts with the socialist ideology (Wei 1999, 2002).

Given its size, diversity, and identity as a transitional and developing country, China provides one of the best laboratories to test theories regarding regional inequality, convergence and uneven regional development (Yao 2009; Gorzelak, Bachtler, and Smętkowski 2014; Herrerías and Monfort 2015; Christiansen and Erdogdu 2016; Cavanaugh and Breau 2017; Wei 2017; Asan Ali Golam Hassan 2018; Haddad 2018; Kahn 2019). The primary objective of the book is to comprehensively analyze changing multi-scalar patterns of regional inequality in China and to deepen our understanding of multiple mechanisms in relation to economic transition. Conceptually, we maintain convergence and divergence theories are overly simplified, masking the complex landscape of regional inequality. We adopt the multi-scale and multi-mechanism framework and pay special attention to the spatiality of regional inequality, with notions of space, scale, place, mobility, and network. Such an approach is more eclectic and provides a middle-ground perspective on regional inequality and development in China beyond the convergence–divergence debate (Wei 2010).

Specifically, we attempt to advance research on regional inequality in China in the following three areas. First, regional inequality changes with time, which requires close monitoring and timely analysis. Although considerable research has been done on regional inequality in China (Wei 1999, 2015, 2017; He, Bayrak, and Lin 2017; He, Fang, and Zhang 2017), rich empirics still need to be more systematically analyzed by using long-run and time-series datasets. As such, we examine uneven development and changing mechanisms both before and after the reform launched in the late 1970s. We also pay attention to changing regional inequality since the recent global financial crisis, which has renewed our attention to the problem of inequality.

Second, the book emphasizes the spatiality of regional inequality (Wei 2015). Conventional theories of convergence and divergence tend to treat space as a container and adopt a black-box approach. This book places spatiality at the center of our studies of regional inequality in China. Multi-scalarity is an essential feature of regional inequality, and we analyze multi-scalar patterns of regional inequality in China: interregional, interprovincial, and intra-provincial scales. We emphasize the relationships between regional inequalities at multiple scales by analyzing recent and more disaggregated county-level data. Regional inequality is also sensitive to the dynamics and trajectories of regions, which can be conceptualized both as space and place. Places are not simply static geographical units, but network with other places and their relative status can also change (place mobility). Regional inequality also relates to geographical agglomeration and spatial polarization.

Third, we also analyze the role of economic transition and adopt a multi-mechanism perspective on sources of regional development and inequality. Following

Wei (2000, 2002), we conceptualize economic transition in China as a triple process of globalization, decentralization, and marketization, during which global investors, state institutions and local agents have emerged as major forces of regional development in China. Together with the notion of multi-scale, this book follows the multi-scale and multi-mechanism framework in the analysis of regional inequality in China. Empirical analyses at the national level could mask the dynamic interplay of global forces, state institutions, and local forces that may provide a more nuanced interpretation of regional development in China. Policy options with respect to balanced development often contradict with those focusing on economic growth (Chen and Groenewold 2011; Chen 2010). For example, preferential policies that emphasize development zones and coastal development are considered as a major cause of uneven development in China as resources are further concentrated in coastal cities and regions (Wei 2000).

Last, regional development processes in China vary from place to place, and recent studies of regional inequality in China have scaled down to intra-provincial analysis (Gu, Zhou, and Ye 2016; Dai *et al.* 2017). Hotspots of studies include Guangdong, Jiangsu, and Zhejiang, and have more recently been expanded to inland provinces such as Henan, Guizhou, and Guangxi (Wei 2004; Wei, Yu, and Chen 2011; Li and Wei 2014; Liao and Wei 2015; Sun *et al.* 2016; Dai *et al.* 2017). This strand of literature has demonstrated a more complex landscape of uneven development. Built upon the authors' previous publications and years of fieldwork in China, this book provides a more nuanced analysis of regional inequalities within provinces, particularly Guangdong and Zhejiang, two coastal provinces that spearhead China's economic reform. We scrutinize representative development models within Guangdong and Zhejiang, emphasizing a more bottom–up approach to regional inequality while adopting the multi-scale and multi-mechanism framework. Our finer analyses of Guangdong and Zhejiang provinces show that regional disparities within provinces are considerably large, and intra-provincial-level analysis could present a more thorough examination of development models and local responses to reforms and globalization in transitional China (Wei and Ye 2009; Liao and Wei 2012). By applying more rigorous modeling approaches such as spatial panel, spatial filtering, and multi-level modelling, the book provides more detailed analyses of spatial and temporal patterns of regional development in China.

1.1 Theories and empirics of regional inequality

Regional inequality has long been an important academic inquiry in economics, geography, sociology, political science, and other disciplines (Richardson 1980; Krugman and Venables 1995; Quah 1996; Rey and Janikas 2005; Wei 2015; Pike, Rodríguez-Pose, and Tomaney 2016; Storper 2018). Neoclassical economics, growth pole theory, and inverted-U models hold that factor mobility and diffusion tend to equalize spatial inequality in regional development (e.g., Borts and Stein 1964; Friedmann 1966; Alonso 1980). Important 'supply' factors of economic growth, such as capital, labor, and technological expertise, are argued to be highly mobile. For example, labor may migrate from low-wage areas to more affluent regions, and capital would be interested in moving away from high-cost regions. The dynamic movement of capital and labor would result in a spatial equilibrium and contribute to regional convergence. Therefore, regional inequality is basically a transitional phenomenon and the differences between rich and poor regions tend to diminish over the long run (Kuznets 1955; Williamson 1965; Lessmann 2014).

The convergence theories, however, were criticized by the divergence school. Structural theories, dependency or world-systems perspectives, and more recently the new economic geography (NEG) model place an emphasis on back-wash effects and maintain that circular cumulative causation and agglomeration tend to reinforce the core–periphery structure of development, and strengthen spatial inequality (Myrdal and Sitohang 1957; Krugman 1981; Smith 1984; Fujita and Hu 2001).

Since the 1990s, liberation and globalization have renewed the scholarly interests in regional inequality and a new generation of regional growth theories were developed. By addressing the β (beta) convergence ratio, the new convergence school has become one of the most influential theories with respect to regional inequality. The central idea of new convergence theory is that poorer regions tend to grow faster than richer regions, leading to the convergence in the long run (Barro *et al.* 1991). Different from the neoclassical growth model, new convergence theory improves the traditional convergence model by adding concepts of conditional convergence and club convergence. It is suggested that there might be convergence among similar groups (clubs) but just a little or no convergence between such groups given the initial conditions such as saving rates, technological innovativeness, and human capital. New convergence theories draw upon empirical evidence in some developed countries, such as the United States, Japan, and European regions (Barro and Sala-i-Martin 1995).

However, empirical studies in developing countries found limited evidence of convergence (Li and Wei 2010), while the concept of club convergence is valuable (Zhang, Xu, and Wang 2019). Under globalization, trade liberalization would worsen the gap between the rich and the poor regions, and countries with more exposure to international trade exhibit more evident territorial inequalities (Rodríguez-Pose 2012). The new convergence theory also underestimates the cyclical effects, different sizes in the units of analysis, and more generally, the spatiality of regional inequality (Petrakos, Rodríguez-Pose, and Rovolis 2005; Yamamoto 2008; Wei 2015; Márquez, Lasarte, and Lufin 2019). Geographers view regional inequality beyond the dichotomy between convergence and divergence and tend to draw upon a more eclectic approach sensitive to space, scale, and place. For example, studies using evidence from China have found a multiscale nature of regional inequality, which could hardly be simplified into either divergence, convergence or inverted-U patterns (Wei 2000, 2015).

When attempting to explain changing patterns of regional inequality, recent studies examine a variety of factors, including spatial division of labor, technological innovation, international trade, decentralization, amenities, and institutional legacy (Lessmann 2012; Rodríguez-Pose 2012; Remington 2015; Wei 2015; Storper 2018). The NEG model, as its subject of research is agglomeration economies, tends to associate the dynamics of firm location or industrial agglomeration with the benefits of agglomeration economies. Focusing on the backward and forward linkages within the manufacturing industries, the NEG model holds that industrial production factors tend to flow centripetally to the industrial core or more developed region, forming a self-reinforcing process due to higher return (Krugman 1990; Fujita *et al.* 1999). The theory is considered as a challenge to the convergence school and is consistent with the work on new industrial districts by economic geographers (e.g., Scott 1988; Storper 1989, 1997; Gordon and McCann 2000; McCann 2014). This book, by addressing the spatial and distributional dynamics of regional development or spatial effects, sheds more lights on the geography or spatiality of regional inequality and the complex mechanism of regional development.

Another frontier of regional inequality studies deals with the role played by institutions or how and to what extent governmental policies influence regional inequality. Kaldor (1970) holds that under Verdoorn's law of circular causation, regional inequality tends to rise over the long run, indicating a process of divergence. However, governmental intervention is necessary to reduce regional inequality. Martin *et al.* (2016) examined the nature of the UK's spatial imbalance and found limited effects of 90 years of regional policy interventions, whereas substantial regional disparities in economic prosperity remain a major pattern of regional development in the UK.

More recent work addresses a set of trade-off questions about why inequality matters (Martin 2015). For example, Chen (2010) suggests reducing inequality might have had a very small negative impact on economic growth and, in the long run, an increase in growth would actually result in a reduction in inequality. Additionally, empirical studies have examined the role of inequality in economic resilience (Lewin, Watson, and Brown 2017). Some policymakers and economists believe that spatial imbalance could de facto enhance national efficiency and, therefore, there is no need for regional policies to deal with regional inequalities. Largely thanks to the recent global financial crisis, there has been more debate on the role of governmental regulation and the significance of institutions in reducing inequality, and the issue of inequality has once again attracted renewed interests (Martin 2015; Cavanaugh and Breau 2017; Wei 2017).

1.2 Regional development and policies in China

The literature has largely agreed upon the shift of spatial development policies before and after the reform. Rooted in the socialist ideology, earlier regional development policies in China emphasize the balanced development model advocated by socialist ideology (Fan 1997; Wei 2007). However, Mao's spatial policies also considered national defense, and economic pragmatism (Ma and Wei 1997). Under the notion of "third-front" construction, many manufacturing industries were relocated from coastal to inland provinces (Wei and Ma 1996), adding considerable industrial capacity to the inland provinces (Lu and Wang 2002). On the other hand, the state also supported the development of established industrial cities and interior investment was less efficient. There were also large gaps between cities and the countryside.

During the post-Mao era, Deng's leadership was more pragmatic and emphasized growth and efficiency, pursuing economic growth through "crossing the river by feeling the stones." The process of China's reform has been conceptualized as a triple process of economic transition, namely, globalization, decentralization, and marketization (Wei 1999, 2000). The control of the central government was reduced in the 1980s and the 1990s, while local states were granted with more decision-making power. The development of a fiscal contract system in the 1980s and the 1990s empowered local governments, who gained greater autonomy in revenue collection and spending and took the main responsibility of balancing the local budget. Marketization strengthens the role of market mechanisms in resource allocation and attracting foreign capital. The reform also resulted in the retreat of stated-owned enterprises (SOEs) in China, and a boom of the township and village enterprises (TVEs) in many rural areas in the 1980s, especially in the coastal region. A more dramatic shift of regional development policies entailed the policies of special economic zones (SEZs), opening-up of coastal cities, and the establishment of development zones (DZs). These preferential policies are spatially biased towards coastal cities and regions (Crane *et al.* 2018). For example, SEZs were designed "to experiment with the development of an outward-looking, market-oriented economic system and to serve the country as a window and a base along these lines" (Ge 1999, p. 49). Because the mobility of production factors was in favor of coastal areas, it is argued that these preferential policies may actually widen the gap between coastal and inland provinces (Li and Haynes 2012; Crane *et al.* 2018).

In the 1990s, even during the heydays of the market reform, the central government took some measures to redirect resources from the coastal region to the western region, aiming at reducing the coastal–inland divide. Such efforts as special funds and preferential bank loans are also accompanied by extending economic reforms and open-door policies to the inland provinces (Wei 2002). The central government has also encouraged coastal provinces and foreign investors to collaborate with inland areas by providing capital and management skills. With the rapid growth of export-oriented manufacturing in the coastal region, the Ninth Five Year Plan (FYP) (1996–2000) considered regional inequality and polarization as one of the most important issues in policymaking. The central government gave a high priority to integrated regional development to reduce regional inequality.

Since the late 1990s, the central government promulgated several specific spatial policies towards interior development and inequality reduction. Examples include the Great Western Development (*xi bu dakaifa*, or the Going West initiative) announced in 1999 during the Ninth FYP, reviving North-eastern Region (*zhenxing dongbei*) and the resurgence of the central region (or *Zhongbu Jueqi*, both during the Tenth FYP, 2000–2005). In the 2000s, large-size infrastructure investments were directed to the western region. The effect of

"Going West" is considered to be more successful than that of the revitalizing northeast project (Lim and Horesh 2017).

In the early 2000s, following the concept of "a harmonious society" (Fan, Kanbur, and Zhang 2011), inequality and poverty alleviation have received more attention in China's Eleventh Five-Year Plan (2006–2010), which addresses regional inequality through the notion of "coordinated development between regions" (Fan and Sun 2008). The idea of a harmonious society is linked to the coordinated development between rural and urban areas to solve the problem of underdevelopment in rural China (Li, Sato, and Sicular 2013).

Under Xi's regime, an ambitious international development program called the "Belt and Road Initiative" came to the fore. This program aims at collaboration with countries across large parts of Eurasia (Ferdinand 2016) and has been associated with large-scale infrastructure investment to support development in inland regions (Shi and Huang 2014). Despite these successive rounds of development policies in reducing regional inequality, patterns and sources of regional inequality in China still need further investigation. Whether the massive investments made to interior regions have had observable effects remains a debatable question (Chen 2010; Chen and Groenewold 2010).

1.3 The significance of Guangdong and Zhejiang Provinces

As mentioned above, this book pays special attention to the multi-scalar nature of regional inequality in China. China can be divided into eastern (or coastal), central, western, and north-eastern regions. Under provinces, there are more than 300 prefectural-level and above units and 2,000 county-level units in China. The multi-scalar pattern of regional inequality provides a valuable perspective and is rooted in a reputable problem in geography, namely the modifiable areal unit problem (MAUP). Indeed, besides provincial-level analysis, county level and prefecture-level inequalities have been the focus of research in the recent literature. With data availability at a finer scale across the whole territory of China, researchers have documented in more details changing regional inequality in China (Li and Fang 2014; He, Bayrak, and Lin 2017; Zhang, Xu, and Wang 2019).

The book includes cases of Guangdong and Zhejiang, which are selected for their importance in China's economic reform and development, as well as inequality studies (Table 1.1 and Figure 1.1). These case studies aim to deepen our understanding of regional inequality and further address the bottom–up process of regional development in China under the triple process of economic transition, namely, globalization, decentralization, and marketization. These provinces are also known for the Pearl River Delta (PRD) model and the Wenzhou model, two representative development models driven by the interplay of the local context, external investment, and thick institutions. In Zhejiang, multiple forces, especially local or grass-root initiatives or the domestic enterprises, are found to be more important. In contrast, Guangdong's regional development tends to rely more heavily on external investments, although the indigenous development model has been strongly

Table 1.1 Economic development in Guangdong and Zhejiang Provinces, 2015

	Zhejiang	% of China	Guangdong	% of China
Land area, 10,000 km²	10.5	1.1	17.9	1.9
hukou population, million	48.7	3.6	90.1	6.7
de facto population, 2010 census, million	54.4	4.1	108.5	7.9
GDP, billion RMB	4,303.8	6.3	7,281.3	10.8
GDP per capita, RMB	88,302	–	67,503	–
Investment in fixed assets, billion RMB	2,661.9	4.7	3,003.1	5.4
Exports, billion US$	276.6	12.2	643.5	28.3
FDI, billion US$	16.9	13.4	26.9	21.3
Local fiscal expenditure, billion RMB	581.8	3.3	1,282.8	8.5
Local fiscal revenue, billion RMB	445.7	2.9	936.7	11.3

Sources: Statistical Yearbook of China, 2016; Guangdong Statistical Yearbook, 2016; Zhejiang Statistical Yearbook, 2016.

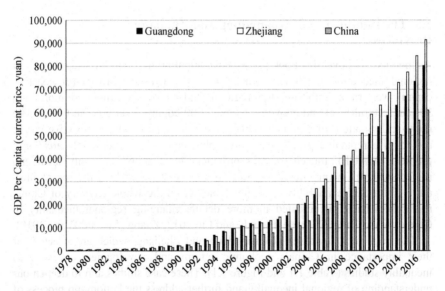

Figure 1.1 GDP per capita in China, Guangdong and Zhejiang, 1978–2017.

advocated in recent years (Lu and Wei 2007; Yang 2012). There have also been evident regional disparities, characterized by the coastal–inland divide in Zhejiang and the core–periphery structure in Guangdong centered on the PRD. Our analysis thus sheds more light on the effects of the formation of new economic space such as the rise of the PRD and the recent changes of the Wenzhou model on regional development and territorial polarization.

1.4 An overview of data and methodology

The data analysis in the book mainly draws upon the compilation of comprehensive historical data reported by the State Statistical Bureau (SSB) of China. We also obtain data from Guangdong Statistical Bureau and Zhejiang Statistical Bureau for county-level statistics. The analysis of data is conducted using both GIS spatial analysis methods, which will be discussed in greater detail in specific chapters. In general, a multi-scale framework is applied and the research addresses the spatiality of regional inequality in different settings (Wei 2015). In addition, we synthesize information gathered from the authors' years of fieldwork and interviews with Chinese officials and companies to understand the process of economic transition, and the underlying mechanisms of regional development.

Scholars working on regional inequality in China have faced challenges regarding data quality and availability (Li and Gibson 2014). Besides gross domestic product (GDP) per capita, many indicators are employed to measure the level of economic development, such as human development index (Li 2012), disposable household income, wage, and level of consumption (Bin and Fracasso 2017). Our analysis mainly relies on the most widely used indicator, namely, GDP per capita (in constant price), partly due to the long-time span of our analyses at both inter- and intra-provincial levels. GDP per capita is also considered as the economic barometer of China, and it is available and readily collected. Besides the residence registration population, the permanent population who live in a place for more than half a year to calculate per capita GDP is also employed. This is particularly related to the case of Guangdong province in which there has been a huge inflow of temporary migrants since the 1980s. In general, GDP and population data are obtained from various versions of China Statistical Yearbook for Regional Economy and China Compendium of Statistics. The data on resident population, if not available, are interpolated using population census statistics.

Besides GDP and population data, various socioeconomic indicators are used as proxies of the triple process of globalization, marketization, and decentralization. For example, foreign direct investment (FDI) is a fundamental feature of globalization and an important force shaping regional inequality as China becomes the largest recipient of FDI among developing countries (Li and Haynes 2012). Fixed assets investment or government expenditure tend to play an important role in China's economic development and are used to understand the role played by investment in general and the role of the state in particular. Market reform in China is closely tied to the rise of private enterprises, which is examined using data in relation to the ownership structure. Regional socioeconomic conditions vary substantially within China and its provinces and may include transportation infrastructure, migration, and development paths. Notably, spatial development policies, such as fiscal policies, regional development policies, and development zone policies, are included for either national level or case studies at the intra-provincial level.

In terms of methodology, traditional analysis of regional inequality relies on aspatial indicators and methods such as coefficient of variation (CV) and global regression. We take full advantage of recent advancements in GIS space–time and exploratory data analytics, including spatial and non-spatial Markov chains, spatial filtering, spMorph, space–time paths, geographically weighted regressions, and multi-level modeling.

1.5 Organization of the book and major results

By integrating a multi-scale and multi-mechanism framework and GIS spatial analysis methods, this book aims at providing a more comprehensive picture of regional inequality in China at both interprovincial and intra-provincial levels. It offers rich empirics with respect to spatial inequality in the context of economic transition relevant to developing countries.

After the introduction, Chapter 2 first overviews how to approach regional inequality from a geographical perspective, and then offers a detailed review of theories of regional inequality. The chapter argues for a more eclectic approach to regional inequality in China. In particular, we hold that regional inequality is sensitive to geographical scales and local contexts, and is influenced by China's triple-process of economic transitions – decentralization, globalization, and marketization. We pay special attention to the spatiality of regional inequality, and in particular, the issues of geographical scales, spatial effects, and bottom–up process, as well as place mobility.

Chapters 3–4 employ a multi-scale framework to guide the analysis of changing patterns of uneven development across China's regions, provinces, prefectures, and counties. These chapters also synthesize state policy and local forces for a better understanding of the drivers of regional inequality in China. In Chapter 3, we show that while interprovincial inequality fluctuated during the period of 1952–2016, interregional inequality has increased in spite of a noticeable drop after the early 2000s. Results of a three-stage spatial decomposition further demonstrate the sensitivity of regional inequality to different scales, and that disparities between prefectures are the largest contributing factor to county-level inequality in China. Hence, national programs that focus on reducing inequality at the macro-region level might have resulted in widening gaps among prefectures and counties. In Chapter 4, we employ time-series and spatial econometric models to gauge the effect of economic transition on the magnitude of regional inequality. We have found the spatial variations of spillover effects. Regional development in the Yangtze River Delta region, for example, has benefited more strongly from the development of Shanghai, but the trickle-down effect of Beijing in the Bohai-rim region would be less evident. Chapters 5–6 apply a multi-scale and multi-mechanism approach to regional disparities in provincial China, through the case study of Guangdong (1980–2014). We have found a new round of regional polarization in Guangdong characterized by the widening gap between the Pearl River Delta (PRD) and the rest of the province (Liao and Wei 2012, 2015). We further summarize the recent changes of the PRD model including the diversification of investment sources, a more knowledge-based growth, and the integration between the PRD, Hong Kong, and Macao. We argue that these changes have reinforced the core–periphery divide in Guangdong, and the efficacy of new programs (e.g., the dual-relocation of industries) that aim to stimulate growth in the periphery remains unclear.

Chapter 7 examines the spatial inequality of regional development in Zhejiang province. Different from Guangdong, Zhejiang's development model is represented by the rise of private enterprises, especially the Wenzhou model. We have revealed the multi-scalar characteristics of regional inequality and identified another round of spatial restructuring in Zhejiang under the "new normal" of the Chinese economy. We explain these changing patterns by emphasizing the Wenzhou model and bottom–up processes. Our results also highlight the importance of fixed asset investment and industrial agglomeration for regional development in Zhejiang. The last chapter summarizes the major findings of this research and discusses their theoretical and policy implications.

References

Alonso, W. 1980. Five bell shapes in development. *Papers in Regional Science* 45 (1): 5–16.

Asan Ali Golam Hassan. 2018. *Growth, structural change, and regional inequality in Malaysia*. Abingdon, Oxon: Routledge, Taylor & Francis Group.

Barro, R. J., and X. Sala-i-Martin. 1995. *Economic growth*. New York: McGraw-Hill.

Barro, R. J., X. Sala-i-Martin, O. J. Blanchard, and R. E. Hall. 1991. Convergence across states and regions. *Brookings Papers on Economic Activity*: 107–182.

Bin, P., and A. Fracasso. 2017. Regional consumption inequality in China: An Oaxaca-Blinder decomposition at the prefectural level. *Growth and Change* 48 (3): 459–486.

Borts, G. H., and J. L. Stein. 1964. *Economic growth in a free market*. New York: Columbia University Press.

Cavanaugh, A., and S. Breau. 2017. Locating geographies of inequality: Publication trends across OECD countries. *Regional Studies* 0 (0): 1–12.

Chen, A. 2010. Reducing China's regional disparities: Is there a growth cost? *China Economic Review* 21 (1): 2–13.

Chen, A., and N. Groenewold. 2010. Reducing regional disparities in China: An evaluation of alternative policies. *Journal of Comparative Economics* 38 (2): 189–198.

Christiansen, B., and M. M. Erdogdu. 2016. *Comparative economics and regional development in Turkey*. Hershey, PA: Business Science Reference.

Crane, B., C. Albrecht, K. M. Duffin, and C. Albrecht. 2018. China's special economic zones: an analysis of policy to reduce regional disparities. *Regional Studies, Regional Science* 5 (1): 98–107.

CSB. 2018. *China Statistical Yearbook*. Beijing: Chinese Statistics Press.

Dai, Q., X. Ye, Y. D. Wei, Y. Ning, and S. Dai. 2017. Geography, ethnicity and regional inequality in Guangxi Zhuang Autonomous Region, China. *Applied Spatial Analysis and Policy*: 1–24.

Diez-Minguela, A., J. Martinez-Galarraga, and D. A. Tirado-Fabregat. 2018. *Regional inequality in Spain, 1860–2015*. Cham: Springer International Publishing.

Fan, C. C. 1997. Uneven development and beyond: Regional development theory in post-Mao China. *International Journal of Urban and Regional Research* 21 (4): 620–639.

Fan, C. C., and M. J. Sun. 2008. Regional inequality in China, 1978–2006. *Eurasian geography and Economics* 49 (1): 1–18.

Fan, S., Kanbur, R., and Zhang, X. 2011. China's regional disparities: Experience and policy. *Review of Development Finance* 1 (1), 47–56.

Ferdinand, P. 2016. Westward ho – the China dream and 'one belt, one road': Chinese foreign policy under Xi Jinping. *International Affairs* 92 (4): 941–957.

Friedmann, J. 1966. *Regional development policy: A case study of Venezuela*. Cambridge: MIT Press.

Fujita, M., and D. P. Hu. 2001. Regional disparity in China 1985–1994: The effects of globalization and economic liberalization. *Annals of Regional Science* 35 (1): 3–37.

Fujita, M., P. R. Krugman, A. J. Venables, and M. Fujita. 1999. *The spatial economy*. Cambridge: MIT Press.

Ge, W. 1999. Special economic zones and the opening of the Chinese economy: Some lessons for economic liberalization. *World Development* 27 (7): 1267–1285.

Gordon, I. R., and P. McCann. 2000. Industrial clusters: Complexes, agglomeration and/or social networks? *Urban Studies* 37 (3): 513–532.

Gorzelak, G., J. Bachtler, and M. Smętkowski. 2014. *Regional development in central and eastern Europe*. London: Routledge.

Gu, J., S. Zhou, and X. Ye. 2016. Uneven regional development under balanced development strategies: Space–time paths of regional development in Guangdong, China. *Tijdschrift voor economische en sociale geografie* 107 (5): 596–610.

Haddad, E. A. 2018. *Regional inequality and structural changes: Lessons from the Brazilian experience*. Abingdon, Oxon: Routledge.

He, S., M. M. Bayrak, and H. Lin. 2017. A comparative analysis of multi-scalar regional inequality in China. *Geoforum* 78: 1–11.

He, S., C. Fang, and W. Zhang. 2017. A geospatial analysis of multi-scalar regional inequality in China and in metropolitan regions. *Applied Geography* 88: 199–212.

Herrerías, M. J., and J. O. Monfort. 2015. Testing stochastic convergence across Chinese provinces, 1952–2008. *Regional Studies* 49 (4): 485–501.

Kahn, T. 2019. *Government-business relations and regional development in post-reform Mexico*. Cham, Switzerland: Palgrave Macmillan.

Kaldor, N. 1970. The case for regional policies. *Scottish Journal of Political Economy* 17 (3): 337–348.

Konsolas, N., A. Papadaskalopoulos, and I. Plaskovitis. 2013. *Regional development in Greece*. Berlin: Springer Berlin.

Krugman, P. 1981. Trade, accumulation, and uneven development. *Journal of Development Economics* 8 (2): 149–161.

Krugman, P. 1990. *Increasing returns and economic geography*. Cambridge, MA: National Bureau of Economic Research.

Krugman, P., and A. J. Venables. 1995. Globalization and the inequality of nations. *Quarterly Journal of Economics* 110 (4): 857–880.

Kuznets, S. 1955. Economic growth and income inequality. *American Economic Review* 45 (1): 1–28.

Lessmann, C. 2012. Regional inequality and decentralization: An empirical analysis. *Environment and Planning A* 44 (6): 1363–1388.

Lessmann, C. 2014. Spatial inequality and development – is there an inverted-U relationship? *Journal of Development Economics* 106: 35–51.

Lewin, P. A., P. Watson, and A. Brown. 2017. Surviving the Great Recession: The influence of income inequality in US urban counties. *Regional Studies* 0 (0): 1–13.

Li, C., and J. Gibson. 2014. Spatial price differences and inequality in the People's Republic of China: Housing market evidence. *Asian Development Review* 31 (1): 92–120.

Li, G., and C. Fang. 2014. Analyzing the multi-mechanism of regional inequality in China. *The Annals of Regional Science* 52 (1): 155–182.

Li, H., and K. Haynes. 2012. Foreign direct investment and China's regional inequality in the era of new regional development strategy. *Regional Science Policy and Practice* 4 (3): 279–300.

Li, S., H. Sato, and T. Sicular. 2013. *Rising inequality in China: Challenges to a harmonious society.* Cambridge: Cambridge University Press.

Li, Y. 2012. The spatial variation of China's regional inequality in human development. *Regional Science Policy and Practice* 4 (3): 263–278.

Li, Y., and Y. D. Wei. 2014. Multidimensional inequalities in health care distribution in provincial China: A case study of Henan Province. *Tijdschrift voor economische en sociale geografie* 105 (1): 91–106.

Li, Y., and Y. H. D. Wei. 2010. The spatial-temporal hierarchy of regional inequality of China. *Applied Geography* 30 (3): 303–316.

Liao, F. H., and Y. D. Wei. 2012. Dynamics, space, and regional inequality in provincial China: A case study of Guangdong province. *Applied Geography* 35 (1): 71–83.

Liao, F. H., and Y. D. Wei. 2015. Space, scale, and regional inequality in provincial China: A spatial filtering approach. *Applied Geography* 61: 94–104.

Lim, K. F., and N. Horesh. 2017. The Chongqing vs. Guangdong developmental 'models' in post-Mao China: Regional and historical perspectives on the dynamics of socio-economic change. *Journal of the Asia Pacific Economy* 22 (3): 372–395.

Lu, L., and Y. D. Wei. 2007. Domesticating globalisation, new economic spaces and regional polarisation in Guangdong Province, China. *Tijdschrift voor economische en sociale geografie* 98 (2): 225–244.

Lu, M., and E. Wang. 2002. Forging ahead and falling behind: Changing regional inequalities in post-reform China. *Growth and Change* 33 (1): 42–71.

Ma, L. J., and Y. Wei. 1997. Determinants of state investment in China, 1953–1990. *Tijdschrift voor economische en sociale geografie* 88 (3): 211–225.

Márquez, M. A., E. Lasarte, and M. Lufin. 2019. The role of neighborhood in the analysis of spatial economic inequality. *Social Indicators Research* 141 (1): 245–273.

Martin, R. 2015. Rebalancing the spatial economy: The challenge for regional theory. *Territory, Politics, Governance* 3 (3): 235–272.

Martin, R., A. Pike, P. Tyler, and B. Gardiner. 2016. Spatially rebalancing the UK economy: Towards a new policy model? *Regional Studies* 50 (2): 342–357.

McCann, P. 2014. Schools of thought on economic geography, institutions, and development. In *Handbook of Regional Science*, eds. M. M. Fischer and P. Nijkamp, 527–538. Berlin, Heidelberg: Springer Berlin Heidelberg.

Myrdal, G., and P. Sitohang. 1957. *Economic theory and under-developed regions.* London: Gerald Duckworth.

Petrakos, G., A. Rodríguez-Pose, and A. Rovolis. 2005. Growth, integration, and regional disparities in the European Union. *Environment and Planning A* 37 (10): 1837–1855.

Pike, A., A. Rodríguez-Pose, and J. Tomaney. 2016. Shifting horizons in local and regional development. *Regional Studies*: 1–12.

Pike, A., A. Rodríguez-Pose, and J. Tomaney. 2017. *Local and regional development.* Second edition. London: Routledge, Taylor & Francis Group.

Piketty, T. 2014. *Capital in the twenty-first century.* Cambridge: Cambridge University Press.

Quah, D. 1996. Regional convergence clusters across Europe. *European Economic Review* 40 (3): 951–958.

Remington, T. F. 2015. Why is interregional inequality in Russia and China not falling? *Communist and Post-Communist Studies* 48 (1): 1–13.

Rey, S. J., and M. V. Janikas. 2005. Regional convergence, inequality, and space. *Journal of Economic Geography* 5 (2): 155–176.

Richardson, W. 1980. Polarization reversal in developing countries. *Papers in Regional Science* 45 (1): 67–85.

Rodríguez-Pose, A. 2012. Trade and regional inequality. *Economic Geography* 88 (2): 109–136.

Scott, A. J. 1988. *New industrial spaces: Flexible production organization and regional development in North America and Western Europe*. London: Pion Ltd.

Shi, H., and S. Huang. 2014. How much infrastructure is too much? A new approach and evidence from China. *World Development* 56: 272–286.

Smith, N. 1984. *Uneven development*. New York: Blackwell.

Stiglitz, J. E. 2012. *The price of inequality: How today's divided society endangers our future*. New York: W. W. Norton & Company.

Storper, M. 1989. The geographical foundations and social regulation of flexible production complexes. *The Power of Geography: How Territory Shapes Social Life*: 21–40.

Storper, M. 1997. *The regional world: Territorial development in a global economy*. New York: Guilford Press.

Storper, M. 2018. Separate worlds? Explaining the current wave of regional economic polarization. *Journal of Economic Geography* 18 (2): 247–270.

Sun, W., X. Lin, Y. Liang, and L. Li. 2016. Regional inequality in underdeveloped areas: A case study of Guizhou Province in China. *Sustainability* 8 (11): 1141.

Tian, X., X. Zhang, Y. Zhou, and X. Yu. 2016. Regional income inequality in China revisited: A perspective from club convergence. *Economic Modelling* 56 (Supplement C): 50–58.

Wei, Y. H. D. 1999. Regional inequality in China. *Progress in Human Geography* 23 (1): 49–59.

Wei, Y. H. D. 2000. *Regional development in China: States, globalization and inequality*. London: Routledge.

Wei, Y. H. D. 2002. Multiscale and multimechanisms of regional inequality in China: Implications for regional policy. *Journal of Contemporary China* 11 (30): 109–124.

Wei, Y. H. D. 2004. Trajectories of ownership transformation in China: Implications for uneven regional development. *Eurasian Geography and Economics* 45 (2): 90–113.

Wei, Y. H. D. 2007. Regional development in China: Transitional institutions, embedded globalization, and hybrid economies. *Eurasian Geography and Economics* 48 (1): 16–36.

Wei, Y. H. D. 2010. Beyond new regionalism, beyond global production networks: Remaking the Sunan Model, China. *Environment and Planning C: Government and Policy* 28 (1): 72–96.

Wei, Y. H. D. 2015. Spatiality of regional inequality. *Applied Geography* 61 (Supplement C): 1–10.

Wei, Y. H. D. 2017. Geography of inequality in Asia. *Geographical Review* 107 (2): 263–275.

Wei, Y. H. D., D. Yu, and X. Chen. 2011. Scale, agglomeration, and regional inequality in provincial China. *Tijdschrift voor economische en sociale geografie* 102 (4): 406–425.

Wei, Y. H. D., and X. Ye. 2009. Beyond convergence: Space, scale, and regional inequality in China. *Tijdschrift Voor Economische En Sociale Geografie* 100 (1): 59–80.

Wei, Y., and L. Ma. 1996. Changing patterns of spatial inequality in China, 1952–1990. *Third World Planning Review* 18 (2): 177.

Wildau, G., and T. Mitchell. 2016, Jan 14. China income inequality among world's worst. *Financial Times.*

Williamson, J. G. 1965. Regional inequality and the process of national development: A description of the patterns. *Economic Development and Cultural Change* 13 (4): 1–84.

World Bank. 2011. *Reducing inequality for shared growth in China: Strategy and policy options for Guangdong Province.* Washington, DC: World Bank.

Xie, Y., and X. Zhou. 2014. Income inequality in today's China. *Proceedings of the National Academy of Sciences* 111 (19): 6928–6933.

Yamamoto, D. 2008. Scales of regional income disparities in the USA, 1955–2003. *Journal of Economic Geography* 8 (1): 79–103.

Yang, C. 2012. Restructuring the export-oriented industrialization in the Pearl River Delta, China: Institutional evolution and emerging tension. *Applied Geography* 32 (1): 143–157.

Yao, Y. 2009. The political economy of government policies toward regional inequality in China. In *Reshaping Economic Geography in East Asia.* Washington, DC: World Bank: 218–240.

Zhang, W., W. Xu, and X. Wang. 2019. Regional convergence clubs in China: Identification and conditioning factors. *The Annals of Regional Science* 62 (2): 327–350.

2 Literature review and analytical framework

This chapter reviews the main theories of regional inequality, including new convergence and new economic geography theories. It also provides the global social and economic contexts in which different theoretical thoughts were dominating the academic inquiry. This chapter then reviews studies of regional inequality in China, with a focus on recent studies of regional inequality within Chinese provinces. We also explain the multi-scale and multi-mechanism framework of analyzing regional inequality in China and summarize the methods or space–time analysis techniques used to measure regional inequality dynamics.

Overall, in light of the size, scale, and complexity of the Chinese economy, the chapter presents key geographical perspectives on regional economic inequality, which are argued to be sensitive to space, scale, place, and complexity. We hold that the evolution of regional inequality is sensitive to the scale of analysis and time periods chosen, and that a multi-scale and multi-mechanism framework is better able to synthesize major agents of regional development and inequality in China.

2.1 Theories of regional inequality

The central topic of regional development theories is the debate of equilibrium or disequilibrium among regions and how they are reached. After World War II, the neoclassical convergence school based on the assumption of a free market emerged as the dominant school of thought in regional inequality (Harris 1957; Borts and Stein 1964). Closely related are the inverted-U model and the growth-pole theory (Perroux 1950; Williamson 1965). However, such a modernization paradigm was heavily criticized for the persistence of poverty and inequality in developing countries. In the 1970s and 1980s, divergence schools became important alternatives, including the structuralism theory and planned economics theory emphasizing disequilibrium in regional development (Richardson 1973; Harvey 1975). Globalization and reforms in former socialist countries renewed the debate on regional inequality since the 1990s. The debate over regional inequality reignited with the rise of new convergence theory and new economic geography theory (Barro et al. 1991; Krugman 1991; Barro and Sala-i-Martin 1992; Krugman and Venables 1995). An increasing interest on the role of spatial process and scale in changes of regional inequality also emerged, trying to overcome the limits of traditional regional development theories treating space merely as a container or a unit of analysis (Soja 2009; Wei and Ye 2009; Rey and Sastré Gutiérrez 2015).

Convergence and divergence theories

Since the 1950s, there has been a dichotomy between the convergence and divergence schools regarding the long-term trajectories of regional inequality. Heavily influenced by neoclassical economics, the convergence school argues that regional disparity will be replaced by spatial equilibrium over time under the assumption of free movement of production factors and full access to information (Borts and Stein 1964). Regional inequality is viewed as a transitory phenomenon because the market would allocate resources efficiently and eventually equalize regional differentials. Hence, if there are two regions with one rich of capital but lacking labor and another one rich of labor but poor with capital, the mobility of capital and labor will lead to the capital flow from developed region to underdeveloped region and vice versa for the labor flow. The relocation process will eventually minimize the gap in wages and the price of capital between regions and reach spatial equilibrium. This process is exemplified in many studies of regional inequality in the United States, European countries, and Japan (Harris 1957; Vining Jr and Strauss 1977; Mera 1978; Tabuchi 1988).

Influenced by the modernization theory and Kuznets' inverted-U theory of income inequality (Rostow 1960; Kuznets and Murphy 1966), the inverted-U model holds the view that regional inequality is an inevitable initial stage before reaching the final stage of equilibrium (Williamson 1965). In modernization theory, all countries occupy positions on a spectrum from "traditional" to "modern" ones, and nations may move to higher development levels by adopting the characteristics of "modern" countries (Rostow 1960). The inverted-U model argues that regional inequality rises in the early stage of development when structural change and specialization happen. But it tends to fall as the economy matures, characterized by advanced structural change and integration, as well as increasing capital movement and labor migration between regions (Williamson 1965). This pattern of regional inequality trajectory is also validated and discussed in recent empirical studies (Ezcurra and Rapún 2006; Barrios and Strobl 2009; Lessmann 2014).

Closely related to the inverted-U model of regional inequality are the growth pole theory (Perroux 1950), the core–periphery model (Friedmann 1966), and the bell-shape development (Alonso 1980). Perroux (1950) argues that entrepreneurial innovation and "propulsive industries" as growth poles serve as the engines for regional development. Though polarization because of agglomeration economies and Myrdalian backwash effect exists in the early phase (Myrdal 1957), diffusion of technologies and innovations will finally cause redistribution and equilibrium. The core–periphery model points out that though development is led by a few core regions and tends to self-reinforce, the trickle-down effects to peripheries will forge functionally interdependent spatial systems (Friedmann 1966). Five bell shapes in regional development are summarized by Alonso (1980): development stages, social inequality, regional inequality, geographic concentration, and demographic transition. These theories discussed above could be categorized under the top–down development or development from the above paradigm (Hansen 1981).

However, the neoclassical convergence school has been criticized since the 1970s (Stöhr and Tödtling 1979; Krebs 1982). The free movement assumption of labor and capital does not hold in most countries (Richardson 1978). The inverted-U model is considered to be exceptional in the U.S. and E.U. because of their special context (Friedmann and Bloch 1990). Controversial patterns are observed based on more recent empirics (Rodríguez-Pose 2012), and the causes of the long-term inverted-U pattern remain elusive (Kim 2008). The rising wage because of out-migration in the periphery is precluded by the high natural population growth rate, and the selective migration of young, skilled, and highly educated groups hampers the potential development of poor regions (Brown and Lawson 1989); the neoclassical theory neglects the cultural, institutional, and geographical factors that influence trade, factor mobility, innovation, and regional development (Wei and Ye 2009).

Inspired by the persistent inequality in most underdeveloped countries and the civil rights movement in the United States, the divergence school emerged in the late 1960s and led to new thinking on inequality (Wei 2015). The divergence school doubts the hypothesis of free market and emphasizes that capital accumulation and cumulative causation could make regional inequality persistent (Smith 1984). The divergence school can be further summarized into two theories – the planned economy theory and the radical theory – which agree that free movement of production factors will enhance the spatial disequilibrium but disagree on the effects of government intervention (Lipshitz 1992). While the planned economy theory postulates that policy intervention is effective to reduce regional inequality, the radical theory holds that government intervention tends to directly or indirectly perpetuate regional inequality.

One common perspective in the planned economy theory is that the widening gap between regions is endogenous in development and exogenous forces like a spatial policy from the government are needed to reduce inequality. In Myrdal (1957), the flow of capital and young and talented labor from the underdeveloped region to the developed region is defined as a "backwash effect" exacerbating regional inequality. Though the opposite flow may occur in a later period, this "spillover effect" is negligible compared with the "backwash effect." Thus, exogenous change is needed to reduce inequality. Hirschman (1958) developed a similar theory in which the two spatial processes are defined as "polarization" and "trickling down" and strongly holds that the efficient intervention from government is the key to closing the interregional gap.

Complementary to Myrdal (1957) and Hirschman (1958), Friedmann (1973) and Richardson (1973, 1978) emphasize the role of technological innovation in regional development. In Friedmann's framework, the inequality between core and periphery is caused by the simultaneous influences of four factors, namely population migration, the flow of capital investment, spatial diffusion of technological innovation, and spatial organization of political power (Friedmann 1973). Like Friedmann, Richardson also considers the spatial distribution of the creation and absorption of technological innovation as the cause of increasing interregional inequality (Richardson 1973, 1978). Spatial policies were undertaken by the government or its authorities, as well as the growth center strategy, which is suggested to target and develop peripheral regions (Richardson 1976, 1980; Friedmann and Douglass 1978; Friedmann and Weaver 1980).

Radical theories, represented by dependency, world system, and Marxian political economy theories, are mainly based on structuralism, rooted in the works of Marx, and emphasize spatial disequilibrium. In a core–periphery structure, the periphery provides low-cost labor force, raw materials, and market for products, while the core exploits the profit by high-priced industrial goods, unequal financial services, and cooperation with local elites, which will exacerbate the stagnation of the periphery and intensify regional inequality (Frank 1967; Griffin 1973). At the national level, the periphery represents rural areas and small urban settlements, and the core represents metropolitan areas. And at the international level, the periphery consists of most underdeveloped countries in Asia, Africa, and Latin America, while the core is made up of developed countries in North America, Europe, and Asia. The dependency between social classes, between regions, and between countries is viewed as the essence of capitalism (Peet 1975; Wallerstein 1979; Soja 1980).

The radical theory is contrary to the neoclassical convergence school and holds that there is not much hope that underdeveloped countries would pass the stages of modernization because of the dependency on the core–periphery structure (Evans 1979). From a Marxist political economy perspective, regional inequality is viewed as a necessary precondition for and unavoidable consequence of capital accumulation (Harvey 1975). The periphery stagnates since it is chronically deprived of investment, less favored by the firms because of the spatial division of labor and lower profit rates (Storper 1989). In the era of flexible production, spatial agglomeration requires the geographic proximity between firms and leads to the convergence of firms at the local level but divergence at the interregional level (Sabel 1984; Scott and Storper 1987). More recent work on post-colonialism and post-structuralism further criticize theories of regional inequality developed in the context of Western countries. However, the radical theory has also been heavily criticized for its reliance on structuralism and the logics of capital accumulation, and the distance to public policies. Their perspectives on the core–periphery structure ignore the interdependence and the dynamics of the structure and capital accumulation and are too strict in practice (Corbridge 1986; Duncan 1989; Knox, Agnew, and McCarthy 2014).

New convergence and new economic geography theories

Since the late 1980s, a renewed interest in regional inequality has been triggered by a new round of thinking on the effects of globalization and liberalization, reforms and transitions in former socialist countries, the rediscovery of space and geography in social sciences, and new developments in the disciplines of economics and geography (Wei and Ye 2009; Wei 2015). Two influential theories, namely new convergence theory and new economic geography, are put forward to respond to the critiques on neoclassical economics and provide a more insightful explanation with relaxed economic assumptions (Barro *et al.* 1991; Krugman 1991, 2011; Barro and Sala-i-Martin 1992; Krugman and Venables 1995).

New convergence theory identifies two concepts of convergence, σ-convergence, and β-convergence. σ-convergence is the most often studied convergence, which refers to the declining dispersion of per capita income or outputs across regions over time (Rey and Janikas 2005). In empirical studies, σ-convergence is usually measured by the coefficient of variance (CV), the ratio between standard deviation and mean value. A decreasing trend indicates that regional inequality is declining. To test σ-convergence, regression of standard deviation over the time trend will be conducted, in which a significant and negative coefficient indicates σ-convergence (Barro and Sala-i-Martin 1992).

Different from the aggregated perspective in σ-convergence, β-convergence refers to the process that poor economies grow faster than wealthier economies, which will ultimately lead to convergence among economies (Barro *et al.* 1991; Barro and Sala-i-Martin 1992). Growth regression that relates the growth rate in per capita income or output over time to the initial level of income or output is extensively used in the validation of β-convergence, which is also called the absolute β-convergence because the steady-state income position of each regional unit is only correlated with its initial state position. The convergence speed, β, is estimated to be about 2% per year in various contexts (Barro and Sala-i-Martin 1995).

In addition to the absolute convergence, concepts of conditional convergence and club convergence are also proposed (Sala-i-Martin 1996). Conditional β-convergence holds that regions tend to converge conditionally on endowments of regions, such as the investment return rate, human capital, population growth rate, technology advancement, and capital depreciation rate (Mankiw, Romer, and Weil 1992; Barro 2015). Club convergence refers to the convergence process in different geographical regions with similar economic conditions, in which economies converge to multiple steady-state equilibrium levels (Lau 2010).

Though new convergence theory has fuelled fresh debates and empirical testing and deserves huge credits for revitalizing the study of regional inequality in mainstream economics, it also receives several criticisms (Wei 2015). It is argued that by focusing only on the aggregated level of dispersion, σ-convergence may conceal important geographical patterns over time, masking any mixing and mobility of individual economies, and ignore other aspects of the income distribution such as skewness and modality (Rey and Montouri 1999; Rey and Janikas 2005; Rey 2016). Exploratory analysis of growth dynamics in the distribution of regional incomes is proposed as an alternative empirical strategy since it does not impose prior restrictive assumptions on the growth processes (Quah 1993, 1996a; Fingleton 1999). Methods like stochastic kernel density estimation and Markov transition matrix are employed to explore the dynamics of regional inequality (Quah 1996b; Magrini 1999; Johnson 2000).

Regarding β-convergence, Lau (2010) argues that cross-section regression in validating β-convergence may commit Galton's fallacy of regression to the mean and implies biased estimates and invalid test statistics. If the technology progress is stochastic, per capita income or output will fail the β-convergence test even if the underlying stochastic process of the economic is convergent and ergodic (Pesaran 2007). Wei and Ye (2009) summarize four limitations of the new convergence theory: (1) it is insensitive to geographical scale since regional inequality is multi-scale layered in nature; (2) it adopts a black-box approach and masks the heterogeneous nature of geographical space; (3) it is devoid of time since it often ignores the temporal process of development and the influence of cyclical effects of economic development; (4) it is weak in understanding the bottom–up forces at work because it stems from the neoclassical economics schools, which are built by a top–down framework.

Without asserting a convergent or divergent trend of regional inequality, new economic geography (NEG) has been proposed to explain regional development by integrating traditional location theory, new trade theory, and transportation cost, forming a set of analytical approaches in economic geography (Krugman 1991; Fujita *et al.* 1999). It adopts a microeconomic lens to consider the effects of imperfect competition in which increasing returns of scale, agglomeration economies, and geographical factors are emphasized (Krugman 1997, 2011). New economic geography serves the significant purpose of bringing geography and economics together and provides insights about how falling trade costs will increasingly integrate the core and periphery regions but also foster a greater concentration of economic activities in the cores (Krugman and Venables 1995; Armstrong and Taylor 2009).

There are three basic elements underlying the new economic geography framework: the relationship between size and variety, factor migration, and the setting of distance costs (McCann 2014). In new economic geography, the profitability of a firm is assumed to be related to the variety of intermediate inputs among which a firm can choose to purchase supplies. Greater city size will increase production welfare because more variety of choices and better matching outcomes are available. Manufacturing goods exhibit increasing returns to scale while constant returns to scale are assigned to agricultural activities. It will affect the factor migration of labor, capital, knowledge, and technology. An "iceberg" form of specification in transportation is defined as the falling value of the good with increasing delivery distance. The costs of distance will increase at the margin with increasing distance under such specification.

Under the new economic geography framework, centripetal and centrifugal forces will be generated between core and periphery regions, which will eventually determine the spatial distribution of economic activities (Krugman 1991; Krugman and Venables 1995). The centripetal forces originate from the advantages of larger cities in which a greater variety of intermediate inputs will provide the efficiency-scale effects in production. Factors will collocate together and the rate and scale of colocation of factors depend in part on the mobility of the factors (Puga 1999). Meanwhile, the iceberg transport cost and localized congestion effects will provide centrifugal forces because of the increasing marginal distance cost and agglomeration diseconomy (Palivos and Wang 1996). The overall observed spatial distribution of economic activities is argued to depend on the balance between the two opposing forces and both regional convergence and divergence are possible.

In new economic geography studies, regionally divergent growth is more often emphasized because the falling trade costs and mutual trade openness in the last 20 years of globalization are seen to generally favor core regions and large urban centers at the expense of other regions (McCann 2007). Approaches in NEG are also criticized for being too sensitive to the actual specification employed and small changes in parameters and assumptions will lead to major empirical change (Bosker and Garretsen 2010). The NEG theory also pays more attention to regional inequality in manufacturing activities. Industrial agglomeration as the core of NEG theory provides an important explanation for patterns of regional development but does not deliver a complete account (Martin 2015). Additionally, recent studies maintain that because of the way the NEG models are formulated, a key implication would be allowing the regional concentration of economic activity will increase growth due to the effect of agglomeration economies, forming a trade-off between efficiency and equity (Gardiner, Martin, and Tyler 2011). Along this line of theoretical thinking, Crozet and Koenning (2005) found some evidence that regions in the EU with a more uneven spatial distribution of production tend to grow faster (see also Iammarino, Rodriguez-Pose, and Storper 2018). In contrast, the case of China shows that in the short run, a reduction in regional inequality reduces growth, while a more equitable distribution can be achieved without a growth sacrifice (Chen 2010). Nevertheless, spatial issues, such as scale, spatial heterogeneity, and autocorrelation, have greatly escaped attention in studies of regional inequality or convergence.

Spatiality and institutions in uneven regional development

The increasing interest in the role of space or spatiality since the mid-1980s reflects how human geographers put geography at the center of understanding the social, economic, and political processes (Massey 1985). Spatiality in regional development could be defined as properties relating to or occupying space such as dimensionality, directionality, and spatial configuration (Wei 2015). In the resurgence of regions and regionalism in development literature, terms such as locality, local context, and scale are associated with local and regional development (Börzel and Risse 2016; Pike, Rodríguez-Pose, and Tomaney 2016). Hence, local endowments of human capital, institutional qualities, or the innovative capacity of firms and individuals are proposed by the evolutionary and institutional schools to understand the local and regional development in certain geographical settings and time periods (Pike, Rodríguez-Pose, and Tomaney 2016).

Unlike the endogenous growth perspective taken by the neoclassical theory and new economic geography, evolutionary and institutional schools focus more on place-based relatedness between regions in technological and institutional terms and how technological "lock-in" and institutional capability affect the differential regional growth (Porter 1990; Aghion and Howitt 1992; Saxenian 1994; Boschma 2005). In empirical models, evolutionary and institutional schools also capture the factors like knowledge spillover, input variety, and human capital, but emphasize that there is no necessarily preordained growth rate or trajectory to which economies should converge. It is argued that the economic growth trajectory of regions depends on how well positioned an economy is to take advantage of the newly emerging technologies (McCann 2014).

The production system and technological innovation play an important role in regional inequality dynamics from the evolutionary economics perspective. The production cycle theory is proposed to explain regional inequality in early studies of the evolutionary school (Norton and Rees 1979; Booth 1986; Amos 1990). The regional economies will show a long-wave pattern consisting of stages from prosperity, stagnancy, decline, recovery, and prosperity again as technological innovation cycles proceed. During the prosperity phase, concentration from the periphery to the core will occur and prompt regional disparity, while the dispersion from the core to periphery will happen and lead to declining regional inequality when the technological innovation declines and loses its competitiveness. The cycling technological innovation causes the rise and fall of regional inequality and several inverted-U patterns as observed in major developed countries (Maxwell and Hite 1992).

Besides the universal impacts of long-wave patterns, the evolutionary perspective attributes the differences in regional growth rate to the different technological profiles of places (Porter 1990; Aghion and Howitt 1992). The proximity in the technological profile of places indicates the degree of congruence of regions to link with and exploit the technological breakthroughs in leading regions, which in turn is determined by the evolutionary processes forging the region's prevailing industrial structure and production capacity. When the region aims to diversify into technological fields that are closer and more related to its current dominant technologies, it will allow the region to better exploit and build upon its existing skills and capabilities, which will eventually lead to stronger growth for the region (Frenken, Van Oort, and Verburg 2007). Empirical evidence shows that both the inflows of new firms and the founding of new local firms are found to be higher in related technological fields in the region, while the outflows of firms or firm failures are likely to be in largely unrelated technological fields (Boschma and Iammarino 2009).

The institutional school argues that the institutional profile of regions also plays an important role in economic development and the historical trajectory of institution and governance systems matters (North 1990; Amin and Thrift 1994). The ability of an institutional system in facilitating regional growth and development depends not only on its architectural design, but also on the interactions between institutional actors, stakeholders, and interested parties. In some cases, the institutional factor is more important than geography or trade (Wei 2000; Acemoglu, Johnson, and Robinson 2002; Rodríguez-Pose 2013). Under a highly centralized state, it will preclude the widespread engagement of local stakeholders and limit endogenous-driven local development, while coordination failures, rent-seeking, duplication, and absence of coordinated strategy will happen in decentralized systems (Barca, McCann, and Rodríguez-Pose 2012).

Empirics show that formal institutional policies, either to the macroeconomic aspect or regional aspect, will impact regional development and inequality. Policies that promote industrialization and foreign investment and trade in developing countries tend to favor the development in core regions and exacerbate regional inequality (Lipton 1977; Gilbert and Gugler 1992). Political factors like officer assignment, corruption, and instability will also cause urban primary and regional inequality (Kim 2008; Wu and Chen 2016). Since the state is also multi-scalar in nature and embedded with dynamics and shifting development philosophy, the role of local government is complex and non-negligible. The local government is empowered with considerable decision-making powers under worldwide decentralization and tends to protect the local interest and cause widening regional inequality (Wei 2000; Agnew and Crobridge 2002). It is suggested that state policies, especially those in developing countries aiming at developing periphery regions and reducing regional inequality, only have limited effects and are often offset by macroeconomic realities, forces from foreign direct investment, and local government in core regions (Wei 2015).

The impacts from the informal institution are also non-negligible, of which social capital is the most important one and brought to contemporary economics discussion about urban and regional systems (Putnam, Leonardi, and Nanetti 1994; Putnam 2001; Westlund 2006). Referred to as all types of social norms, social rules, and social conventions that operate within a society, social capital, especially social trust in government institutions, is suggested to be highly correlated with levels of economic activities over time and influence a region's ability to adapt to changes, which therefore implies that the institutional history of the regions also determines the long-term development of a region (Putnam, Leonardi, and Nanetti 1994; Putnam 2001). Like the evolutionary school, the institutional school points out that the technological, institutional, and social profile of the region is crucial in understanding its growth pattern and economic development over time beyond the questions of geographical proximity and economic scales and agglomeration (McCann 2014).

Scalarity is an important concept closely related to spatiality. Regional development differs across scales, indicating that regional inequality is multi-scalar in nature (Wei 1999; Kim 2008). With the advent of new regionalism, multi-scalar geographical analysis covering the global and local, the macro and micro, the exogenous and endogenous development processes are intensively encouraged (He, Fang, and Zhang 2017). Scale is also socially constructed and subject to the rescaling process which underlies the dynamic mechanisms of spatial inequality. First, representative theories in support of regional convergence tend to neglect the spatiality of regional inequality (Wei 2015). Second, the divergent trend persists through the process of circular and cumulative causation. Capital doesn't move to lagging regions while labor migration from the poor to the rich has further strengthened rather than weakened the prosperity of more developed regions. Persistent core–periphery structure limits the mobility of relatively poor regions and places. For example, regional inequality in Europe has attracted considerable attention due to the expansion of the E.U. and the concern regarding economic development in Eastern and Central Europe. However, inequality among regions has sharply been intensified in the new millennium (Iammarino, Rodriguez-Pose, and Storper 2018). There is never a convergence trend among regions in the E.U. as the new convergence theory would predict (Haughton 2012).

2.2 Regional inequality in China

Scholarly interests regarding regional development and inequality in China can be traced back to the Lardy–Donnithorne debate in the 1970s, which emphasizes the association between changing spatial allocation of investment funds during the Mao period and the change in regional economic disparity (Wei 1999). Scholars have found that before the establishment of the PRC in 1949, uneven development in China was already evident, characterized by a more developed coastal region due to its geographical location and legacy of colonialism (He, Bayrak, and Lin 2017; Wei 2007; Yu and Wei 2003). Works in the mid-1990s presented a more complete landscape of uneven regional development in China and extended to data in the 1980s (Wei and Ma 1996). In the 1980s, development policies had been experimental, and encouraging coastal regions to 'get rich first' was a more critical concern. Consequently, the economic reform unleashed new forces that led to the spatial restructuring of industries, whereas coastal provinces have benefited more from these changes (Wei and Ma 1996).

Since the 1990s, many regional economists employed neoclassical growth models to analyze the change in regional inequality in China. The modeling specifically adopts two concepts of convergence: (1) σ convergence, which occurs when the divergence of per capita income or output across regions decline over time; and (2) β convergence that refers to the tendency for initially poorer regions to develop more rapidly than richer areas (Barro and Sala-i-Martin 1995).

Lyons (1991) conducted a pioneering study and found that the economic status of Chinese provinces diverged from 1966 to 1976, resulting in rising regional disparities during the period of "Mao radicalism." Using a neoclassical convergence paradigm, scholars identified regional convergence among Chinese provinces in the early stage of the reform (1978–1985), and a divergence trend in the late 1980s and the early 1990s (Chen and Fleisher 1996; Jian, Sachs, and Warner 1996). Although convergence or divergence following the neoclassical thoughts remains prevalent (Yao and Zhang 2001), researchers tend to agree that the coastal and inland divide has persisted during the reform era, but findings from most recent literature have been inconclusive (Sakamoto and Islam 2008; Li and Gibson 2013).

Focusing on the different "ergodic distributions" before and after the reform, additional evidence has been provided about uncertainties towards convergence at the provincial level (Sakamoto and Islam 2008). In contrast, using the indicators of capital intensity, labor productivity, and total factor productivity (TFP), Herrerías and Monfort (2015) found that convergence among provinces is evident when analyzing the data for the period of 1952–2008 (Herrerías and Monfort 2015). Scholarly attention has also been directed to the notion of *club convergence*, which refers to the convergence process in different regions or locales with similar economic conditions. Studies applying the concept tend to define clubs based on the predefined coastal–inland divide (Phillips and Sul 2007; Lau 2010). However, some empirical work found that dual-convergence club based on usual and coastal-versus-interior classification could hardly explain the spatial patterns of provincial-level economic growth differentials (Pedroni and Yao 2006).

More studies further analyze county-level data within particular provinces. In this realm, more attention is paid to coastal provinces as they experienced more rapid change and benefit most from the economic development since the reform. Special regional development trajectories and models are emphasized in intra-provincial studies, like the Wenzhou model in Zhejiang Province centered on the private enterprises (Wei and Ye 2004, 2009; Yue *et al.* 2014), the Sunan model in Jiangsu Province based on the development of township and village enterprises (TVEs) (Wei and Fan 2000; Wei and Kim 2002; Wei, Yu, and Chen 2011), and the Pearl River Delta (PRD) model in Guangdong Province driven by export-oriented manufacturing and overseas investments (Lu and Wei 2007; Liao and Wei 2012, 2015). The Greater Beijing region in northern coastal China also received scholars' attention because of its persistent core–periphery structure and weak linkage between the capital and nearby regions (Yu 2006; Yu and Wei 2008). To fill the gap that there is limited understanding about the intra-provincial inequality in central and western China, several studies analyze the inequality trend and mechanisms of less developed regions like Henan Province (Li and Wei 2014), Guangxi province (Dai *et al.* 2017), Gansu Province (Wei and Fang 2006), and other inland and mountainous regions (Zhang and Deng 2016).

Studies on regional inequality in China keep pace with the development of spatial analysis methods to reveal the importance of scale and spatial effects. By applying techniques in exploratory spatial data analysis (ESDA), scholars highlight the existence of spatial dependence at both national and local scales (Yu and Wei 2003; Wei, Yu, and Chen 2011; Li and Fang 2014; Liao and Wei 2015). In Li and Fang (2014), a positive spatial autocorrelation and an inverted-U shape Global Moran's *I* are found for the county-level inequality in China from 1992 to 2010. By using global and local spatial association indexes, scholars find that the positive spatial dependence of county-level GDP per capita rose consistently since the reform and the core–periphery is consistent in coastal provinces like Zhejiang (Wei and Ye 2009; Yue *et al.* 2014). Similar patterns are also observed for cases of Jiangsu (Wei, Yu, and Chen 2011), Guangdong (Liao and Wei 2012, 2015), and the Greater Beijing area (Yu and Wei 2008).

Spatial modeling approaches have been intensively utilized in regional inequality studies in China. Geographically explicit methods like spatial filtering, multi-level modeling, spatial Markov chain, spatial panel regression, spatial regime model, and geographically weighted regression are used to integrate and advance the understanding of geographical and spatial effects in regional inequality (Yu 2006; Yu and Wei 2008; Li and Wei 2010b; Liao and Wei 2012; Dai *et al.* 2017). Because spatial dependency in cross-sectional data on geographic units will violate the assumption of ordinary least squares (OLS) estimation and lead to mis-specified models, ignoring the spatial effects might lead to biased coefficients and thus misleading interpretation of regional inequality determinants (Anselin and Rey 1991; Yu and Wei 2008). In analyzing the absolute and conditional β-convergence across urban and county economies in China, Li and Fang (2016) find that the OLS framework may lead to estimation errors or invalid estimates, while the spatial econometric models like spatial autoregressive (SAR) and spatial error models (SEM) are superior in performance after comparison.

Recent work has also extended the analysis of spatiality of inequality to the spatiotemporal dynamics of inequality. Space–time analysis methods and frameworks are proposed to deal with the temporal dynamics of geographic processes and spatial dynamics of economic development across scales and dimensions (Ye and Rey 2013). The exploratory space–time analysis framework, originating from ESDA, attempts to extend ESDA into a dynamic context and explores data from a systematic perspective. Methods like space–time path and rank statistics are implemented to exploratorily analyze the local and adjacent regions' development trajectories in the context of China (Gu, Zhou, and Ye 2016; Wu *et al.* 2019). The popularity of social media provides new tools to study the nature of human behavior and spatial interaction. Social media has also produced a new space of inequality, which has yet to be fully understood (Wei 2015).

The multi-scale and multi-mechanism framework

The neoclassical account for uneven development mentioned above was founded upon assumptions of economic rationality, perfect mobility, perfect information, and perfect competition, basically drawing upon the thinking of equilibrium. Economic geographers or other researches would like to focus on the spatiality or multi-scalar nature of regional inequality (Wei 2002; Li and Wei 2010b); a multi-mechanism framework has been found more applicable to China by conceptualizing underlying forces into a triple process of globalization, marketization, and decentralization (Wei 2002, 2007).

Table 2.1 Scales and timespan of regional inequality studies in China

Studies	Study area	Regions	Timespan	Scale
National scale				
Fan and Sun (2008)	China	Eastern, central, and western	1978–2006	Provincial
Kanbur and Zhang (2005)		Coastal and inland	1952–2000	Provincial
Wang (2007)		Four-region division	1978–2007	Provincial
Ye and Xie (2012)		Six-region division	1960–2000	Prefectural
Huang and Wei (2019)		Eastern, central, and western	1990–2010	Prefectural
He, Fang, and Zhang (2017)		Four-region division	1997–2010	County
Li and Fang (2014)		Four-region division (not explicitly applied in analysis)	1992–2010	County
Gao et al. (2019)		Eastern, central, and western	2000–2015	Rural and county
Intra-provincial scale				
Wei and Fan (2000)	Jiangsu	Sunan, Suzhong, and Subei	1950–1995	County
Wei and Kim (2002)			1950–1995	County
Wei et al. (2011)			1978–2005	County
Liu et al. (2019)			2000–2014	County
Wei and Ye (2004)	Zhejiang	Northeast Zhejiang and southwest Zhejiang	1978–1998	County
Ye and Wei (2005)			1978–1998	County
Wei and Ye (2009)			1978–2004	County
Yue et al. (2014)			1990–2010	County
Gu et al. (2001)	Guangdong	Pearl River Delta (PRD) and Mountainous rim	1980–1995	County
Lu and Wei (2007)			1978–2003	Prefectural
Liao and Wei (2012)			1979–2009	County
Liao and Wei (2015)			1988–2012	County
Gu et al. (2016)			1978–2013	Prefectural
Zhang et al. (2018)			1990–2012	Prefectural

Reference	Study area	Detail	Period	Scale
Wei and Fang (2006)	Gansu	Northwestern Hexi Corridor and southeast Gansu	1952–2002	County
Dai et al. (2017)	Guangxi	The Beibu Gulf Economic Zone (BGEZ), the Xijiang River Economic Belt (XREB) and the Guangxi (WG)	1989–2012	County
Sun et al. (2016)	Guizhou	Northeast, West, South, and Central Guizhou	2000–2012	County
Ye et al. (2017)	Chongqing	Seven function areas in Chongqing	1997–2015	County
Hybrid scales				
He et al. (2017)	China	Seven state-level metropolitan regions	1997–2010	County
Yu et al. (2018)		Nineteen urban agglomerations	2004–2016	Prefecture
Wang and Shen (2017)	Yangtze River Delta (YRD) and Pearl River Delta	Jiangsu, Shanghai, and Zhejiang; and PRD	2000–2010	Prefectural
Sheng and Liu (2018)	Mega-urban regions along Yangtze River	YRD, Middle Yangtze River, and Chengdu-Chongqing	2000–2012	Prefecture
Yu and Wei (2008)	Greater Beijing area	Beijing, Tianjin, Hebei	1978–2001	County
Li (2012)			1990–2004	County
Zhang and Deng (2016)	Junction area in southwest China	Sichuan, Yunnan, and Guizhou	1995–2010	County

Based on the administrative hierarchy in China (Figure 2.1), the multi-scalarity of regional inequality mainly covers three levels, namely the regional level, the provincial level, and the county level. Studies have documented that regional inequality in China is sensitive to geographical scales. Interregional inequalities have been intensified since the reform, but there was a noticeable drop of inter-provincial inequality in the 1980s (Fan 1997).

At the provincial level, regional inequality in China shows a fluctuating pattern after the reform. Peaks and troughs of inequality are observed by scholars and they support the notion that policy changes are critical factors in explaining the interprovincial inequality trend. The period of rural reform in 1978 to 1984 saw a decline in inequality which gathered pace in the early 1980s and interprovincial inequality reached its trough in 1984. The economic reforms that began in the late 1970s boosted the development of several provinces in the eastern region that had previously been laggards, thus reducing interprovincial inequality in the 1980s. In the post-rural reform period after 1984, when China decentralized, opened up, and experienced an explosion of trade and foreign direct investment, interprovincial inequality rose steadily and then sharply until the 2000s. After the negative ramifications of Tiananmen in 1989, Deng Xiaoping's southern tour in 1992 to further the open-door policy stimulated full-throttle

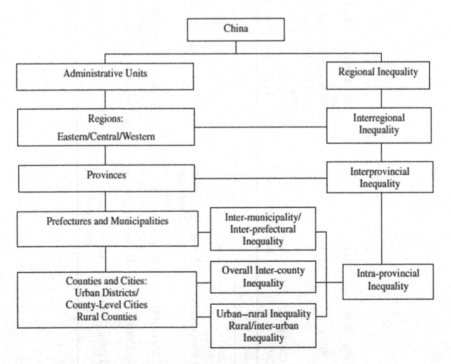

Figure 2.1 A typology of multi-scalar regional inequalities in China.

Source: Adapted from Wei and Ye (2009).

development of the eastern region, thus also increasing interprovincial inequality in the 1990s. After the late 1990s, the interprovincial inequality was relatively stable and has even declined since the early 2000s, which hints at a downward trend. The year 2004 could be viewed as a turning point for interprovincial inequality as well as interregional inequality, indicating the initial success of government policies for reducing regional inequality. The severe regional inequality since the reform has alarmed policymakers and seen them implement policies aiming to alleviate inequality nationally and regionally.

Because of data availability and development of spatial analysis techniques, recent studies have attempted to "scale down" the analysis to "county-level" economic inequality in China (see Figure 2.1). He, Bayrak, and Lin (2017) comprehensively analyze inter-county inequality. A wave-shaped pattern characterized by a broad inverted-U shape is observed for counties in China from the 1990s to 2010. Inter-county inequality in China increased in the 1990s and declined in most of the years in the 2000s. After 2009, a slightly upward trend is found until 2010 with no further observation after 2010. Regarding the economic growth convergence of counties in China, scholars reach different conclusions on inter-county inequality. By using spatial econometric analysis, Li and Fang (2016) find significant absolute and conditional β-convergence across counties and county-level cities in China from 1992 to 2010. Cheong and Wu (2013) suggest that the income distribution of counties in China is highly likely to be persistent based on the analysis of the transitional dynamics of panel data from 1997 to 2007. However, both studies agree that spatial effect is nonnegligible in deciding convergence or divergence in county-level inequality and club convergence exists for regions in China because of geographic location and spatial proximity.

In addition to the multi-scalarity of regional inequality in China, scholars are also increasingly concerned about the underlying mechanism that drives uneven development. Several factors have been investigated to inquire their effects on regional inequality, including human capital (Fleisher, Li, and Zhao 2010), fiscal decentralization (Wang 2010; Chen and Groenewold 2013; Liu, Martinez-Vazquez, and Wu 2017), foreign investment (Yao, Wei, and Liu 2010; Yu *et al.* 2011; Li and Haynes 2012; Huang and Wei 2016; Greaney and Li 2017), trade openness and globalization (Fujita and Hu 2001; Zhang and Zhang 2003; Wan, Lu, and Chen 2007; He, Wei, and Xie 2008), fixed-asset investment (Yu and Wei 2003), state-owned enterprises (SOEs) (Fujita and Hu 2001), the ratio of heavy industry to gross output value (Kanbur and Zhang 2005), industrial agglomeration (Ge 2009; Ke 2010), total factor productivity (TFP) (Tsui 2007; Hao and Wei 2009), public investment (Zhang and Fan 2004), population growth rate (Li and Wei 2010a), economic structures and agglomeration economies (Li and Haynes 2011; Cheong and Wu 2014), and biased policy and political forces (Ho and Li 2008; He 2016).

The multi-mechanism framework, centered on the triple transitional processes of globalization, marketization, and decentralization, is developed and implemented to analyze the underlying driving forces of regional inequality in

China (Wei 2000, 2007; He, Wei, and Xie 2008). With the economic and administrative decentralization to local governments and enterprises, local authorities have been given considerable power in decision-making, resource allocation, enterprise management, revenue collection, and local spending (Qiao, Martinez-Vazquez, and Xu 2008). Local governments constantly bargain with the central government in revenue-sharing rates, expenditure responsibilities, and investment locations (Chen and Groenewold 2013). More profitable enterprises and coastal regions tend to retain more funds for investment, with the increasing investment from private and foreign sources, which leads to economic growth as well as a significant increase in regional inequality (Song 2013; Liu, Martinez-Vazquez, and Wu 2017). The revenue transfer between surplus coastal provinces and deficit inland provinces has diminished and it hampered inland development and contributed to the widening coastal–inland gap (Huang and Chen 2012). Decentralization has also put increased pressure on local governments to implement successful development policies as a measure of political performance (He and Zhu 2007). Interregional competition stimulates localities to duplicate industries that could rapidly improve local revenues or growth through a rational imitation process of successful strategies elsewhere (Thun 2004). This imitation process leads to local protectionism and economic fragmentation in China, therefore promotes the spatial dispersion of industries (Poncet 2005; He and Pan 2010).

The marketization process has reduced the role of the planned economy and the market economy has been rapidly developed in China (Fujita and Hu 2001; Wei 2002). The dominant role of state-owned enterprises (SOEs) has been challenged with a variety of ownership structures such as collective-owned enterprises (COEs), individual-owned (private) enterprises (IOEs), foreign-invested enterprise (FIEs), and shareholding enterprises (SHEs). The SOEs used to be distributed more heavily in interior regions and enjoyed subsidies and low-price raw materials during Mao's period, but were also more strictly controlled by governments, had to pay higher taxes and administrative fees, and were burdened with inefficient productivity and social services compared with non-state enterprises (Cao, Qian, and Weingast 1999). Since the reform, the advantages of SOEs have been reduced and most of them have become less competitive in a marketized economy (Wei 2004; Li and Wei 2010b). Thus, the regions used to be dominated by SOEs and slow to adapt reform policies, like the north-eastern industrial base and inland provinces targeted by the "third front project," lagged behind in economic development, while on the contrary coastal regions have been one step ahead in reforms and developed quickly based on the growth of non-SOEs and the agglomeration of FDI (Hao and Wei 2010; He, Zhou, and Zhu 2017). Besides the formation of mixed ownership structure and competition mechanism in the market economy, the marketization process has also lifted the limits on factor mobility and commodity exchanges. The central government has eased labor migration, which used to be constrained by the household registration system (*hukou* system) to reallocate the abundant rural labor force to higher wage areas aligning the coastal line (Zhang and Tan 2007; Fang 2010).

Under globalization, coastal areas have been provided with preferential policies. A series of reform policies in investment, finance, and trade were implemented and provided more decentralized and more open policies to the coastal region (Yao 2009). Special economic zones (SEZ), coastal open cities, and numerous economic and technological development districts have been established in coastal China to provide private and foreign-invested firms with a number of benefits to make them flourish (Yeung, Lee, and Kee 2009). FDI promotion policies cover a wide range of areas including the ownership, duration, sector choice, size, location, tax rate, land use, management, employment and wage system, pricing, and financing and remittance of profits. Again, the coastal provinces are unevenly favored by FDI and export-oriented industries due to factors like preferential policies from central government in dealing with foreign investment, currency exchange, and foreign trade, advantages in location, resources, networks, infrastructure, labor forces, and local policies, as well as the long-established closer kinship ties with foreign countries and investors. Empiric studies reveal that globalization, articulated by the unbalanced concentration of FDI and multinational enterprises in the coastal region, contributes significantly to the widening regional inequality since the reform (Zhang and Zhang 2003; Wan, Lu, and Chen 2007; Lessmann 2013; Greaney and Li 2017).

Scholars also find that the uneven industrialization process and China's transition from an agricultural society to the industrial society is an important factor in regional inequality. Huang *et al.* (2003) find that the development in the secondary sector contributes half of the overall inequality in China. Kanbur and Zhang (2005) identify the ratio of heavy industry to gross output as one of the three key policy variables in China's regional inequality. Tsui (2007) shows that the uneven provincial distribution of secondary industry sector share led to regional disparities in growth and interprovincial inequality in China. Li and Haynes (2011) find that the differential rate of transition in economic structure toward the secondary and tertiary sectors has contributed to the widening gap between the coastal and the inland provinces. Cheong and Wu (2014) validate that industrialization is the largest contributor to regional inequality and the high value-added industries contribute the most to the overall regional inequality.

2.3 Conclusion

This chapter has reviewed mainstream theoretical perspectives regarding the evolution of regional inequality and studies of regional inequality in China. While neoclassical growth models suggest convergence in income levels and growth rates, empirical findings are inclusive. While regional inequality declines in some more developed countries, regional polarization and poverty persist in many developing countries and regions. Income inequality has even intensified in many developed countries since the recent global financial crisis, which has reignited the debate on inequality. Theories of regional inequality have been dominated by neoclassical growth theories, and have been further advanced by new convergence and new economic geography theories. Alternative theories of regional inequality have also enriched our thinking on regional inequality, including dependence, the world system, and Marxian political economy theories. Western theories of regional inequality have been heavily criticized by radical and critical theories, including post-colonialist and post-structuralist theories.

Geographers have long been actively involved in the study of regional inequality. While earlier work followed regionalism and neoclassical economics, the field has also been heavily influenced by alternative thinking and even turned to radical/critical theories in the 1970s and 1980s. The notion of divergence and new economic geography models have appealed to geographers. However, geographers have been cautious with the ways geography is being treated in mainstream economic and sociological theories, largely as a unit of analysis. They have criticized neoclassical theories of regional inequality for treating space as a container, a unit of analysis, and adopting a black-box approach based on the assumption of free market by ignoring institutions and agents of regional development and spatiality of regional inequality. Other theoretical perspectives, such as institutional and evolutionary economics and the political-economy approach, are integrated into recent studies but rarely connected to the sources of regional inequality in a rigorous manner.

More recent work has emphasized the role of geography and institutions in regional development and inequality by emphasizing notions of space, place, scale, network, mobility, and complexity. With the aid of GIS spatial analysis techniques, patterns of regional inequality in China and its dynamics were also analyzed in greater details. Scholars have scaled down to provinces to study intra-provincial inequality. More attention has also been paid to the time dimension and effects of globalization, including the recent global financial crisis, on regional inequality.

In this book, by adopting an eclectic approach to regional inequality, we hold that both divergence or convergence schools might have missed some important features of regional inequality. We place the notion of spatiality at the center of our academic inquiry. The book also adopts a multi-scale and multi-mechanism framework to guide empirical studies of regional inequality in China in the following chapters.

References

Acemoglu, D., S. Johnson, and J. A. Robinson. 2002. Reversal of fortune: Geography and institutions in the making of the modern world income distribution. *Quarterly Journal of Economics* 117 (4): 1231–1294.

Aghion, P., and P. Howitt. 1992. A model of growth through creative destruction. *Econometrica* 60: 323–351.

Agnew, J., and S. Crobridge. 2002. *Mastering space: Hegemony, territory and international political economy*. London: Routledge.

Alonso, W. 1980. Five bell shapes in development. *Papers in Regional Science* 45 (1): 5–16.

Amin, A., and N. Thrift. 1994. Living in the global. *Globalization, Institutions, and Regional Development in Europe*: 1–22.

Amos, O. M. 1990. Growth pole cycles: A synthesis of growth pole and long wave theories. *The Review of Regional Studies* 20 (1): 37.

Anselin, L., and S. Rey. 1991. Properties of tests for spatial dependence in linear regression models. *Geographical Analysis* 23 (2): 112–131.

Armstrong, H., and J. Taylor. 2009. *Regional economics and policy.* 3rd ed., reprint. Malden, MA: Blackwell.

Barca, F., P. McCann, and A. Rodríguez-Pose. 2012. The case for regional development intervention: Place-based versus place-neutral approaches. *Journal of Regional Science* 52 (1): 134–152.

Barrios, S., and E. Strobl. 2009. The dynamics of regional inequalities. *Regional Science and Urban Economics* 39 (5): 575–591.

Barro, R. J. 2015. Convergence and modernisation. *The Economic Journal* 125 (585): 911–942.

Barro, R. J., and X. Sala-i-Martin. 1992. Convergence. *Journal of Political Economy* 100 (2): 223–251.

Barro, R. J., and X. Sala-i-Martin. 1995. *Economic Growth*. New York: McGraw-Hill.

Barro, R. J., X. Sala-i-Martin, O. J. Blanchard, and R. E. Hall. 1991. Convergence across states and regions. *Brookings Papers on Economic Activity*: 107–182.

Booth, D. E. 1986. Long waves and uneven regional growth. *Southern Economic Journal*: 448–460.

Borts, G. H., and J. L. Stein. 1964. *Economic growth in a free market*. New York: Columbia University Press.

Börzel, T. A., and T. Risse. 2016. *The Oxford handbook of comparative regionalism*. Oxford: Oxford University Press.

Boschma, R. 2005. Proximity and innovation: A critical assessment. *Regional Studies* 39 (1): 61–74.

Boschma, R., and S. Iammarino. 2009. Related variety, trade linkages, and regional growth in Italy. *Economic Geography* 85 (3): 289–311.

Bosker, M., and H. Garretsen. 2010. Trade costs in empirical new economic geography. *Papers in Regional Science* 89 (3): 485–511.

Brown, L. A., and V. A. Lawson. 1989. Polarization reversal, migration related shifts in human resource profiles, and spatial growth policies: A Venezuelan study. *International Regional Science Review* 12 (2): 165–188.

Cao, Y., Y. Qian, and B. R. Weingast. 1999. From federalism, Chinese style to privatization, Chinese style. *Economics of Transition* 7 (1): 103–131.

Chen, A. 2010. Reducing China's regional disparities: Is there a growth cost? *China Economic Review* 21 (1): 2–13.

Chen, A., and N. Groenewold. 2013. The national and regional effects of fiscal decentralisation in China. *The Annals of Regional Science* 51 (3): 731–760.

Chen, J., and B. M. Fleisher. 1996. Regional income inequality and economic growth in China. *Journal of Comparative Economics* 22 (2): 141–164.

Cheong, T. S., and Y. Wu. 2013. Regional disparity, transitional dynamics and convergence in China. *Journal of Asian Economics* 29 (Supplement C): 1–14.

Cheong, T. S., and Y. Wu. 2014. The impacts of structural transformation and industrial upgrading on regional inequality in China. *China Economic Review* 31 (Supplement C): 339–350.

Corbridge, S. 1986. *Capitalist world development: A critique of radical development geography*. Boston: Rowman & Littlefield.

Crozet, M., and P. Koenig. 2005. *The cohesion vs growth tradeoff: Evidence from EU regions (1980–2000)*. Louvain-la-Neuve: European Regional Science Association (ERSA).

Dai, Q., X. Ye, Y. D. Wei, Y. Ning, and S. Dai. 2017. Geography, ethnicity and regional inequality in Guangxi Zhuang Autonomous Region, China. *Applied Spatial Analysis and Policy*: 1–24.

Duncan, S. S. 1989. Uneven development and the difference that space makes. *Geoforum* 20 (2): 131–139.

Evans, P. B. 1979. *Dependent development: The alliance of multinational, state, and local capital in Brazil*. Princeton, NJ: Princeton University Press.

Ezcurra, R., and M. Rapún. 2006. Regional disparities and national development revisited: The case of Western Europe. *European Urban and Regional Studies* 13 (4): 355–369.

Fan, C. C. 1997. Uneven development and beyond: Regional development theory in post-Mao China. *International Journal of Urban and Regional Research* 21 (4): 620–639.

Fan, C. C., and M. Sun. 2008. Regional inequality in China, 1978–2006. *Eurasian Geography and Economics* 49 (1): 1–18.

Fang, C. C. 2010. The formation and evolution of China's migrant labor policy. *Narratives of Chinese Economic Reforms: How Does China Cross the River?* 5: 71.

Fingleton, B. 1999. Estimates of time to economic convergence: An analysis of regions of the European Union. *International Regional Science Review* 22 (1): 5–34.

Fleisher, B., H. Li, and M. Q. Zhao. 2010. Human capital, economic growth, and regional inequality in China. *Journal of Development Economics* 92 (2): 215–231.

Frank, A. G. 1967. *Capitalism and underdevelopment in Latin America*. New York: NYU Press.

Frenken, K., F. Van Oort, and T. Verburg. 2007. Related variety, unrelated variety and regional economic growth. *Regional Studies* 41 (5): 685–697.

Friedmann, J. 1966. *Regional development policy: A case study of Venezuela*. Cambridge: MIT Press.

Friedmann, J. 1973. *Urbanization, planning, and national development*. London: Sage Publications.

Friedmann, J., and R. Bloch. 1990. American exceptionalism in regional planning, 1933–2000. *International Journal of Urban and Regional Research* 14 (4): 576–601.

Friedmann, J., and M. Douglass. 1978. *Agropolitan development: Towards a new strategy for regional planning in Asia*. Los Angeles: University of California.

Friedmann, J., and C. Weaver. 1980. *Territory and function: The evolution of regional planning*. Berkeley, CA: University of California Press.

Fujita, M., and D. P. Hu. 2001. Regional disparity in China 1985–1994: The effects of globalization and economic liberalization. *Annals of Regional Science* 35 (1): 3–37.

Fujita, M., P. R. Krugman, A. J. Venables, and M. Fujita. 1999. *The spatial economy: Cities, regions and international trade*. London: Wiley Online Library.

Gao, J., Y. Liu, J. Chen, and Y. Cai. 2019. Demystifying the geography of income inequality in rural China: A transitional framework. *Journal of Rural Studies*. https://doi.org/10.1016/j.jrurstud.2019.01.010

Gardiner, B., R. Martin, and P. Tyler. 2011. Does spatial agglomeration increase national growth? Some evidence from Europe. *Journal of Economic Geography* 11 (6): 979–1006.

Ge, Y. 2009. Globalization and industry agglomeration in China. *World Development* 37 (3): 550–559.

Gilbert, A., and J. Gugler. 1992. Cities, poverty and development: Urbanization in the third world. In *Cities, poverty and development: Urbanization in the third world.* Oxford: Oxford University Press.

Greaney, T. M., and Y. Li. 2017. Multinational enterprises and regional inequality in China. *Journal of Asian Economics* 48 (Supplement C): 120–133.

Griffin, K. 1973. Underdevelopment in history. In Charles K. Weber (ed.) *The political economy of development and underdevelopment*, 69. New York: Random House.

Gu, C., J. Shen, K. Y. Wong, and F. Zhen. 2001. Regional polarization under the socialist-market system since 1978: A case study of Guangdong province in south China. *Environment and Planning A* 33 (1): 97–119.

Gu, J., S. Zhou, and X. Ye. 2016. Uneven regional development under balanced development strategies: Space–time paths of regional development in Guangdong, China. *Tijdschrift voor economische en sociale geografie.*

Hansen, N. M. 1981. Development from above. In *Development from above or below? The dialectics of regional planning in developing countries*, 15–38. New York: John Wiley.

Hao, R., and Z. Wei. 2009. Sources of income differences across Chinese provinces during the reform period: A development accounting exercise. *Developing Economies* 47 (1): 1–29.

Hao, R., and Z. Wei. 2010. Fundamental causes of inland-coastal income inequality in post-reform China. *Annals of Regional Science* 45 (1): 181–206.

Harris, S. E. 1957. *International and interregional economics.* New York: McGraw-Hill.

Harvey, D. 1975. The geography of capitalist accumulation: A reconstruction of the Marxian theory. *Antipode* 7 (2): 9–21.

Haughton, G. 2012. *Regional development and spatial planning in an enlarged European Union.* Farnham, UK: Ashgate Publishing, Ltd.

He, C., and F. Pan. 2010. Economic transition, dynamic externalities and city-industry growth in China. *Urban Studies* 47 (1): 121–144.

He, C., Y. D. Wei, and X. Xie. 2008. Globalization, institutional change, and industrial location: Economic transition and industrial concentration in China. *Regional Studies* 42 (7): 923–945.

He, C., Y. Zhou, and S. Zhu. 2017. Firm dynamics, institutional context, and regional inequality of productivity in China. *Geographical Review* 107 (2): 296–316.

He, C., and S. Zhu. 2007. Economic transition and industrial restructuring in China: Structural convergence or divergence? *Post-Communist Economies* 19 (3): 317–342.

He, Q. 2016. Do political factors cause the regional inequality in the reform-era China? *Review of Development Economics* 20 (2): 387–398.

He, S., M. M. Bayrak, and H. Lin. 2017. A comparative analysis of multi-scalar regional inequality in China. *Geoforum* 78: 1–11.

He, S., C. Fang, and W. Zhang. 2017. A geospatial analysis of multi-scalar regional inequality in China and in metropolitan regions. *Applied Geography* 88: 199–212.

Herrerías, M. J., and J. O. Monfort. 2015. Testing stochastic convergence across Chinese provinces, 1952–2008. *Regional Studies* 49 (4): 485–501.

Ho, C.-Y., and D. Li. 2008. Rising regional inequality in China: Policy regimes and structural changes. *Papers in Regional Science* 87 (2): 245–259.

Huang, B., and K. Chen. 2012. Are intergovernmental transfers in China equalizing? *China Economic Review* 23 (3): 534–551.

Huang, H., and Y. Wei. 2016. Spatial inequality of foreign direct investment in China: Institutional change, agglomeration economies, and market access. *Applied Geography* 69 (Supplement C): 99–111.

Huang, H., and Y. D. Wei. 2019. The spatial–temporal hierarchy of inequality in urban China: A prefectural city-level study. *The Professional Geographer*, 71 (3): 391–407.

Huang, J.-T., C.-C. Kuo, and A.-P. Kao. 2003. The inequality of regional economic development in China between 1991 and 2001. *Journal of Chinese Economic and Business Studies* 1 (3): 273–285.

Iammarino, S., A. Rodriguez-Pose, and M. Storper. 2018. Regional inequality in Europe: Evidence, theory and policy implications. *Journal of Economic Geography* 19 (2): 273–298.

Jian, T. L., J. D. Sachs, and A. M. Warner. 1996. Trends in regional inequality in China. *China Economic Review* 7 (1): 1–21.

Johnson, P. A. 2000. A nonparametric analysis of income convergence across the US states. *Economics Letters* 69 (2): 219–223.

Kanbur, R., and X. B. Zhang. 2005. Fifty years of regional inequality in China: A journey through central planning, reform, and openness. *Review of Development Economics* 9 (1): 87–106.

Ke, S. 2010. Agglomeration, productivity, and spatial spillovers across Chinese cities. *The Annals of Regional Science* 45 (1): 157–179.

Kim, S. 2008. *Spatial inequality and economic development: Theories, facts, and policies.* Washington, DC: World Bank Publications.

Knox, P., J. A. Agnew, and L. McCarthy. 2014. *The geography of the world economy.* London: Routledge.

Krebs, G. 1982. Regional inequalities during the process of national economic development: A critical approach. *Geoforum* 13 (2): 71–81.

Krugman, P. 1991. Increasing returns and economic geography. *Journal of Political Economy* 99 (3): 483–499.

Krugman, P. 1997. *Development, geography, and economic theory.* Boston: MIT Press.

Krugman, P. 2011. The new economic geography, now middle-aged. *Regional Studies* 45 (1): 1–7.

Krugman, P., and A. J. Venables. 1995. Globalization and the inequality of nations. *Quarterly Journal of Economics* 110 (4): 857–880.

Kuznets, S., and J. T. Murphy. 1966. *Modern economic growth: Rate, structure, and spread.* New Haven, CT: Yale University Press.

Lau, C. K. M. 2010. New evidence about regional income divergence in China. *China Economic Review* 21 (2): 293–309.

Lessmann, C. 2013. Foreign direct investment and regional inequality: A panel data analysis. *China Economic Review* 24: 129–149.

Lessmann, C. 2014. Spatial inequality and development: Is there an inverted-U relationship? *Journal of Development Economics* 106: 35–51.

Li, C., and J. Gibson. 2013. Rising regional inequality in China: Fact or artifact? *World Development* 47: 16–29.

Li, G., and C. Fang. 2014. Analyzing the multi-mechanism of regional inequality in China. *The Annals of Regional Science* 52 (1): 155–182.

Li, G., and C. Fang. 2016. Spatial econometric analysis of urban and county-level economic growth convergence in China. *International Regional Science Review* 41 (4): 410–447.

Li, H., and K. E. Haynes. 2011. Economic structure and regional disparity in China: Beyond the Kuznets transition. *International Regional Science Review* 34 (2): 157–190.

Li, Y. 2012. The spatial variation of China's regional inequality in human development. *Regional Science Policy & Practice* 4 (3): 263–278.

Li, Y., and Y. Wei. 2010a. A spatial-temporal analysis of health care and mortality inequalities in China. *Eurasian Geography and Economics* 51 (6): 767–787.

Li, Y., and Y. H. D. Wei. 2010b. The spatial-temporal hierarchy of regional inequality of China. *Applied Geography* 30 (3): 303–316.

Li, Y., and Y. D. Wei. 2014. Multidimensional inequalities in health care distribution in provincial China: A case study of Henan Province. *Tijdschrift voor economische en sociale geografie* 105 (1): 91–106.

Liao, F. H., and Y. D. Wei. 2012. Dynamics, space, and regional inequality in provincial China: A case study of Guangdong Province. *Applied Geography* 35 (1): 71–83.

Liao, F. H., and Y. D. Wei. 2015. Space, scale, and regional inequality in provincial China: A spatial filtering approach. *Applied Geography* 61: 94–104.

Lipshitz, G. 1992. Divergence versus convergence in regional development. *Journal of Planning Literature* 7 (2): 123–138.

Lipton, M. 1977. *Why poor people stay poor: A study of urban bias in world development*. Canberra: Australian University Press.

Liu, B., M. Xu, J. Wang, L. Zhao, and S. Xie. 2019. Spatio-temporal evolution of regional inequality and contribution decomposition of economic growth: A case study of Jiangsu Province, China. *Papers in Regional Science* 98 (3): 1485–1498.

Liu, Y., J. Martinez-Vazquez, and A. M. Wu. 2017. Fiscal decentralization, equalization, and intra-provincial inequality in China. *International Tax and Public Finance* 24 (2): 248–281.

Lu, L., and Y. D. Wei. 2007. Domesticating globalisation, new economic spaces and regional polarisation in Guangdong Province, China. *Tijdschrift voor economische en sociale geografie* 98 (2): 225–244.

Magrini, S. 1999. The evolution of income disparities among the regions of the European Union. *Regional Science and Urban Economics* 29 (2): 257–281.

Mankiw, N. G., D. Romer, and D. N. Weil. 1992. A contribution to the empirics of economic growth. *Quarterly Journal of Economics* 107 (2): 407–437.

Martin, R. 2015. Rebalancing the spatial economy: The challenge for regional theory. *Territory, Politics, Governance* 3 (3): 235–272.

Massey, D. 1985. New directions in space. In D. Gregory and J. Urry (eds.) *Social relations and spatial structures*, Critical Human Geography, 9–19. London: Macmillan Education UK.

Maxwell, P., and J. C. Hite. 1992. The recent divergence of regional per capita incomes: some evidence from Australia. *Growth and Change* 23 (1): 37–53.

McCann, P. 2007. Observational equivalence? Regional studies and regional science. *Regional Studies* 41 (9): 1209–1222.

McCann, P. 2014. Schools of thought on economic geography, institutions, and development. In M. M. Fischer and P. Nijkamp (eds.) *Handbook of Regional Science*, 527–538. Berlin, Heidelberg: Springer Berlin Heidelberg.

Mera, K. 1978. Population concentration and regional income disparities: A comparative analysis of Japan and Korea. In N. Hansen (ed.) *Human settlement systems*, 155–176. Cambridge: Ballinger Publishing Company.

Myrdal, G. 1957. *Economic theory and under-developed regions*. London: Methuen.

North, D. C. 1990. *Institutions, institutional change and economic performance*. Cambridge: Cambridge University Press.

Norton, R. D., and J. Rees. 1979. The product cycle and the spatial decentralization of American manufacturing. *Regional Studies* 13 (2): 141–151.

Palivos, T., and P. Wang. 1996. Spatial agglomeration and endogenous growth. *Regional Science and Urban Economics* 26 (6): 645–669.

Pedroni, P., and J. Y. Yao. 2006. Regional income divergence in China. *Journal of Asian Economics* 17 (2): 294–315.

Peet, R. 1975. Inequality and poverty: A Marxist-geographic theory. *Annals of the Association of American Geographers* 65 (4): 564–571.

Perroux, F. 1950. Economic space: Theory and applications. *Quarterly Journal of Economics* 64 (1): 89–104.

Pesaran, M. H. 2007. A simple panel unit root test in the presence of cross-section dependence. *Journal of Applied Econometrics* 22 (2): 265–312.

Phillips, P. C., and D. Sul. 2007. Transition modeling and econometric convergence tests. *Econometrica* 75 (6): 1771–1855.

Pike, A., A. Rodríguez-Pose, and J. Tomaney. 2016. Shifting horizons in local and regional development. *Regional Studies*: 1–12.

Poncet, S. 2005. A fragmented China: Measures and determinants of Chinese domestic market disintegration. *Review of International Economics* 13 (3): 409–430.

Porter, M. E. 1990. The competitive advantage of nations. *Harvard Business Review* 68 (2): 73–93.

Puga, D. 1999. The rise and fall of regional inequalities. *European Economic Review* 43 (2): 303–334.

Putnam, R. D. 2001. *Bowling alone: The collapse and revival of American community*. New York: Simon & Schuster.

Putnam, R. D., R. Leonardi, and R. Y. Nanetti. 1994. *Making democracy work: Civic traditions in modern Italy*. Princeton, NJ: Princeton University Press.

Qiao, B., J. Martinez-Vazquez, and Y. Xu. 2008. The tradeoff between growth and equity in decentralization policy: China's experience. *Journal of Development Economics* 86 (1): 112–128.

Quah, D. 1993. Empirical cross-section dynamics in economic growth. *European Economic Review* 37 (2–3): 426–434.

Quah, D. 1996a. Regional convergence clusters across Europe. *European Economic Review* 40 (3): 951–958.

Quah, D. 1996b. Twin peaks: Growth and convergence in models of distribution dynamics. *The Economic Journal*: 1045–1055.

Rey, S. J. 2016. Space–time patterns of rank concordance: Local indicators of mobility association with application to spatial income inequality dynamics. *Annals of the American Association of Geographers* 106 (4): 788–803.

Rey, S. J., and M. V. Janikas. 2005. Regional convergence, inequality, and space. *Journal of Economic Geography* 5 (2): 155–176.

Rey, S. J., and B. D. Montouri. 1999. US regional income convergence: A spatial econometric perspective. *Regional Studies* 33 (2): 143–156.

Rey, S. J., and M. L. Sastré Gutiérrez. 2015. Comparative spatial inequality dynamics: The case of Mexico and the United States. *Applied Geography* 61: 70–80.

Richardson, W. 1973. *Regional growth theory*. London: Macmillan.

Richardson, W. 1976. Growth pole spillovers: The dynamics of backwash and spread. *Regional Studies* 10 (1): 1–9.

Richardson, W. 1978. Growth centers, rural development and national urban policy: A defense. *International Regional Science Review* 3 (2): 133–152.

Richardson, W. 1980. Polarization reversal in developing countries. *Papers in Regional Science* 45 (1): 67–85.

Rodríguez-Pose, A. 2012. Trade and regional inequality. *Economic Geography* 88 (2): 109–136.

Rodríguez-Pose, A. 2013. Do institutions matter for regional development? *Regional Studies* 47 (7): 1034–1047.

Rostow, W. W. 1960. The stages of economic growth. *The Economic History Review* 12 (1): 1–16.

Sabel, C. F. 1984. *The second industrial divide: Possibilities for prosperity.* New York: Basic Books.

Sakamoto, H., and N. Islam. 2008. Convergence across Chinese provinces: An analysis using Markov transition matrix. *China Economic Review* 19 (1): 66–79.

Sala-i-Martin, X. X. 1996. The classical approach to convergence analysis. *The Economic Journal*: 1019–1036.

Saxenian, A. 1994. *Regional advantage: Culture and competition in Silicon Valley and Route 128.* Cambridge, MA: Harvard University Press.

Scott, A. J., and M. Storper. 1987. High technology industry and regional development: A theoretical critique and reconstruction. *International Social Science Journal* 39: 215–232.

Sheng, R., and S. L. Liu. 2018. Evolution on regional disparities in China from 2000 to 2012: Evidence from 74 cities within three mega-urban regions along Yangtze River. *Quality & Quantity* 52: 1989–2006. https://doi.org/10.1007/s11135-017-0560-1

Smith, N. 1984. *Uneven development: Nature, capital, and the production of space.* Athens. GA: University of Georgia Press.

Soja, E. W. 1980. The socio-spatial dialectic. *Annals of the Association of American geographers* 70 (2): 207–225.

Soja, E. W. 2009. Regional planning and development theories. In *International Encyclopedia of Human Geography*, 259–270. London: Elsevier Ltd.

Song, Y. 2013. Rising Chinese regional income inequality: The role of fiscal decentralization. *China Economic Review* 27: 294–309.

Stöhr, W., and F. Tödtling. 1979. Spatial equity: Some anti-theses to current regional development doctrine. In *Spatial inequalities and regional development*, 133–160. Berlin: Springer.

Storper, M. 1989. The geographical foundations and social regulation of flexible production complexes. In *The power of geography: how territory shapes social life* (RLE Social & Cultural Geography), 37–56. London: Routledge.

Sun, W., X. Lin, Y. Liang, and L. Li. 2016. Regional inequality in underdeveloped areas: A case study of Guizhou Province in China. *Sustainability* 8 (11): 1141.

Tabuchi, T. 1988. Interregional income differentials and migration: Their interrelationships. *Regional Studies* 22 (1): 1–10.

Thun, E. 2004. Keeping up with the Jones': Decentralization, policy imitation, and industrial development in China. *World Development* 32 (8): 1289–1308.

Tsui, K. 2007. Forces shaping China's interprovincial inequality. *Review of Income and Wealth* 53 (1): 60–92.

Vining Jr., D. R., and A. Strauss. 1977. A demonstration that the current deconcentration of population in the United States is a clean break with the past. *Environment and Planning A* 9 (7): 751–758.

Wallerstein, I. 1979. *The capitalist world-economy.* Cambridge: Cambridge University Press.

Wan, G., M. Lu, and Z. Chen. 2007. Globalization and regional income inequality: Empirical evidence from within China. *Review of Income and Wealth* 53 (1): 35–59.

Wang, E. 2010. Fiscal decentralization and revenue/expenditure disparities in China. *Eurasian Geography and Economics* 51 (6): 744–766.

Wang, L., and J. Shen. 2017. Comparative analysis of urban competitiveness in the Yangtze River Delta and Pearl River Delta regions of China, 2000–2010. *Applied Spatial Analysis* 10: 401–419. https://doi.org/10.1007/s12061-016-9210-6

Wang, S. 2007. *The great transformation in China: From economic policy to social policy*. Paper presented at the Conference on the Future of U.S.–China Relations, University of Southern California.

Wei, Y. H. D. 1999. Regional inequality in China. *Progress in Human Geography* 23 (1): 49–59.

Wei, Y. H. D. 2000. *Regional development in China: States, globalization and inequality*. London: Routledge.

Wei, Y. H. D. 2002. Multiscale and multimechanisms of regional inequality in China: Implications for regional policy. *Journal of Contemporary China* 11 (30): 109–124.

Wei, Y. H. D. 2004. Trajectories of ownership transformation in China: Implications for uneven regional development. *Eurasian Geography and Economics* 45 (2): 90–113.

Wei, Y. H. D. 2007. Regional development in China: Transitional institutions, embedded globalization, and hybrid economies. *Eurasian Geography and Economics* 48 (1): 16–36.

Wei, Y. H. D. 2015. Spatiality of regional inequality. *Applied Geography* 61 (Supplement C): 1–10.

Wei, Y. H. D., and C. C. Fang. 2000. Regional inequality in China: A case study of Jiangsu Province. *Professional Geographer* 52 (3): 455–469.

Wei, Y. D., and C. Fang. 2006. Geographical and structural constraints of regional development in western China: A study of Gansu Province. *Issues and Studies – English Edition* 42: 131.

Wei, Y. H. D., and S. Kim. 2002. Widening inter-county inequality in Jiangsu Province, China, 1950–95. *Journal of Development Studies* 38 (6): 142–164.

Wei, Y., and L. Ma. 1996. Changing patterns of spatial inequality in China, 1952–1990. *Third World Planning Review* 18 (2): 177.

Wei, Y. H. D., and X. Ye. 2004. Regional inequality in China: A case study of Zhejiang Province. *Tijdschrift Voor Economische En Sociale Geografie* 95 (1): 44–60.

Wei, Y. H. D., and X. Ye. 2009. Beyond convergence: Space, scale, and regional inequality in China. *Tijdschrift voor economische en sociale geografie* 100 (1): 59–80.

Wei, Y. H. D., D. Yu, and X. Chen. 2011. Scale, agglomeration, and regional inequality in provincial China. *Tijdschrift voor economische en sociale geografie* 102 (4): 406–425.

Westlund, H. 2006. *Social capital in the knowledge economy: Theory and empirics*. Berlin: Springer.

Williamson, J. G. 1965. Regional inequality and the process of national development: A description of the patterns. *Economic Development and Cultural Change* 13 (4): 1–84.

Wu, C., F. Ren, X. Ye, X. Liang, and Q. Du. 2019. Spatiotemporal analysis of multiscale income mobility in China. *Applied Geography* 111: 102060.

Wu, M., and B. Chen. 2016. Assignment of provincial officials based on economic performance: Evidence from China. *China Economic Review* 38 (Supplement C): 60–75.

Yao, S., K. Wei, and A. Liu. 2010. Economic growth, foreign investment and regional inequality in China. In *China and the World Economy*, 194–225. London: Palgrave Macmillan.

Yao, S., and Z. Zhang. 2001. On regional inequality and diverging clubs: A case study of contemporary China. *Journal of Comparative Economics* 29 (3): 466–484.

Yao, Y. 2009. The political economy of government policies toward regional inequality in China. In *Reshaping economic geography in East Asia*, 218–240. Washington, DC: World Bank.

Ye, X., and S. Rey. 2013. A framework for exploratory space–time analysis of economic data. *The Annals of Regional Science* 50 (1): 315–339.

Ye, X., and Y. D. Wei. 2005. Geospatial analysis of regional development in China: The case of Zhejiang Province and the Wenzhou model. *Eurasian Geography and Economics* 46 (6): 445–464.

Ye, X., and Y. Xie. 2012. Re-examination of Zipf's law and urban dynamic in China: A regional approach. *The Annals of Regional Science*, 49 (1): 135–156.

Ye, X., L. Ma, K. Ye, J. Chen, and Q. Xie. 2017. Analysis of regional inequality from sectoral structure, spatial policy and economic development: A case study of Chongqing, China. *Sustainability* 9 (4): 633.

Yeung, Y., J. Lee, and G. Kee. 2009. China's special economic zones at 30. *Eurasian Geography and Economics* 50 (2): 222–240.

Yu, D.-L. 2006. Spatially varying development mechanisms in the Greater Beijing Area: A geographically weighted regression investigation. *The Annals of Regional Science* 40 (1): 173–190.

Yu, D. L., and Y. H. D. Wei. 2003. Analyzing regional inequality in post-Mao China in a GIS environment. *Eurasian Geography and Economics* 44 (7): 514–534.

Yu, D., and Y. D. Wei. 2008. Spatial data analysis of regional development in Greater Beijing, China, in a GIS environment. *Papers in Regional Science* 87 (1): 97–117.

Yu, H., Y. Liu, C. Liu, F. Fan. 2018. Spatiotemporal variation and inequality in China's economic resilience across cities and urban agglomerations. *Sustainability* 10: 4754.

Yu, K., X. Xin, P. Guo, and X. Liu. 2011. Foreign direct investment and China's regional income inequality. *Economic Modelling* 28 (3): 1348–1353.

Yue, W., Y. Zhang, X. Ye, Y. Cheng, and M. R. Leipnik. 2014. Dynamics of multi-scale intra-provincial regional inequality in Zhejiang, China. *Sustainability* 6 (9): 5763–5784.

Zhang, J., and W. Deng. 2016. Multiscale spatio-temporal dynamics of economic development in an interprovincial boundary region: Junction area of Tibetan Plateau, Hengduan Mountain, Yungui Plateau and Sichuan Basin, Southwestern China Case. *Sustainability* 8 (3): 215.

Zhang, X., and S. Fan. 2004. Public investment and regional inequality in rural China. *Agricultural Economics* 30 (2): 89–100.

Zhang, X., and K.-Y. Tan. 2007. Incremental reform and distortions in China's product and factor markets. *The World Bank Economic Review* 21 (2): 279–299.

Zhang, X., and K. H. Zhang. 2003. How does globalisation affect regional inequality within a developing country? Evidence from China. *Journal of Development Studies* 39 (4): 47–67.

Zhang, Y., D. Tong, and X. Liang. 2018. New perspective on regional inequality: Theory and evidence from Guangdong, China. *Journal of Urban Planning and Development* 144 (1): 04018002.

3   Multi-scalar patterns of regional inequality

In Chapter 2, we argued that regional inequality in China is multi-scalar in nature and the scales are socially constructed in essence (Wei 2015). Drawing upon a multi-scalar perspective, this chapter carries out a comprehensive empirical analysis of regional (economic) inequality in China. We first analyze the changes and the level of regional inequality at the provincial scale by using a long-run (60 years) economic dataset covering both pre-reform and post-reform eras. Through the application of a three-stage nested spatial decomposition technique, we further research the patterns of spatial inequality at the county, prefecture, and provincial levels, following the Chinese administrative hierarchy. The chapter also compares the distributional dynamics and ergodic distributions of regional income at multiple scales of province, prefectures, and counties, as well as in the four economic regions. The last section summarizes the findings and policy implications.

3.1 Data and methodology

As mentioned in previous chapters, research on regional inequality in China faces challenges with respect to data availability and quality. Publications in the 1970s and 1980s were constrained by the incomplete dataset that could not even cover all of the Chinese provinces (Lyons 1991). Publications in the 1990s focused on the gross value of industrial and agricultural output (GVIAO) rather than GDP, which may result in the problem of double counting (Fan and Sun 2008).

GDP is still regarded as the best indicator in the studies of regional (economic or income) inequality in China, as it provides the most continuity data that covers a longer time span. Specifically, due to the lack of consistent deflators, studies have to employ current-price or nominal GDP data. As wealthier places appear to have a higher cost of living and using nominal GDP data could overestimate the degree of regional inequality (Brandt and Holz 2006). Based on the study done by Li and Gibson (2013), if interprovincial inequality is measured using nominal GDP data, there would be a 20–40% increase of the Theil index values. Recent work has been able to employ nationwide and comparable price deflators at the provincial level across a longer period, but intra-provincial studies are largely constrained by the nominal GDP data. Constant prices are comparable over time so are more often used in the study of regional inequality. In this chapter, the GDP data were converted to the 1978 constant price.

Similarly, the key indicator of economic development, i.e., GDP per capita, is often calculated using the *hukou* (household registration system) population, which refers to the population with residence status in China's household registration system. Because coastal provinces have hosted a large number of non-*hukou* migrants, the degree of regional inequality could be overestimated. Some studies demonstrated the calculation using different population data could even change the judgment of divergence or convergence (Li and Gibson 2013). However, because the registered population has better access to jobs and public services, the two types of population might be complementary. Inequality between *hukou* and residential populations actually reflects the nature of China's institutionally created inequality (Wei 2017). With respect to the Chinese population data, a set of data using statistical yearbooks of China on GDP and the *hukou* population were compiled for the study period of 1952–2016. Recent literature suggests a *hukou* population-based GDPPC may overestimate the level of regional inequality. While the permanent population or resident population (hereafter) represents the real population residing in a city, the *hukou* population is also important, since it represents the people living in cities who can fully benefit from services provided by local governments. Most rural migrants have their household registration in the countryside, and they are largely excluded from formal jobs and public services in the cities where they live. For the analysis of regional inequality in the post-reform era, we employ both *hukou* and resident population data to explore multi-scalar characteristics of regional inequality in China.

Because GDP and population statistics are aggregated using administrative boundaries, studies on regional inequality have recognized the influence of using different administrative boundaries and regional participation schema on inequality measures (He *et al.* 2016). Li and Wei (2010) compared the regional inequality with and without consideration of centrally administered municipalities, and results showed that regional inequality has dropped down significantly after removing the four centrally administered municipalities of Beijing, Shanghai, Tianjin, and Chongqing. This issue could be more pressing for finer-scale investigations as the economic transition has strong effects on changes in administrative boundaries. More recent work has documented that different findings regarding the extent of regional inequality could be attributable to different spatial partitioning systems, because there has been a trend of merging suburban counties into central urban districts since the early 2000s (Zhang and Wu 2006; He *et al.* 2016).

In this chapter, we draw upon a comprehensive dataset of economic data covering the 31 provincial-level administrative units (hereafter provinces), 341 prefectures, and 2,179 counties in China (Figure 3.1). At the provincial level, we employ a dataset over the period of 1952–2013. County-level data from 1997 to 2016 is adopted to construct the measurements of regional inequality across the

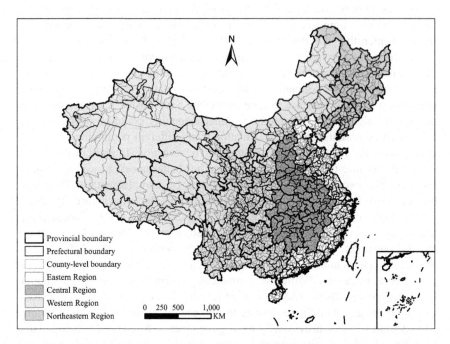

Figure 3.1 The spatial hierarchy of regions and localities in China.

regional, provincial, prefectural, and county levels. Previous studies have employed different grouping schemes of the provinces. In our analyses, 31 provinces are grouped into the four regions of Western, Central, Eastern and North-eastern China. Hong Kong, Macao, and Taiwan are not included due to data availability and different political and economic systems. Though the eastern–central–western division and the coastal–inland division have been used in previous studies (Fan and Sun 2008), the four-region division is adopted in recent studies, which better reflects the macroeconomic linkages and the development policy of central government (He, Bayrak, and Lin 2017; Zhang, Xu, and Wang 2019).[1]

Eastern provinces include Beijing, Tianjin, Hebei, Shanghai, Jiangsu, Zhejiang, Guangdong, Fujian, Shandong, and Hainan. North-eastern provinces include Jilin, Heilongjiang, and Liaoning. The central region consists of Shanxi, Anhui, Jiangxi, Henan, Hubei, and Hunan. Provinces in the western region include Guangxi, Sichuan, Guizhou, Yunan, Tibet (or *Xizang*), Shaanxi, Gansu, Qinghai, Ningxia, Xinjiang, and Inner Mongolia (or *Neimenggu*). The administrative boundary changes are salient at the county level and thus may affect the prefectural units and inequality measures (He *et al.* 2018). The county-level boundary in 2016 is used and aggregated into the prefectural-level boundary to ensure boundary consistency, following the statistics units issued by the National Bureau of Statistics.

To explore regional inequality, several statistical indexes, such as coefficient of variation (CV), the GINI coefficient, and the Theil index, have been widely employed in previous studies. These indexes are different in terms of their properties and sensitivity to outliners. One advantage of the Theil index is that as a type of entropy indices, it can be decomposed into additive terms that quantify the inequality among and within groups. Therefore, in some of the empirical analysis in the rest of the chapter, we use the Theil index to decompose regional inequality into interregional and intraregional inequalities based on the different groups of provinces and counties.

For the regional inequality measures, they could be generally categorized into three types: dispersion indices, Lorenz Curve indices, and entropy or information-theoretic indices. The dispersion indices include mean deviation, standard deviation, and coefficient of variation. They are straightforward and easy to compute, but since the absolute (in)equality is measured, they are scale-dependent and sensitive to outliers. Among the dispersion indices, the coefficient of variation (CV) is the most popular index, which could be presented as:

$$\frac{\sigma_Z}{\mu_Z}$$

where Z is the per capita GDP, σ is the standard deviation, and μ is the mean.

The Lorenz curve indices are associated with the GINI coefficient and most frequently used by economists and geographers, but they are difficult to compute and unduly influenced by high values at the upper end of the Lorenz curve. The GINI coefficient represents twice the area between the Lorenz curve, a cumulative proportion curve of the overall income distribution, and the equality curve when individuals have the same income:

$$Gini = \frac{1}{2n^2 \mu_Z} \sum_{i=1}^{n} \sum_{j=1}^{n} | Z_i - Z_j |$$

where n is the number of areas, Z_i and Z_j are the per capita GDP of ith and jth area.

Compared with the dispersion and Lorenz curve indices, the entropy indices are reasonably tractable and not affected by extreme values. Besides, the entropy indices, like the Theil index, are readily decomposable into components that measure the inequality between and within groups of observations by regions. The Theil index T and its decomposition components, between-region inequality T_{bg} and within-region inequality T_{wg}, could be depicted as:

$$T = \sum_{i=1}^{n} y_i \log\left(\frac{y_i}{x_i}\right)$$

$$T = T_{wg} + T_{bg} = \sum_{g=1}^{G} Y_g \sum_{i \in S_g} \frac{y_i}{Y_i} \log\left(\frac{y_i / Y_g}{x_i / X_g}\right) + \sum_{g=1}^{G} Y_g \log\left(\frac{Y_g}{X_g}\right)$$

where y_i and x_i are the GDP and population share of ith area, and Y_g and X_g are the GDP and population share of gth group of areas (say, gth region).

As an entropy-based method, it satisfies several properties like mean independence, population-size independence, and the Pigou–Dalton principle of transfers (Shorrocks 1980). More importantly, the Theil index is readily decomposable into within-region inequality, T_{wr}, and between-region inequality, T_{br}, thus making it possible to measure the contribution of the two (Theil 1967):

$$T = \sum_i \sum_j \frac{y_{ij}}{y} \log\left(\frac{y_{ij}/y}{x_{ij}/x}\right)$$

$$T = \sum_i \frac{y_i}{y} \sum_j \frac{y_{ij}}{y_i} \log\left(\frac{y_{ij}/y_i}{x_{ij}/x_i}\right) + \sum_i \frac{y_i}{y} \log\left(\frac{y_i/y}{x_i/x}\right) = T_{wr} + T_{br}$$

where y and x are total GDP and population, y_i and x_i are GDP and population in a region or county i, and y_{ij} and x_{ij} are GDP and population of province or county j in region i.

In Akita (2003), the decomposable advantage of the Theil index is improved by developing the one-stage decomposition into a two-stage one. The two-stage decomposition using county-level data can include a finer scale at the prefectural level, k:

$$T = \sum_i \sum_j \sum_k \frac{y_{ijk}}{y} \log(\frac{y_{ijk}/y}{x_{ijk}/x}) = \sum_i \frac{y_i}{y} T_i + T_{br}$$

$$T_i = \sum_j \sum_k \frac{y_{ijk}}{y_i} \log\left(\frac{\dfrac{y_{ijk}}{y_i}}{\dfrac{x_{ijk}}{x_i}}\right)$$

$$T_i = \sum_j \frac{y_{ij}}{y_i} \sum_k \frac{y_{ijk}}{y_{ij}} \log(\frac{y_{ijk}/y_{ij}}{x_{ijk}/x_{ij}}) + \sum_j \frac{y_{ij}}{y_i} \log(\frac{y_{ij}/y_i}{x_{ij}/x_i}) = T_{i\_wp} + T_{i_{bp}}$$

$$T = \sum_i \frac{y_i}{y} T_{i\_wp} + \sum_i \frac{y_i}{y} T_{i\_bp} + T_{br} = T_{wp} + T_{bp} + T_{br}$$

where y_{ijk} and x_{ijk} are GDP and population of prefecture k in province j, region i. For each region i, T_i is the overall inequality measure based on prefectural units, and T_{iwp} and T_{ibp} are within-province inequality and between-province inequality components in region i. T_{wp} and T_{bp} are a weighted sum of within-province inequality and between-province inequality for all regions.

Akita's idea was further expanded into a three-stage decomposition by Paredes *et al.* (2016). The three-stage decomposition is more relevant for policy issues in China because it fits the spatial hierarchy of region–province–prefecture–county in China and is not constrained to any specific scale level. After integrating the county level, *c*, the overall inequality is measured as:

$$T = \sum_{i=1}^{n} y_i \log\left(\frac{y_i}{x_i}\right)$$

$$T = \sum_i \sum_j \sum_k \sum_c \frac{y_{ijkc}}{y} \log(\frac{y_{ijkc}/y}{x_{ijkc}/x}) = \sum_i \frac{y_i}{y} T_i + T_{br}$$

$$T_i = \sum_j \sum_k \sum_c \frac{y_{ijkc}}{y_i} \log(\frac{y_{ijkc}/y_i}{x_{ijkc}/x_i})$$

$$T_i = \sum_j \frac{y_{ij}}{y_i} T_{ij} + T_{i\_bp}$$

$$T_{ij} = \sum_k \sum_c \frac{y_{ijkc}}{y_{ij}} \log\left(\frac{\dfrac{y_{ijkc}}{y_{ij}}}{\dfrac{x_{ijkc}}{x_{ij}}}\right)$$

$$T_{ij} = \sum_k \frac{y_{ijk}}{y_{ij}} \sum_c \frac{y_{ijkc}}{y_{ijk}} \log(\frac{y_{ijkc}/y_{ijk}}{x_{ijkc}/x_{ijk}}) + \sum_k \frac{y_{ijk}}{y_{ij}} \log(\frac{y_{ijk}/y_{ij}}{x_{ijk}/x_{ij}}) = T_{ij\_wm} + T_{ij\_bm}$$

$$T = \sum_i \frac{y_i}{y} \sum_j \frac{y_{ij}}{y_i} T_{ij\_wm} + \sum_i \frac{y_i}{y} \sum_j \frac{y_{ij}}{y_i} T_{ij\_bm} + \sum_i \frac{y_i}{y} T_{i\_bp} + T_{br}$$

$$T = T_{wm} + T_{bm} + T_{bp} + T_{br}$$

where y_{ijkc} and x_{ijkc} are GDP and population of county *c* in prefecture *k*, province *j*, region *i*. For each province *j* in region *i*, T_{ij} is the overall inequality measure based on county units, and T_{ijwm} and T_{ijbm} are within-municipality[2] inequality and between-municipality inequality components. T_{wm} and $T_{bm,}$ are a weighted sum of within-municipality inequality and between-municipality inequality for all provinces in each region.

3.2 Analyzing multi-scalar patterns of regional inequality at the provincial level

Interprovincial inequalities, measured by CV, the Theil index and the Gini coefficient, suggest that over the 60 years of 1952–2013, regional inequality at the provincial level has generally exhibited a triple-peak pattern (Figure 3.2), matching the different phases of China's economic development and market reform. As compared with those based on the Gini coefficient and the Theil index, the values of CV fluctuated more strongly during the whole study period (1952–2013). Interprovincial inequality was relatively low and increased during the First Five-Year Plan (1953–1957) and the Great Leap Forward (1958–1960), reaching a peak in 1960. The extent of interprovincial inequality experienced an abrupt decline after 1961, partly owing to the Great Famine (1959–1961). This crisis led to relatively sluggish statuses of Beijing, Shanghai, and other provincial economies dominated by state-owned enterprises (SOEs), resulting in declining regional inequality (Figure 3.2).

During the 1960s and the Cultural Revolution (1966–1976), regional inequality increased and peaked in the late 1970s. The CV for the year 1978 is the second-highest in the past six decades, which implies that income gaps among China's provinces actually widened during the Maoist period (Wei and Ma 1996). The earlier years of economic reforms and rural reforms in the early 1980s benefitted some less developed coastal provinces in China, and regional inequality declined (Figure 3.2). China's deeper reform in the early 1990s, triggered by the Xiaoping Deng's South China trip in 1992 and the accession to the WTO in 2001 marked changes of interprovincial inequality in the 1990s and the 2000s. Coastal provinces that benefited from marketization and liberalization during this period and regional inequality rose until the mid-2000s (Fujita and Hu 2001; Hao and Wei 2010; Ezcurra and Rodríguez-Pose 2013). This result also echoes recent work that indicates the strengthening effect of globalization or trade liberalization on the level of regional inequality in low- and middle-income countries (Rodríguez-Pose 2012). Nevertheless, Figure 3.2 shows that since the mid-2000s, facilitated by several development programs toward reducing regional disparities, on par with the rise of production cost in coastal provinces,

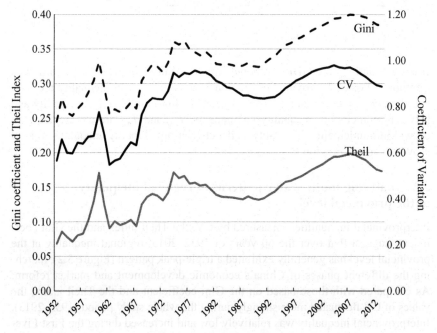

Figure 3.2 Interprovincial regional inequality, 1952–2013 (*hukou* population).

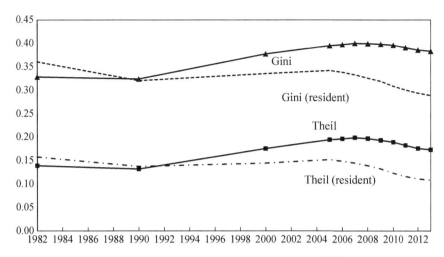

Figure 3.3 Interprovincial regional inequality, 1982–2013 (resident population).

regional inequality at the provincial level has declined (Li and Gibson 2013). The overall trend of regional inequality at the provincial level over the past six decades could hardly follow either convergence or divergence assumptions.

When analyzing regional inequality using the GDP per capita based on the resident population, changes in regional inequality have largely followed the same trajectory in comparison with the patterns based on the *hukou* population (Figure 3.3). GDP per capita based on the permanent population, however, changes more proactively. The divergence between these two sets of GDP per capita statistics is more apparent after the mid-2000s. For instance, from 2005 to 2013, the *hukou* population-based GDP per capita data shows a decreasing Theil index of 13%, but its counterpart using the resident population was 40% (Figure 3.3). Our results are consistent with other studies focusing on this issue and reveal that the overall spatial inequality of economic development between wealthier and poor provinces keeps being closed in recent years and these trends are more evident when the interprovincial migration population is considered.

In addition to interprovincial-level inequality, regional inequality between the macro-regions in China is of particular concern given its significance for regional development policies. In comparison with regional income gaps among provinces, interregional inequality consistently increases over the past 60 years. Values of the Theil index, CV, and the Gini coefficient increased by 798%, 284%, and 276% during the period of 1952–2013 (Table 3.1). In contrast, interprovincial inequality rose by 253%, 157%, and 156% with respect to the values of the Theil index, CV, and the Gini coefficient.

Decomposition analysis using the Theil index quantifies contributions of interregional and intraregional inequalities to the regional inequality at the provincial

Table 3.1 Interprovincial and interregional inequalities in China, 1952–2015

Year	Interprovincial inequality			Interregional inequality		
	Theil	*CV*	*Gini*	*Theil*	*CV*	*Gini*
1952	0.121	0.566	0.245	0.012	0.315	0.081
1960	0.171	0.775	0.331	0.019	0.199	0.108
1965	0.098	0.612	0.263	0.010	0.142	0.077
1970	0.140	0.837	0.328	0.023	0.222	0.121
1975	0.163	0.929	0.356	0.033	0.265	0.141
1980	0.154	0.949	0.346	0.038	0.282	0.146
1985	0.135	0.879	0.327	0.041	0.295	0.152
1990	0.132	0.837	0.324	0.050	0.326	0.164
1995	0.158	0.880	0.355	0.089	0.438	0.217
2000	0.175	0.951	0.377	0.102	0.469	0.232
2005	0.194	0.970	0.395	0.115	0.501	0.246
2010	0.189	0.928	0.396	0.111	0.424	0.240
2013	0.173	0.887	0.383	0.109	0.458	0.223

Notes
GDP per capita is calculated based on 1978 constant price GDP and *hukou* population

level. As evident in Figure 3.4, interprovincial inequality actually fluctuated but interregional inequality tends to increase consistently since 1952, despite a noticeable drop after 2007. Moreover, interregional inequality increased in most of the time during the past six decades, but due to the recent decrease after 2007, interregional inequality in 2013 returned to the same level in 1998. Figure 3.4 also shows that the level of spatial inequality within regions also fluctuates in

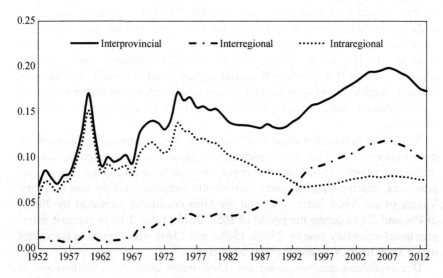

Figure 3.4 Decomposition of interprovincial inequality using Theil index, 1952–2013.

the pre-reform era (1952–1978) and generally follows the trajectory of interprovincial inequalities before the reform. The level of intraregional inequality peaked in 1975 and substantially declined during the reform period as proven in previous literature (Tsui 2007; Fan and Sun 2008; Fan, Kanbur, and Zhang 2011). The results partially reflect a *club convergence* process among Chinese provinces especially in the 1990s (Herrerías and Monfort 2015). It is also worthwhile pointing out that intraregional inequality's contributions to the total inequality at the provincial level were overtaken by interregional inequality after the early 1990s (Figure 3.4). Findings using resident population-based GDP per capita confirm that between-group inequality was overestimated by approximately 37% in the 2000s if GDP per capita is calculated based on the *hukou* population, in spite of the fact that both datasets reveal a declining trajectory of interregional inequality after the mid-2000s (Figure 3.5).

The general declining intraregional inequality masks the changes in intraregional inequality within each region. In Figure 3.6, intraregional inequality is further decomposed into respective contributions by the four regions. Throughout the period from 1952 to 2013, intraregional inequality in the eastern region was considerably high and was obviously a primary contributor to the total intraregional inequality (Figure 3.6). But similar to the recent drop of interregional inequality, it had declined since the mid-2000s. Intraregional inequality in the north-eastern and central regions declined slightly in recent years and remained small over the past six decades. In contrast, intraregional inequality within the western region experienced an increase after 2002. In short, regional inequality in China is sensitive to geographical scales, and patterns focusing on different components such as intraregional inequality and interregional inequality could result in different judgments of either convergence or divergence trends.

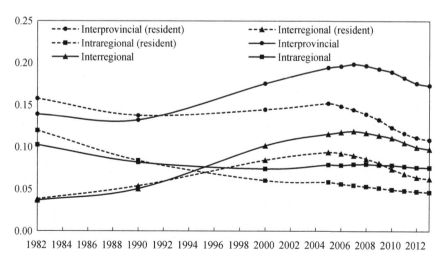

Figure 3.5 Decomposition of interprovincial inequality using Theil index (resident population), 1982–2013.

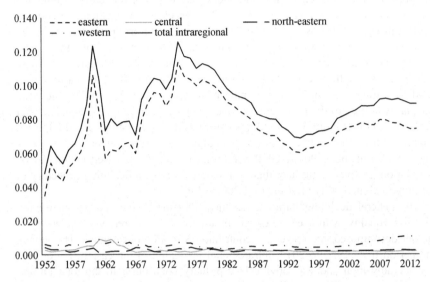

Figure 3.6 Decomposition of intraregional inequality using Theil index, 1952–2013.

3.3 A three-stage decomposition analysis using county-level data

The previous section mainly addresses the interregional, interprovincial, and intraregional inequalities in China. While most studies focus on the interregional and interprovincial scales, only a few provide comprehensive empirics regarding regional inequality at the county level or inequalities below provinces (He, Bayrak, and Lin 2017; He, Fang, and Zhang 2017). In this section, as mentioned earlier, we apply a three-stage nested Theil decomposition method (Akita 2003; Paredes, Iturra, and Lufin 2016) to the county-level dataset in China. The nested decomposition method takes the four-level and multi-scalar region–province–prefecture–county administrative hierarchy in China into consideration. By doing so, it investigates and assists clarification of the sources of spatial inequalities in economic development at the county level, which is also the most disaggregated level of the administrative unit in China.

As also discussed above, since the impact of population migration on economic development is evident in China, the registered population, also called the *hukou* or de jure population, may cause biased inequality measures. The de facto or *resident* population is estimated by using the ratio between de facto and de jure population interpolated from the census data in 2000 and 2010 (Liao and Wei 2012). The impacts of population migration on regional inequality are confirmed by the comparative analysis of using de facto and de jure population in the Theil index (Figure 3.7). Similar to the provincial-level analysis, though, both the population measures show an inverted-U pattern of regional inequality

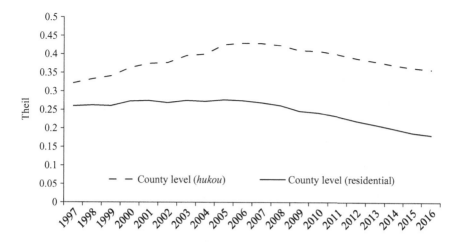

Figure 3.7 Theil index based on *hukou* population and residential population.

at the county level, the Theil index by the de jure population is greater than the de facto population. The gap between the *de jure* and de facto measures was small at the beginning of the study period (1997–2016) when the migration was not evident. With the rapid economic growth in developed regions in China, the demand for migrant workers increases and the higher income level attracts the population from the agricultural sector in the less developed regions to the coastal region and provincial capitals (Li and Gibson 2013). Meanwhile, the restriction on the *hukou* system has been greatly loosened by the central government, which strengthens the human capital mobility (Fan, Kanbur, and Zhang 2011). As a result, the gap between two Theil measures increases continuously in the study period and reached as high as 0.18 in 2016.

By using the de facto population, the multi-scalar regional inequality was researched, which has generated several interesting findings (Figure 3.8). First, regional inequality in China is sensitive to scales, manifested by the increasing levels of inequality, measured by the values of the Theil index, when moving from the coarse scales to the finer scales. The average Theil index is 0.07, 0.1, 0.19, and 0.25 at the regional, provincial, prefectural, and county levels, respectively. Second, an overall inverted-U pattern is observed across the four scales in China, showing that regional inequality first increased from the late-1990s to the mid-2000s and then declined continuously until the mid-2010s. The temporal trend provides updated empirical evidence and matches previous findings which suggest a turning point of regional inequality in China around 2005 (He, Bayrak, and Lin 2017; Ravi, Yue, and Xiaobo 2017).

The reasons for the declining regional inequality after 2005 are complex, which could be associated with the outcome of economic restructuring, global market, and government policy. Since the 2000s, besides such regional

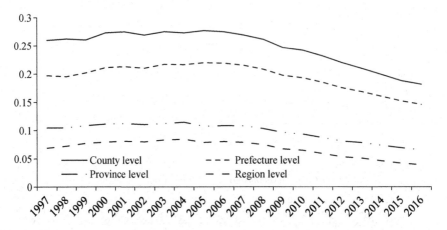

Figure 3.8 Multi-scale regional inequality from 1997 to 2016 (Theil index).

development policies as the Western Development Plan, the Revitalization Program of Northeast China's Old Industrial Base, the Rise of Central China Program, which have been mentioned in previous provincial-level analysis, the central government has launched several development policies, like the Enhancing County-Level Economy Plan, to support the economic growth in the disadvantaged interior, especially the county economy in rural China (Chen and Groenewold 2010; Groenewold, Chen, and Lee 2010). Moreover, rising production costs in the coastal region and improving consumption levels in the interior have also resulted in new investments in the interior, including some industries relocated from the coastal region.

A further investigation by the nested Theil decomposition method reveals more nuanced patterns of regional inequality by comparing the contributions of different sources, including the between-prefecture, within-prefecture, between-region, and between-province components (Figure 3.9). First, the inequality among prefectures or the between-prefecture component contributes the most in the overall inter-county inequalities, followed by the between-region inequality, the within-prefecture inequality, and the inequality among provinces within each region. It should be noted that if between-region and between-province level inequalities are accounted for, the inequality at the prefectural and county levels contributes more than half of the overall inequalities across counties. Meanwhile, between-province inequalities only occupy the smallest shares among all of the four components. The comparison was made possible by using the three-stage decomposition technique, which confirms the importance of analyzing regional inequality below provinces (Wei and Fang 2006; Wei, Yu, and Chen 2011; Liao and Wei 2012; Dai *et al.* 2017; Ye *et al.* 2017).

Second, the changes of the between-region components are identical to the region-level inequality using the provincial-level dataset (see Figure 3.8). The

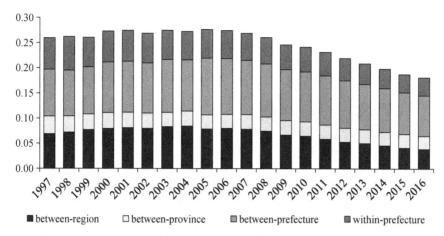

Figure 3.9 Nested decomposition of the Theil index.

inequality between four regions first increased from 1997 to 2005 and then declined, which confirms the previous discussion about the inward and northern-ward shift of economic gravity (Ng and Tuan 2006). China's regional development in the last decade has witnessed an inward and northward shift due to rising labor costs in the coastal and southern regions and relatively low capital prices in inland and northern China (Ye 2012; Wu *et al.* 2018). The spatial agglomera-tion of economic development in north China has been strengthened because of the rise of Beijing and the Bohai-rim region in recent years and other major economic centers in the northern part of China (He, Fang, and Zhang 2017). While the high-tech and capital-intensive industries remain in the coastal region, some labor-intensive and resource-based sectors have moved toward the periphery of China (Wu *et al.* 2018). The global financial crisis in 2008 has dampened the export-oriented industries, triggering a slower economic growth in the coastal cities and strengthen the tendencies of convergence across coun-ties, prefectures, and provinces.

Third, the decline of the overall inequality after 2005 is mainly attributed to the change in the between-region and within-prefecture components, as com-pared with the contributions derived from the between-province and between-prefecture components. The between-region component has declined from 0.069 to 0.039 during the period and the within-prefecture one has decreased from 0.063 to 0.036, while the between-province one only decreased from 0.036 to 0.026 and the between-prefecture one dropped from 0.093 to 0.081 during the study period of 1997–2016. It implies that the economic restructuring and urban-ization at the national level has narrowed the gap among regions and among urban–rural counties within prefectures in recent years. However, the divide between provinces in each region and the gap between prefectures within each province persists or remains salient. Furthermore, the convergence trend is

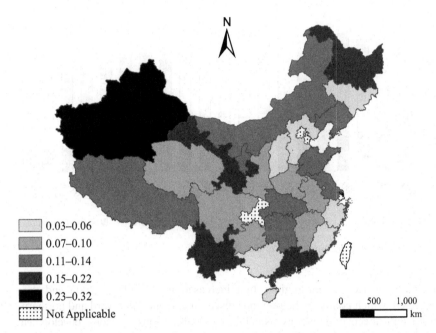

Figure 3.10 Spatial distribution of between-prefecture Theil values (average of the period of 1997–2016).

observed for all the four scales, but the between-prefecture inequalities, which is the largest source of spatial inequality in economic development, have declined by less than 13%, while the component is the largest source of regional inequality in China across counties.

As the largest component in the overall inequality, the between-prefecture inequality is further decomposed into the contribution of each province based on the average value of the between-prefecture components from 1997 to 2016, which considers both their weight in China's economy and the gap among prefectures within each province (Figure 3.10 and Figure 3.11).[3]

Three coastal provinces, i.e., Guangdong, Jiangsu, and Shandong, are the three most important contributing provinces to the between-prefecture inequality when their sizes of economies are considered. The three provinces are not only important sources of uneven development in China but they are also characterized by internal unevenness of regional development (e.g., Guangdong). Furthermore, the prefectural-level inequalities within several interior provinces, e.g., Xinjiang, Gansu, Heilongjiang, and Yunnan, are also large (Figure 3.10), which is greatly attributed to the geographical conditions and structural constraints of regional development within these inland provinces (Wei and Fang 2006).

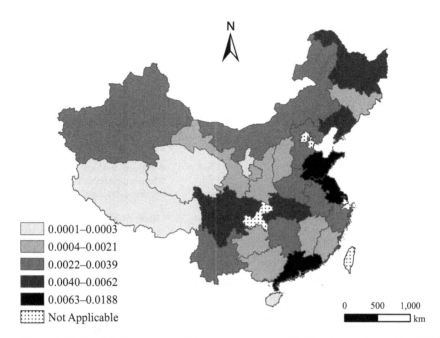

Figure 3.11 Spatial distribution of between-prefecture Theil values weighted by GDP (average of the period of 1997–2016).

As shown in Figure 3.12, the nested spatial decomposition method is applied to each region to quantify the relationship between inequalities across scales in different geographical contexts. Specifically, the contribution is decomposed into the inequality between provinces in each region, the inequality among prefectures in each province within specific regions, and the gap among counties in each prefecture (Figure 3.12). We have found several interesting patterns regarding multi-scalar characteristics.

First, like the multi-scalar inequality in China, the inequality in four regions is also sensitive to scales, manifested by the increasing inequality as the focusing scale changes from the provincial level to the prefectural and county levels, regardless of regions. However, different temporal patterns are observed in four regions, which may be masked, again, by the analysis at the national level or analysis using the provincial-level dataset. For example, even though regional inequality at the national level exhibits an inverted-U pattern across different scales, there have been differentiated trends or magnitudes of changes in the four regions.

Regional inequality in the eastern region has decreased regardless of spatial scales. In other words, the convergence in the eastern region is not only the result of a narrowing gap among the coastal provinces, but also attributed to narrowing gaps among the prefectures and counties in the region (Zhang, Xu, and Wang 2019).

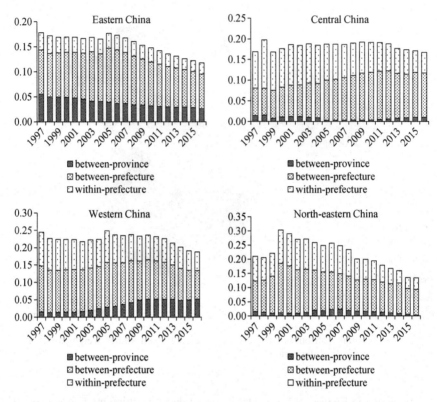

Figure 3.12 Nested decomposition of the Theil index for regions in China.

However, similar to other regions, the between-prefectural scale remained the largest source of regional inequality and its decline is less evident as compared with the between-province and the within-prefecture components. Researchers have found several core–periphery structures in the coastal provinces, like the coastal–inland divide in Zhejiang (Wei and Ye 2009; Yue *et al.* 2014), the Sunan–Suzhong–Subei gradient in Jiangsu (Wei, Yu, and Chen 2011; Liu *et al.* 2019), and the gap between the Pearl River Delta and the periphery Guangdong (Liao and Wei 2012; Zhang, Tong, and Liang 2018). The concentration of resources, i.e., labor, fixed investment, foreign capital, and technology and information, in the core areas, especially prefectures, has been reinforced and has a counter effect on the overall trend of convergence in the eastern region (Liao and Wei 2015).

For the central region, the changes in regional inequality across counties have remained stable during 1997–2016. There has been a U-shape pattern when focusing on provincial-level inequalities, while its contribution was very small. However, the most important source of regional inequality, i.e., the between-prefecture component, has exhibited a divergence trend. This finding indicates that the divide between the prefectures in central China has been widening from 1997 to 2016, while there has been narrowing gaps among counties within each prefecture. Hence, overall inter-county inequality remained stable. Recent studies of regional development and inequality in the central region indicate that provincial-level regional development strategy tends to favor the provincial capital and gradually cultivate the growth pole around the capital city (Ke and Feser 2010). Meanwhile, the rapid urbanization in China and in the region has played an important role in narrowing the vast gap between the urban and rural counties, leading to the decline of within-prefecture inequality.

As shown in Figure 3.12, the between-province component has made a larger contribution to the overall county-level inequalities in the western region, as compared with the other three regions. There have been declining inequalities across counties and prefectures when the between-province component is controlled for. In contrast, between-province inequality has increased by almost 200%. As discussed in He *et al.* (2017a), the Western Development Program since 2000 aims to enhance infrastructure construction and industrial modernization in the western provinces. But the development strategy is geographically uneven, favoring provincial economies with rich resources. Provinces like Inner Mongolia have achieved rapid economic growth during the period, but provinces with geographic constraints, poor natural resources, and low-skilled human capital have been lagging behind. Hence, the decline of overall county-level inequality in western China is greatly attributed to the narrowing gap among prefectures and counties within each province rather than the gaps among provinces.

Different from the western and eastern regions, the between-province component has made less contribution to the overall county-level inequalities. The inter-county inequalities are mainly determined by the within-province inequality, namely the between-prefecture and within-prefecture components, which both have increased rapidly from 1997 to 2001 and gradually decreased from 2002 to 2016. These results suggest that despite the implementation of the Revitalization of the North-eastern Old Industrial Bases Program, industrial restructuring in the north-eastern region has suffered from the decline of original leading industrial cities in the Chinese rust belt, which are burdened with the inefficient SOEs (Huang *et al.* 2018), resulting in convergence among counties and prefectures in the region.

3.4 The distributional dynamics of regional inequality at multiple scales

The analyses so far have revealed the temporal pattern of regional inequality by the administrative hierarchy and a multi-scalar perspective. In order to investigate and compare the long-run properties of the regional income distribution, the Markov chain method is used in the section. Four classes, namely poor (P), less-developed (L), developed (D), and rich (R), are adopted to represent different development levels. The results of the Markov method contain the gridline of development level, the transitional probabilities among classes and the long-run ergodic distribution, which provides a holistic picture of the development processes at three scales (Table 3.2).

First, the gridline, which is used to divide the ratio of income level to the national average of each county into four development levels, indicates the gap across the spatial units and how it changes with scales. At the provincial level, the variance of per capita GDP is relatively small, with the highest one as 3.5 times the national average and the lowest one less than 0.6. As it moves to finer scales of the prefectural and county ones, the disparity becomes evident and the richest county could be 15 times more than the national average and the poorest one be less than half. Since the quartile division is used in the Markov method, the number of spatial units within each development level, listed after the abbreviation, is similar.

The transitional matrix implies the probability of certain spatial units to stay in the current class or move towards other classes in the diagonal and non-diagonal values, respectively. Together with the long-run ergodic distribution, it indicates how the regional inequality evolves and the convergence/divergence trend if the current development process sustains. The sensitivity to scales is also observed in the long-run income distribution (see Table 3.2). While the ergodic distribution at the provincial level implies a strong convergence trend within the developed and rich classes, the prefectural and county level indicates a more even distribution in the long term. This observation also coincides with previous studies suggesting that convergence among provinces may mask the consistent

Table 3.2 Markov chain transitional probability at three scales, 1997–2016

Scale	Grid line [upper bound]			
Province	P [0.612]	L [0.727]	D [1.337]	R [3.495]
P (150)	0.940	0.060	0.000	0.000
L (149)	0.040	0.899	0.060	0.000
D (142)	0.000	0.021	0.944	0.035
R (148)	0.000	0.000	0.027	0.973
Ergodic	0.081	0.121	0.346	0.451
Prefecture	P [0.541]	L [0.811]	D [1.198]	R [8.099]
P (1,634)	0.947	0.050	0.002	0.001
L (1,619)	0.043	0.904	0.053	0.001
D (1,615)	0.003	0.048	0.901	0.048
R (1,611)	0.001	0.000	0.047	0.953
Ergodic	0.217	0.242	0.263	0.278
County	P [0.492]	L [0.766]	D [1.246]	R [15.69]
P (10,439)	0.923	0.072	0.004	0.001
L (10,310)	0.068	0.856	0.075	0.001
D (10,304)	0.003	0.074	0.869	0.054
R (10,348)	0.002	0.003	0.049	0.946
Ergodic	0.237	0.252	0.25	0.26

or widening disparity within provinces and among prefectures and counties (Zhang, Xu, and Wang 2019).

A closer look at the matrix reveals that the probability of a spatial unit, either a provincial, prefectural, or county one, to stay in the current class is relatively high in general. The highest diagonal value is 97.3% for rich provinces and the lowest one is 85.6% for less-developed counties to remain the same class during the transition. At the provincial level, no leap-frog, e.g., from poor to developed or from developed to poor, is found. The probability of upward movement is more possible than the downward one since the upward probabilities are slightly larger than their counterparts for all transitions, which could be attributed to the recent convergence trend at the provincial level. For the prefectural and county level, the upward probabilities are only slightly higher than their counterparts, implying the stable economic structure and the persistent inequality in the long run (He, Fang, and Zhang 2017). Table 3.3 further depicts the distributional dynamics in different regions. It shows that upward mobility at the county level is highest in the eastern region, followed by north-eastern regions. This is consistent with the previous discussion on the convergence of county-level economy within the eastern region, which also contributes to the increasing interprovincial and interregional inequality at the national level (Figure 3.4 and Figure 3.5). In contrast, upward mobility is much lower for counties in the western region, which even shows some inclination of downward movement. The result implies the declining regional inequality at the national level might be attributed to convergence between counties in the coastal region, characterized by a trend of club convergence. Localities in inland provinces still face challenges of catching up, and spatial inequalities or the formation of poverty trap therein should warrant more attention.

3.5 Conclusion

This chapter investigates the multi-scalar patterns of regional inequality in China by analyzing the long-run dataset of per capita GDP during the period of 1952–2016 and a comprehensive spatial dataset of county-level economic dataset during 1997–2016. We have found that changes in regional inequality coincide with different phases of China's regional development and the reform. The evolution of regional inequality could hardly be simplified into convergence or divergence patterns and regional inequality is sensitive to geographical scales. For example, interprovincial inequality fluctuated, and by the early 2010s, it was similar to the magnitude of regional inequality at the provincial level in the 1960s. In contrast, interregional inequality has risen despite a noticeable drop after 2005. Our results show that convergence, divergence, and inverted-U theories are overly simplified, and therefore rarely applicable in the case of China during our study period.

The chapter also employs a three-stage spatial decomposition technique to tackle the sources of regional inequalities by decomposing county-level inequalities in China into between-region, between-province, between-prefecture, and within-prefecture components. The results not only confirm that regional

Table 3.3 Markov chain transitional probabilities in different regions, 1997–2016

Scale	P [−INF., 0.492]	L [0.492, 0.766]	D [0.766, 1.246]	R [1.246, 15.69]
Eastern region				
P (381)	0.850	0.142	0.008	0.000
L (1,465)	0.051	0.872	0.076	0.001
D (3,046)	0.001	0.048	0.902	0.050
R (4,874)	0.000	0.000	0.034	0.965
Ergodic	0.067	0.188	0.304	0.441
Central region				
P (2,455)	0.918	0.079	0.002	0.000
L (3,619)	0.066	0.873	0.061	0.001
D (2,823)	0.001	0.092	0.866	0.041
R (1,895)	0.001	0.003	0.068	0.929
Ergodic	0.283	0.347	0.232	0.138
Western region				
P (7,301)	0.934	0.062	0.003	0.001
L (4,610)	0.074	0.850	0.075	0.000
D (3,266)	0.004	0.080	0.858	0.059
R (2,303)	0.004	0.004	0.056	0.936
Ergodic	0.310	0.254	0.224	0.212
North-eastern region				
P (302)	0.778	0.169	0.04	0.013
L (616)	0.071	0.766	0.156	0.006
D (1,169)	0.010	0.081	0.825	0.083
R (1,276)	0.006	0.010	0.067	0.916
Ergodic	0.091	0.200	0.341	0.368

inequality in China is sensitive to scales but also deepen our understanding of the sensitivity of regional inequality to different scales and comparing the sources of regional inequality in the four regions, including eastern, western, central and north-eastern regions.

The obtained results demonstrated the contributions of the four individual components, including between-prefecture, between-region, between-province, and within-prefecture, to overall inequality at the county level, which is the most disaggregated level administrative unit in China. The between-prefecture component, which measures the inequality among prefectures within each province, contributes most to the overall inequality at the county level, followed by the between-region component, the intra-prefecture, and the between-province ones. Notably, inequalities among prefectures are the largest contributing factor to regional inequalities across counties. The declining between-region inequality in recent years has been accompanied by the spatial expansion of economic gravity centers including those rising regions in northern and interior China due to economic restructuring and the impacts from the global market (He, Bayrak, and Lin 2017). When considering the gap among prefectures within each province, the interior provinces are in general higher than the coastal provinces except for Guangdong Province.

The spatial heterogeneous development processes are identified. We have found that the overall trend of convergence might mask the detailed geographies of regional inequality especially when focusing on the contributions of different components. For instance, counties in the eastern region have experienced convergence whereas downward mobilities of counties in the western and central regions are relatively higher, contributing to the persistent coastal–inland inequality in China. Furthermore, the between-prefecture component has been the major contributor to county-level inequality in the eastern region, but their contributions are smaller in the western region, in which between-province components should warrant more attention too if compared with the other three regions.

It is also noticeable that the probability of a spatial unit, either a provincial, prefectural, or county one, to stay in the current class is relatively high in general. This indicates the existence of a relatively stable, fragmented regional structure in China, where rich regions tend to stay rich and poor regions tend to stay poor. It is concerning that upward mobility is much lower for counties in the western region, which even shows some inclination of downward movement.

To summarize, spatial development or planning strategies that favor the growth pole and the provincial capital could be helpful in stimulating economic growth but may widen the gap among prefectures and counties within the province. National and provincial programs are still needed in regional development to reduce disparities among regions, more attention should be given to address spatial effects and the problem of such policies since they tend to intensify gaps among counties within provinces and between prefectures or cities. More reform and open-door policies such as development zones should be used to target the less developed western cities, rather than favoring coastal cities. More efforts should also be made by the interior provinces to promote economic reforms and more effectively initiate local policies to promote regional development and reduce inequalities among cities and counties.

Notes

1 The three-region division originates from the Seventh Five-Year Plan (1986–1990), while the four-region division is based on the Eleventh Five-Year Plan (2006–2010) (Fan and Sun 2008). For development policies of central government, the Western Development Program includes Guangxi and Inner Mongolia as the western region but not coastal or central region in some studies. The Revitalization Program of Northeast China's Old Industrial Base is concentrated in Liaoning, Jilin, and Heilong Jiang Provinces. The central provinces in the four-region division matches the target provinces in the Rise of Central China program.
2 Municipality and the abbreviation m is used equivalently with prefecture to avoid ambiguous abbreviation for province and its abbreviation p.
3 Four directly administrated municipalities, namely Beijing, Tianjin, Shanghai, and Chongqing, are not included because, as a special provincial unit, they are also considered to be consisted of only one prefecture in analysis. For their role in regional inequality in China, see Li and Wei (2010).

References

Akita, T. 2003. Decomposing regional income inequality in China and Indonesia using two-stage nested Theil decomposition method. *The Annals of Regional Science* 37 (1): 55–77.

Brandt, L., and C. A. Holz. 2006. Spatial price differences in China: Estimates and implications. *Economic Development and Cultural Change* 55 (1): 43–86.

Chen, A., and N. Groenewold. 2010. Reducing regional disparities in China: An evaluation of alternative policies. *Journal of Comparative Economics* 38 (2): 189–198.

Dai, Q., X. Ye, Y. D. Wei, Y. Ning, and S. Dai. 2017. Geography, ethnicity and regional inequality in Guangxi Zhuang Autonomous Region, China. *Applied Spatial Analysis and Policy*: 1–24.

Ezcurra, R., and A. Rodríguez-Pose. 2013. Political decentralization, economic growth and regional disparities in the OECD. *Regional Studies* 47 (3): 388–401.

Fan, C. C., and M. J. Sun. 2008. Regional inequality in China, 1978–2006. *Eurasian Geography and Economics* 49 (1): 1–18.

Fan, S., R. Kanbur, and X. Zhang. 2011. China's regional disparities: Experience and policy. *Review of Development Finance* 1 (1): 47–56.

Fujita, M., and D. P. Hu. 2001. Regional disparity in China 1985–1994: The effects of globalization and economic liberalization. *Annals of Regional Science* 35 (1): 3–37.

Groenewold, N., A. Chen, and G. Lee. 2010. Interregional spillovers of policy shocks in China. *Regional Studies* 44 (1): 87–101.

Hao, R., and and Z. Wei. 2010. Fundamental causes of inland-coastal income inequality in post-reform China. *Annals of Regional Science* 45 (1): 181–206.

He, S., M. M. Bayrak, and H. Lin. 2017. A comparative analysis of multi-scalar regional inequality in China. *Geoforum* 78: 1–11.

He, S., C. K. L. Chung, M. M. Bayrak, and W. Wang. 2016. Administrative boundary changes and regional inequality in provincial China. *Applied Spatial Analysis and Policy*: 1–18.

He, S., C. K. L. Chung, M. M. Bayrak, and W. Wang. 2018. Administrative boundary changes and regional inequality in provincial China. *Applied Spatial Analysis and Policy* 11 (1): 103–120.

He, S., C. Fang, and W. Zhang. 2017. A geospatial analysis of multi-scalar regional inequality in China and in metropolitan regions. *Applied Geography* 88: 199–212.

Herrerías, M. J., and J. O. Monfort. 2015. Testing stochastic convergence across Chinese provinces, 1952–2008. *Regional Studies* 49 (4): 485–501.

Huang, Y., Y. Fang, G. Gu, and J. Liu. 2018. The evolution and differentiation of economic convergence of resource-based cities in northeast China. *Chinese Geographical Science* 28 (3): 495–504.

Ke, S., and E. Feser. 2010. Count on the growth pole strategy for regional economic growth? Spread–backwash effects in greater central China. *Regional Studies* 44 (9): 1131–1147.

Li, C., and J. Gibson. 2013. Rising regional inequality in China: Fact or artifact? *World Development* 47: 16–29.

Li, Y., and Y. H. D. Wei. 2010. The spatial-temporal hierarchy of regional inequality of China. *Applied Geography* 30 (3): 303–316.

Liao, F. H., and Y. D. Wei. 2012. Dynamics, space, and regional inequality in provincial China: A case study of Guangdong province. *Applied Geography* 35 (1): 71–83.

Liao, F. H., and Y. D. Wei. 2015. Space, scale, and regional inequality in provincial China: A spatial filtering approach. *Applied Geography* 61: 94–104.

Liu, B., M. Xu, J. Wang, L. Zhao, and S. Xie. 2019. Spatio-temporal evolution of regional inequality and contribution decomposition of economic growth: A case study of Jiangsu Province, China. *Papers in Regional Science* 98(3), 1485–1498.

Lyons, T. P. 1991. Interprovincial disparities in China: Output and consumption, 1952–1987. *Economic Development and Cultural Change* 39 (3): 471–506.

Ng, L. F.-Y., and C. Tuan. 2006. Spatial agglomeration, FDI, and regional growth in China: Locality of local and foreign manufacturing investments. *Journal of Asian Economics* 17 (4): 691–713.

Paredes, D., V. Iturra, and M. Lufin. 2016. A spatial decomposition of income inequality in Chile. *Regional Studies* 50 (5): 771–789.

Ravi, K., W. Yue, and Z. Xiaobo. 2017. *The great Chinese inequality turnaround.* Washington, DC: International Food Policy Research Institute.

Rodríguez-Pose, A. 2012. Trade and regional inequality. *Economic Geography* 88 (2): 109–136.

Shorrocks, A. F. 1980. The class of additively decomposable inequality measures. *Econometrica* 48 (3): 613–625.

Theil, H. 1967. *Economics and information theory.* Amsterdam: North-Holland Publishing Company.

Tsui, K. 2007. Forces shaping China's interprovincial inequality. *Review of Income and Wealth* 53 (1): 60–92.

Wei, Y. 2017. Geography of inequality in Asia. *Geographical Review* 107 (2): 263–275.

Wei, Y. D. 2015. Spatiality of regional inequality. *Applied Geography* 61 (Supplement C): 1–10.

Wei, Y. D., D. Yu, and X. Chen. 2011. Scale, agglomeration, and regional inequality in provincial China. *Tijdschrift voor economische en sociale geografie* 102 (4): 406–425.

Wei, Y., and C. Fang. 2006. Geographical and structural constraints of regional development in western China: a study of Gansu Province. *Issues and Studies* 42 (2): 131–170.

Wei, Y. H. D., and X. Ye. 2009. Beyond convergence: Space, scale, and regional inequality in China. *Tijdschrift voor economische en sociale geografie* 100 (1): 59–80.

Wei, Y., and L. Ma J. C. 1996. Changing patterns of spatial inequality in China, 1952–1990. *Third World Planning Review* 18 (2): 177.

Wu, J., Y. Wei, Q. Li, and F. Yuan. 2018. Economic transition and changing location of manufacturing industry in China: A study of the Yangtze River Delta. *Sustainability* 10 (8): 2624.

Ye, M. Q. 2012. Characteristics and influence factors analysis of gravity movement for China's economy from 1978 to 2008. *Economic Geography* 32 (4): 12–18.

Ye, X., L. Ma, K. Ye, J. Chen, and Q. Xie. 2017. Analysis of regional inequality from sectoral structure, spatial policy and economic development: A case study of Chongqing, China. *Sustainability* 9 (4): 633.

Yue, W., Y. Zhang, X. Ye, Y. Cheng, and M. R. Leipnik. 2014. Dynamics of multi-scale intra-provincial regional inequality in Zhejiang, China. *Sustainability* 6 (9): 5763–5784.

Zhang, J., and F. Wu. 2006. China's changing economic governance: Administrative annexation and the reorganization of local governments in the Yangtze River Delta. *Regional Studies* 40 (1): 3–21.

Zhang, W., W. Xu, and X. Wang. 2019. Regional convergence clubs in China: identification and conditioning factors. *The Annals of Regional Science*. 62(2), 327–350.

Zhang, Y., D. Tong, and X. Liang. 2018. New perspective on regional inequality: Theory and evidence from Guangdong, China. *Journal of Urban Planning and Development* 144 (1): 04018002.

4 Provincial dynamics and multi-mechanism process of regional inequality

In Chapter 3, we have characterized the multi-scalar patterns and distribution dynamics of regional inequality in China. This chapter aims to deepen our understanding of the dynamics and multi-mechanism process of China's uneven development. Specifically, we use both traditional locational quotient and a newly developed exploratory spatial-temporal data analysis (ESTDA) method, namely space–time paths, to investigate the development trajectories of selected provinces and their spatial dependence on neighboring regions. By doing so, we examine how individual province's growth trajectories and spatial spillovers might have influenced the changes in spatial inequality in economic development across regions and provinces. Lastly, both spatial and time-series and spatial econometric techniques were employed to model the underlying forces of regional development following the multi-mechanism framework and to assess the impacts of triple processes, namely globalization, marketization, and decentralization, on uneven regional development in China.

4.1 Changing statuses of regions, provinces, and municipalities

In order to depict how an individual region's development status has an influence on regional inequality, the location quotient method is used to evaluate the trend of an individual region's status as compared with the national average.

$$LQ = \frac{\dfrac{X_i}{\sum X_i}}{\dfrac{Y_i}{\sum Y_i}}$$

Where X_i and $\sum X_i$ are the regional and total value of the indicator, like GDP, export, fixed asset investment, local fiscal expenditure, and industrial output, and Y_i and $\sum Y_i$ are the regional and total population base. Therefore, LQ over 1 means that a region's status is above the average level, while LQ less than 1 indicates the opposite. As evident in Figure 3.6, the Eastern region was generally

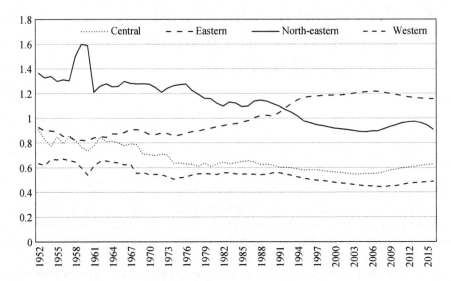

Figure 4.1 Location quotients of different regions in China.

better off during the reform era, contributing to the rise of between-region inequality during the post-reform era (see Figure 3.4). In contrast, LQs of the north-eastern, central, and western regions declined substantially until the mid-2000s, which contributed to the rise of interregional inequality in the past three decades. The interregional inequality in China has declined slightly, which could be attributed to the recent catch-up of the inland regions (see Figure 4.1).

Development trajectories of individual provinces also have a profound influence on regional inequality in China. In this section, LQs of GDP per capita for specific provincial units were calculated to elaborate on how individual provinces could have an impact on regional inequality. As shown in Table 4.1, these provinces are selected based on their geographical location and significance for regional inequality as discussed in the previous literature (Yu and Wei 2003).

In the pre-reform era (1952–1978), the economic statuses of municipalities such as Beijing and Shanghai had been superior to other coastal provinces

Table 4.1 Representative provincial-level units

Region	Centrally Administered Municipalities	Provinces
Eastern	Beijing, Shanghai	Jiangsu, Guangdong
Central		Henan, Hunan, Jiangxi
North-eastern		Heilongjiang, Jilin, Liaoning
Western		Sichuan, Gansu, Inner Mongolia

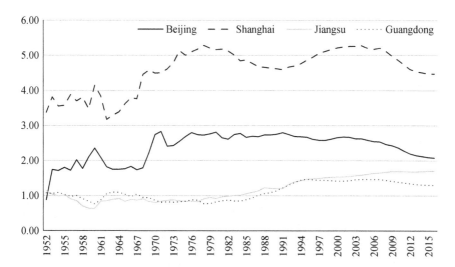

Figure 4.2 LQ changes of selected provinces in the eastern region.

(Figure 4.2). Partly due to the central planning system and interests of national defense during the pre-reform period, LQs of Jiangsu and Guangdong Provinces were approximately 1 between 1952 and the late 1970s (Figure 4.2). In the 1980s and 1990s, Jiangsu and Guangdong Provinces within the eastern region had relatively higher growth rates in comparison with the two most developed municipalities. The rise of these coastal provinces contributed to declining intraregional inequality and interprovincial inequality particularly in the 1980s and the 1990s (see Figure 3.4 and Figure 3.6).

LQs of specific inland provinces, such as Hunan in the central region and Gansu in the western region, had maintained their positions before the reform (Figure 4.3 and Figure 4.4). However, a number of provinces at the border, such as Inner Mongolia or Neimenggu in the western region and Heilongjiang in the north-eastern region, fell in the pre-reform period (Figure 4.4 and Figure 4.5). The evident spatial variations of regional development trajectories resulted in a significantly high level of intraregional-level spatial inequalities of economic development in the pre-reform period (Figure 3.4).

In the reform era, LQs of some originally more developed provinces in the north-eastern and western regions, such as Liaoning and Gansu Provinces, have declined (Figure 4.4 and Figure 4.5). For example, the LQ of Gansu Province dropped from 0.74 in 1978 to 0.54 in 2015 (Figure 4.4). Liaoning Province in the north-eastern region, which used to be an important industrial province, suffered from the historic burden of state-owned enterprises (SOE), and its LQ descended from 1.59 in 1975 to 1.09 in 2015 (Figure 4.5). In contrast, during the reform era, some inland provinces with an abundance of natural resources have gained momentum due to the increased demand for energy from the booming

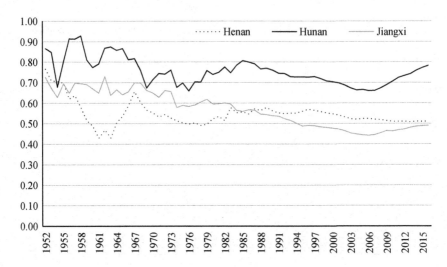

Figure 4.3 LQ changes in selected provinces in the central region.

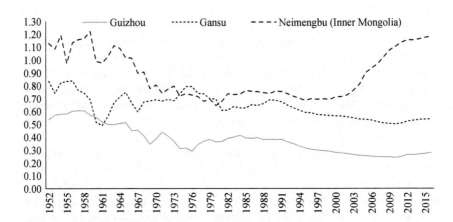

Figure 4.4 LQ changes in selected provinces in the western region.

manufacturing industries in the coastal region. A typical case would be Inner Mongolia, whose LQ rose from 0.84 in 2002 to 1.37 in 2015 (Figure 4.4).

To shed further light on regional development in China, we also calculated growth rates of provincial GDP per capita (Table 4.2) and mapped the provincial GDP per capita in specific cross-sections (Figure 4.6). Four important sub-periods were selected: (1) 1952–1978, which was the pre-reform era; (2) 1980–1990 when the economic reform was implemented in specific regions and provinces; (3) 1990–2000, which marked the deepening of reform; (4) 2000–2015, when the economy grew fast after China's accession into the WTO. In 1952, municipalities

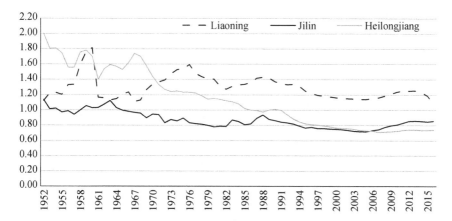

Figure 4.5 LQ changes in selected provinces in the north-eastern region.

and some industrial provinces in the northern part of China had higher GDP per capita, followed by coastal provinces in the south-eastern region. This pattern remained largely the same in 1980 when the reform just began (Figure 4.5). In the 1980s, the average growth rates of Beijing and Shanghai were much lower than the coastal provinces. The growth rate of Shanghai was even lower than the national average, which results in declining interprovincial inequality in the 1980s (Figure 3.4 and Table 4.2).

Since the early 1990s when more open-door policies were implemented in Shanghai and the Yangtze River Delta, economic growth in Shanghai accelerated and growth rates of most coastal provinces were higher than the growth rates of other provinces in the western and central regions (Table 4.2). This contributes to the increase of both interprovincial and interregional inequalities in the 1990s. By 2000, the provinces with the highest GDP per capita were mostly located in the coastal region (Figure 4.6). The spatial pattern of provincial-level GDP per capita in 2015 was similar to that in 2000 and most western provinces remained the poorest provinces in China (Figure 4.6). Therefore, the gap between the coastal and interior regions increased consistently in most of the reform period.

Nevertheless, with the efforts to develop the interior since the late 1990s, it is worth highlighting that in the 2000s, provinces in the western region had grown faster than the provinces in the eastern region (Table 4.2). The average growth rate of per capita GDP was 11.50, as compared with 11.07 in the eastern provinces. The highest growth rate of GDP per capita occurred in such western provinces as Neimengbo (Inner Mongolia), where natural resources such as coal and oil are abundant (Table 4.2 and Figure 4.5). As the only centrally administrated municipality in the western region, Chongqing has exhibited a catching-up trajectory in recent years, with an annual growth rate of 12.79%. Although recent growth rates of some western provinces had been apparently high, we hold that

Table 4.2 Level and growth of per capita GDP in Chinese provinces

Provinces	Level (1978 constant yuan)					Annual growth rate (%)			
	1952	1978	1990	2000	2015	1952–1978	1978–1990	1990–2000	2000–2015
Eastern Region	154	485	1,262	4,031	18,344	4.51	8.30	12.31	10.63
Beijing	140	1,249	3,000	7,953	28,395	8.78	7.58	10.24	8.85
Tianjin	304	1,141	2,315	6,525	42,381	5.22	6.07	10.92	13.29
Hebei	129	362	794	2,431	9,398	4.05	6.76	11.84	9.43
Shanghai	537	2,484	5,035	15,614	60,656	6.07	6.06	11.98	9.47
Jiangsu	180	427	1,311	4,605	23,087	3.38	9.80	13.39	11.35
Zhejiang	133	330	1,105	4,197	18,507	3.56	10.60	14.28	10.40
Fujian	116	271	817	2,961	13,764	3.32	9.63	13.74	10.79
Shandong	100	315	837	2,810	13,762	4.51	8.48	12.88	11.17
Guangdong	171	367	1,256	4,308	17,719	2.98	10.80	13.12	9.89
Hainan	–	310	795	2,211	5,280	–	8.16	10.77	5.97
North-eastern Region	217	560	1,218	2,748	12,796	3.71	6.69	8.48	10.80
Liaoning	178	675	1,495	3,479	16,097	5.26	6.85	8.81	10.75
Heilongjiang	319	559	1,103	2,293	9,970	2.18	5.83	7.59	10.29
Jilin	181	382	938	2,239	11,467	2.91	7.77	9.09	11.50
Central Region	149	311	718	1,758	7,510	2.87	7.22	9.37	10.16
Shanxi	130	363	799	1,869	7,826	4.03	6.80	8.87	10.02
Anhui	157	242	586	1,528	7,145	1.68	7.65	10.06	10.83
Jiangxi	175	273	651	1,508	6,732	1.73	7.51	8.76	10.49
Henan	122	231	613	1,641	6,925	2.49	8.47	10.35	10.08
Hubei	138	330	829	2,108	10,480	3.41	7.98	9.78	11.28
Hunan	115	285	587	1,439	6,626	3.55	6.21	9.38	10.72
Western Region	106	262	621	1,494	7,137	3.54	7.46	9.18	10.99
Inner Mongolia	179	318	827	2,132	15,915	2.23	8.29	9.93	14.34
Guangxi	74	223	408	1,113	4,929	4.33	5.16	10.56	10.43

Chongqing	113	255	609	1,667	10,145	3.18	7.52	10.59	12.79
Sichuan	106	261	630	1,569	7,756	3.53	7.62	9.55	11.24
Guizhou	85	174	415	843	3,696	2.79	7.51	7.34	10.36
Yunnan	88	223	570	1,293	5,157	3.64	8.13	8.54	9.66
Tibet	123	372	745	1,928	8,624	4.35	5.96	9.98	10.50
Shaanxi	96	292	741	1,769	9,287	4.37	8.07	9.09	11.69
Gansu	133	346	749	1,689	7,294	3.75	6.65	8.47	10.24
Qinghai	116	426	759	1,503	6,796	5.13	4.93	7.07	10.58
Ningxia	98	366	805	1,567	6,403	5.20	6.79	6.89	9.84
Xinjiang	190	317	906	1,914	6,568	1.99	9.15	7.77	8.57

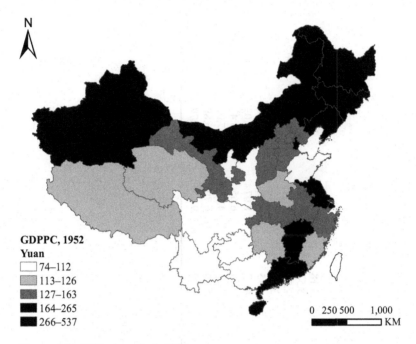

Figure 4.6a GDP per capita in 1952.

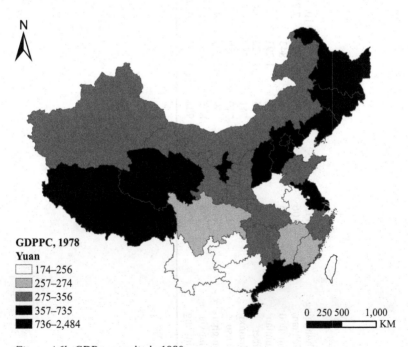

Figure 4.6b GDP per capita in 1980.

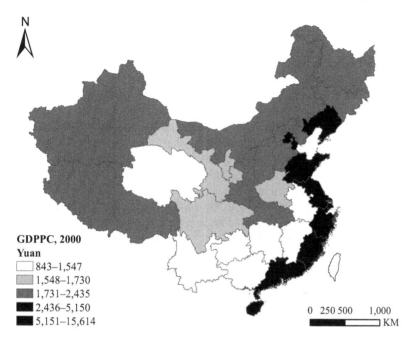

Figure 4.6c GDP per capita in 2000.

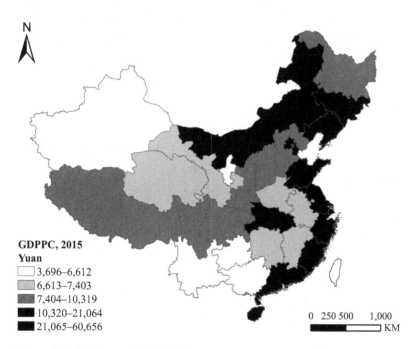

Figure 4.6d GDP per capita in 2015.

the noticeable decline of interregional and interprovincial inequalities after 2005 may be caused by both development policies and market forces, which changed the status of the coastal region.

Moreover, under the global economic crisis, the central government did invest heavily in infrastructure development and those inland areas benefited from these giant infrastructure projects, such as the construction of high-speed railway (Shi and Huang 2014). Meanwhile, the 2008 global economic crisis has negatively affected the development status of coastal provinces where exports played a key role in their economic growth. In short, recent declining regional inequality should be more carefully examined when longer-time data become available. The efforts made by the Chinese government may only have certain impact on regional development in specific localities such as Chongqing in the western region and some provinces in the central region, but the coastal areas have still been far ahead of the inland regions as a whole in terms of economic development (Hao and Wei 2010).

4.2 Space–time analysis of provincial dynamics

Aided by the GIS techniques, this section researches the bottom–up provincial-level dynamics of regional inequality with a focus on the spatial effects (Yu and Wei 2003). Specifically, a novel ESTDA method called space–time path was employed to reveal the trajectories and spatial effects, and more generally in the evolution of regional development in China. As evident in Figure 4.7, the global Moran's *I* of regional development measured by per capita GDP at the provincial level increased consistently from less than 0.1 to 0.4 during the past six decades, a rise of 400%. This result indicates the spatial clustering or concentration of regional economic development in China across provinces has been evident. Specifically, these trends are not detected using conventional

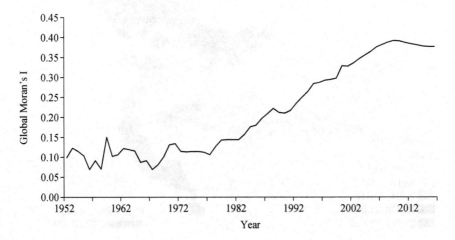

Figure 4.7 Global Moran's *I* of provincial-level GDP per capita, 1952–2016.

inequality measures. For instance, the results of CV or Theil statistics indicate the declining regional inequality in the 1980s, while the results of spatial auto-correlation or Moran's I imply a strengthening tendency of local clusters.

Although the global Moran's I statistic could identify the increasingly spatial clustering of regional development in China, those bottom–up paths of the indi-vidual province and detailed local hotspots are not fully examined. The space–time paths, an ESTDA tool, can depict the trajectory of individual provinces in a two-dimensional economic space, of which the x-axis represents the relative GDP per capita of the focal region's economy and the y-axis is the spatially weighted GDP per capita of the adjacent regions. By investigating the path's trend in the economic space, the space–time path method reveals the develop-ment modes, either the local economy develops or declines as its neighbors develop or decline, and the role of spatial effects (Figure 4.8).

Specifically, as shown in Figure 4.8 each quadrant refers to the case that local areas and the neighbors are below or above the average level, and each pattern

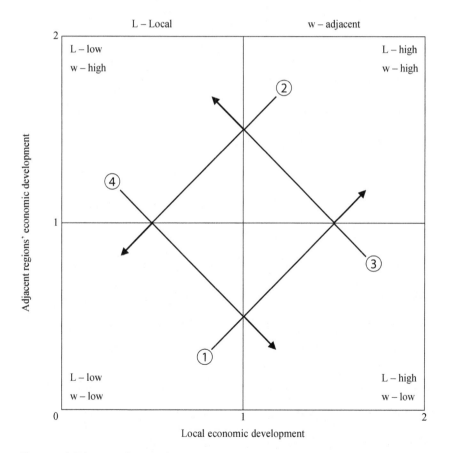

Figure 4.8 Diagram of space–time method. Adapted from Gu *et al.* (2016).

refers to the situation if the relative status of the local or the neighbors is improving or exacerbating. Taking the Type IV pattern, for example, the path indicates that the focal region is developing but the economies of its neighbors are lagging behind. The method extends the static view of local spatial dependence into the dynamic context (Ye and Rey 2013). It can be considered as a continuous representation of spatial dynamics and a powerful exploratory tool to understand the local system's stability and dynamics in practice (Rey and Janikas 2005).

Space–time paths of regional development of provinces in the coastal region

Following Yu and Wei (2003), four coastal provinces, namely Jiangsu, Shanghai, Zhejiang, and Guangdong, are selected to unfold the individual development trajectories and patterns during the rise of coastal China using space–time paths (Figure 4.9). The x values of the trajectories of Jiangsu, Zhejiang, and Guangdong Provinces are less than 1 before 1980, which implies that their economic performance was below the national average. Since Shanghai is the neighbor for both Jiangsu and Zhejiang provinces, the two coastal provinces have partially benefited from its spillovers and the values of its neighboring provinces were above the national average before the reform. In contrast, Guangdong province is adjacent to either other coastal provinces like Fujian and Guangxi or the less developed interior provinces like Hunan and Jiangxi. Both Guangdong's and its neighborhoods' relative GDP were below the national average before the reform (Figure 4.9).

As discussed earlier, the development trajectories since the reform in 1978 indicate that the coastal provinces have moved upward except for Shanghai during China's transition to a market economy. The trajectory of Shanghai indicates that its relative advantageous economic status has declined since the reform (Figure 4.9), which is attributed to the rise of Guangdong and other originally poorer coastal provinces (Tian *et al.* 2016). The adjacent regions of Shanghai experienced a stronger growth before 2000 and stabilized after 2000, reflecting the development of private enterprises in these provinces and the increasingly integrated development of the Yangtze River Delta (YRD), which comprises Zhejiang, Shanghai, and Jiangsu. Zhejiang Province, known for the development of private enterprises, experienced relatively faster economic growth in the first two decades of the reform of the 1980s and the 1990s, but its status has relatively stabilized since 2000 (Figure 4.9). For Jiangsu Province, the local economy consistently outperformed the national average during the reform era, while its adjacent provinces have gone through slight descent, rapid ascent, rapid descent, and slight re-ascent stages in the four decades after 1980. Guangdong Province represents a third mode of development trajectory when spatial spillover is considered. While the development of Guangdong experienced a similar ascent–descent process before and after 2000 like Zhejiang, its adjacent regions have consistently moved upward since 1990.

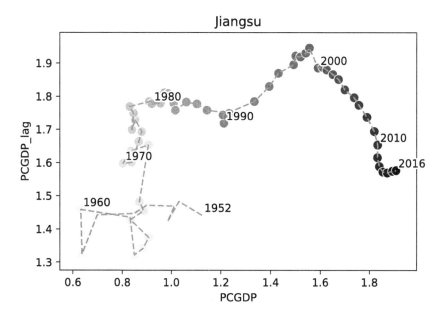

Figure 4.9a Space–time paths of selected coastal provinces: Jiangsu.

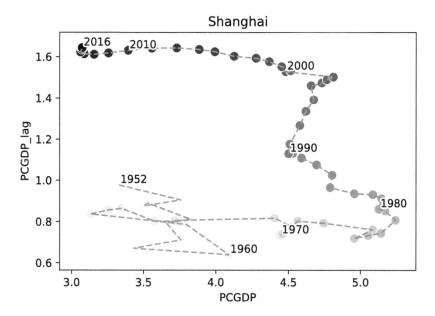

Figure 4.9b Space–time paths of selected coastal provinces: Shanghai.

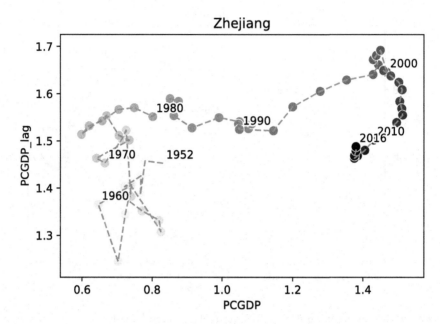

Figure 4.9c Space–time paths of selected coastal provinces: Zhejiang.

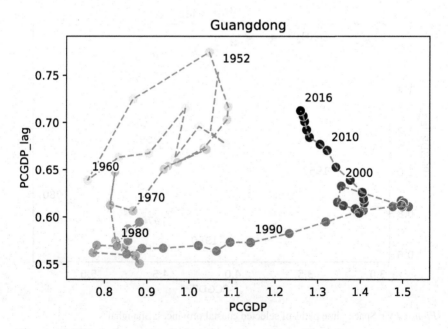

Figure 4.9d Space–time paths of selected coastal provinces: Guangdong.

Space–time paths of regional development of provinces in the north-eastern region

In line with the rise of coastal provinces, north-east China has lost its favored status and declined during the transition (Kanbur and Zhang 2005; Fan, Kanbur, and Zhang 2009). The three north-eastern provinces, Heilongjiang, Jilin, and Liaoning, as well as Inner Mongolia in the western region, are selected to investigate their development patterns before and after the reform. Though the north-eastern provinces have formed and maintained a developed club before the reform (Figure 4.10). At the beginning of the study period, the economic performance of four provinces was above the national average, as well as for the adjacent provinces since they are neighbors to each other. But the four provinces have lost their advantageous status before the reform partly due to the concern about national defense. Inner Mongolia, Heilongjiang, and Jilin Provinces have consistently declined from 1952 to 1980. Liaoning Province was the only province that managed to achieve growth during the period. The pre-reform policies favor the development of heavy industries and SOEs, especially in Liaoning.

During the 1980s and the 1990s, all of the four provinces experienced a period of stagnation and decline. Specifically, in Liaoning Province, though the SOEs were still dominant in heavy industries and capital-intensive sectors at the beginning of the reform in 1978, the supporting pillars, like the trinity system, have gradually collapsed during China's transition from a planned

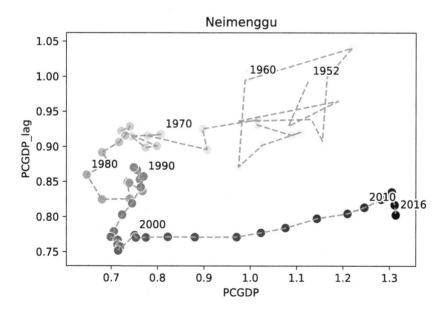

Figure 4.10a Space–time paths of north-eastern provinces and Inner Mongolia: Inner Mongolia.

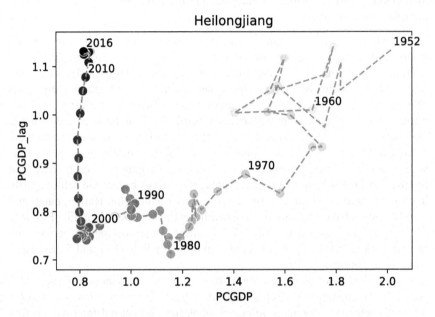

Figure 4.10b Space–time paths of north-eastern provinces and Inner Mongolia: Heilongjiang.

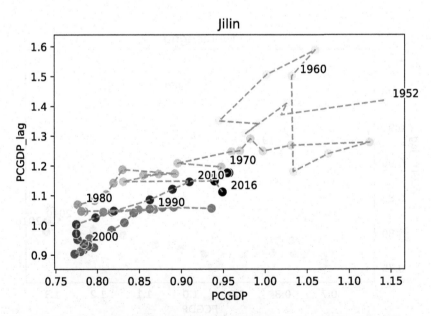

Figure 4.10c Space–time paths of north-eastern provinces and Inner Mongolia: Jilin.

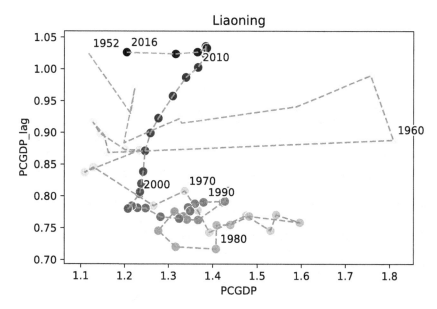

Figure 4.10d Space–time paths of north-eastern provinces and Inner Mongolia: Liaoning.

economy to a market economy (Hu 2007; Hu and Lin 2013). However, the issues related with the poor performance of SOEs have remained, which include the insufficient motivation of workers or managers because of the ambiguous property rights under socialism, the erosion of SOEs' monopolistic profits, the competition from the non-SOE sectors, and the heavy socio-economic obligations of SOEs like the tribute revenue transferred to the central government and the housing, medical, pension, and other social welfare to their employees (Hu 2005). As a result, the north-eastern provinces, as the most concentrated region of China's old industrial bases and unproductive SOEs, have further declined during the 1980s and 1990s.

As mentioned earlier, the economic gravity center in China has moved northward since the 2000s, due to complex global and domestic contexts, spatial restructuring and transformation in economic activities, and the spatial shifting of favored foreign investment locations (He, Bayrak, and Lin 2017; He, Fang, and Zhang 2017). Together with the revitalization of the north-eastern old industrial bases program launched by the central government, these four provinces have achieved substantial economic growth after 2000; their neighbors have experienced steady growth until the slowdown after 2010.

Space–time paths of regional development in the Bohai-rim region

The individual trajectories of provinces around the Bohai Bay area, namely Beijing, Tianjin, Hebei, and Shandong, are also the focal provinces for several reasons. First, the Bohai-rim economic zone ranks as the third-largest metropolitan region after the Pearl River Delta (PRD) and the YRD. Second, the intensifying inequality and core–periphery structure in the Greater Beijing area has drawn considerable scholarly attention in recent years (Yu 2006, 2014; Yu and Wei 2008). Third, as two directly administrated municipalities, Beijing and Tianjin show strong economic performance, and their neighboring provinces, Hebei and Shandong Provinces, have transitioned from a very poor region to a poor region.

As shown in Figure 4.11, Beijing and Tianjin have potentially developed during the pre-reform era when the development policies were urban- and industrial-biased. The relative GDP per capita of Beijing and Tianjin reached as high as 2.5 times the national average on the eve of the reform. In contrast, the economic statuses of Hebei and Shandong Provinces remained stable or declined during the pre-reform period. After the reform, the advantageous status of Beijing has faded and converged to the national average, especially after the mid-1990s. The adjacent regions of Beijing were characterized by the rapid declining phase from 1980 to 1995, the rapid rising phase from 1995 to 2005, and the stable phase from 2005 to 2016. The trajectory of Hebei Province after the reform indicates that the spatial effects are dependent on the study period.

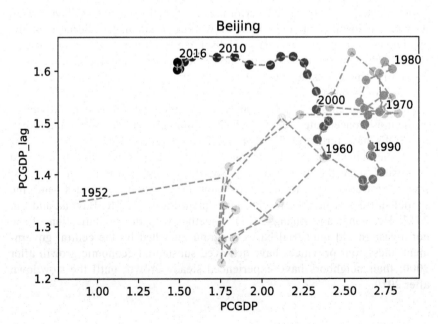

Figure 4.11a Space–time paths of provincial economies in the Bohai-rim region: Beijing.

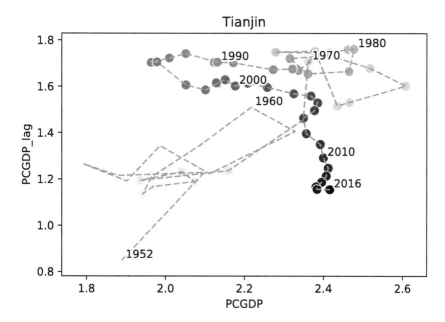

Figure 4.11b Space–time paths of provincial economies in the Bohai-rim region: Tianjin.

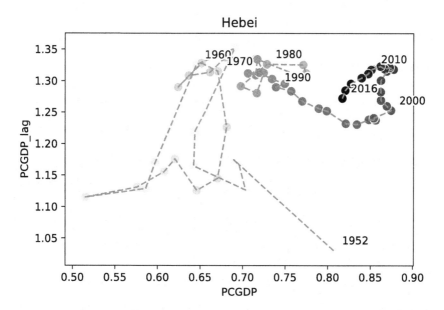

Figure 4.11c Space–time paths of provincial economies in the Bohai-rim region: Hebei.

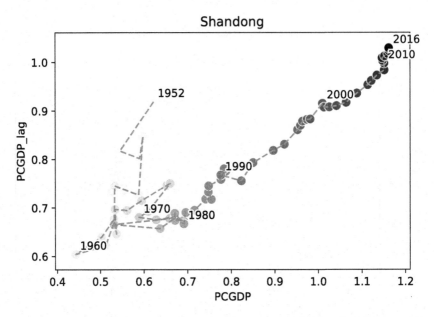

Figure 4.11d Space–time paths of provincial economies in the Bohai-rim region: Shandong.

From the 1980s to the 2000s, the spatial spillovers from Beijing and Tianjin had positive impacts on promoting Hebei's economic development. But the spillover effects declined since 2000, which partially leads to the stagnation and relatively declining status in the 2000s and 2010s. For the case of Shandong, it has achieved a typical win-win mode for the economic development of the local and adjacent regions, because it could take the advantages of locating in the coastal portion of the Bohai-rim economic zone and geographical proximity to South Korea and Japan (Kim and Zhang 2008).

The space–time path results also help to deepen the understanding of economic dynamics and transformations in the Greater Beijing area (Figure 4.11). The diverging trend between Beijing and Tianjin as the core and Hebei Province as the periphery in the pre-reform period is attributed to the "urban-industrialization" process under the planned economy, which has made the industrialized urban areas in Beijing and Tianjin grow at a relatively high speed while rural Hebei was less developed (Yu 2006). Since the reform, the economic performance in Hebei Province has been promoted because the trickle-down effects and benefits from the reform policies have become evident after the early 1990s (Yu and Wei 2008).

But the temporary converging trend in the Greater Beijing area has been replaced by the divergence trend after 2000. The different development trajectories are due to the specific geopolitical context of Beijing and Tianjin and Hebei as a province geographically containing the two. Beijing as China's capital and Tianjin as a centrally administrated municipality are more preferred not only in the urbanization and industrialization processes but also with more resources and preferential policies during China's reform (Wei and Yu 2006; Yu 2006, 2014; Yu and Wei 2008). Beijing and Tianjin took one step ahead of Hebei Province to implement the reform policies after the validation in the southern provinces. The governmental supports, fixed asset investment, and capital from the foreign investors are all concentrated in Beijing and Tianjin rather than Hebei Province. At the same time, Beijing and Tianjin have evident backwash effects on Hebei Province since 2000 by drawing labor, capital, and resources, which has impeded the local economic development. Hebei's support or sacrifice, partly as the political task, has guaranteed the stable economic development in Beijing and Tianjin but also created a "poverty belt" around the country's capital (Yuan and Wang 2014; Sun, Xu, *et al.* 2016).

Space–time paths of regional development in the western and central regions

Two central provinces, Henan and Gansu, and two western provinces, Guizhou and Guangxi, are selected to be compared with the coastal provinces discussed above (Figure 4.12). The four interior provinces share several characteristics in common regarding economic development, e.g., low urbanization level, dominant SOEs sector as the legacy of "Third Front Construction" program, remote and mountainous geographical locations, and as the target of poverty alleviation policies from the central government (Wei and Fang 2006; Li and Wei 2014; Sun, Lin, *et al.* 2016; Dai *et al.* 2017). Like the other regions, the trajectory of interior provinces also shows a fluctuating economic development process during the pre-reform period. A general descent trend is observed for GDP per capita and its spatial lag from 1952 to 1980, indicating that beginning with a relatively low economic status, the four provinces and their adjacent regions had further diverged away from the national average. The trajectories in the 1980s and 1990s imply that the interior provinces and their adjacent provinces have experienced stagnation or a moderate decline in regional development when the economy in the coastal provinces has substantially developed. Since 2000, the trends of four provinces have been reversed, with both the local and the adjacent economies being promoted to reach or surpass the pre-reform level.

Further scrutiny on the regional development processes reveals the underlying forces behind the space–time path trajectory. Driven by the desire to alter the historically uneven spatial pattern of regional development and the national security concerns, the central government has allocated considerable investment and resources to the interior provinces, which has reached the peak during the "Third Front Construction" program from 1965 to 1971 (Ma and Wei 1997; Wei 2000). Consequently, the economic status of the interior provinces has been promoted to a certain degree within the descent trend in the pre-reform period. After the reform, the interior provinces lagged behind in implementing reform

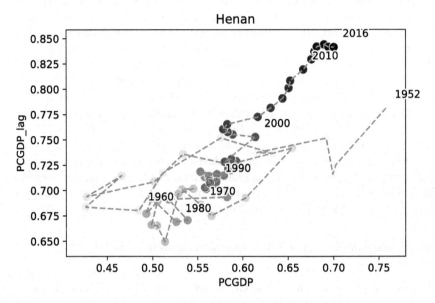

Figure 4.12a Space–time paths of selected interior provinces: Henan.

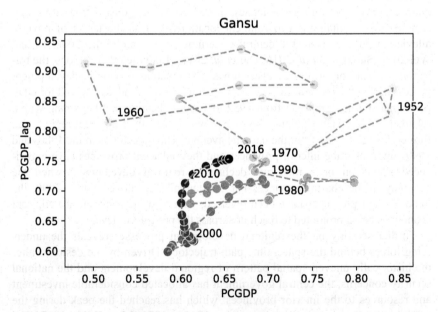

Figure 4.12b Space–time paths of selected interior provinces: Gansu.

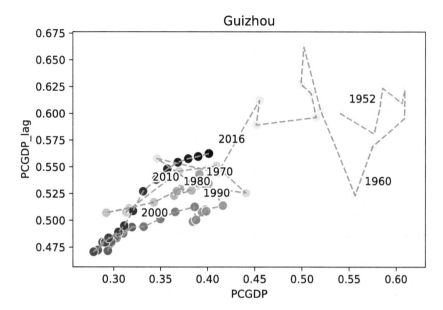

Figure 4.12c Space–time paths of selected interior provinces: Guizhou.

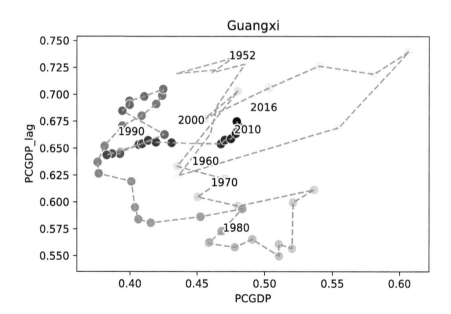

Figure 4.12d Space–time paths of selected interior provinces: Guangxi.

policies and were slow in the transition to a market economy, which results in the stagnation or moderate decline in the 1980s and 1990s (Wei and Fang 2006). But the reversed ascent trend since 2000 implies that the poverty alleviation policies, i.e., the Western Development program and the Rise of Central China program, have gradually taken effect and promoted the central and western regions in China. However, the relative income level of selected provinces was still low, with the highest one of Henan as 70% and the lowest one of Guizhou as 40% of the national average in 2016 (Figure 4.12).

4.3 Modeling multi-mechanisms of regional inequality

Sigma convergence and time-series analysis of the multi-mechanism process

As discussed in Section 4.2, the evolution of regional inequalities in China, especially since the implementation of reform, has been driven by economic transition and market reform (Wei 2002). Recent studies found that the three policy variables, including globalization, marketization, and decentralization, are also fundamental causes of inland–coastal disparities or regional inequality across both pre-reform and post-reform periods (Kanbur and Zhang 2005; Hao and Wei 2010). Two regression exercises are carried out using the time-series data in the period of 1952–2013. Table 4.3 presents the major independent variables based on the triple-process transition framework mentioned above. Decentralization is measured by the ratio of local government expenditure to the total government expenditure. The effect of globalization is represented by the ratio of total trade volume to total GDP in each year. We also employed the share of total employment from non-state-owned enterprises to capture the process of marketization.

Table 4.3 Trends of trade, marketization, and decentralization in China, 1952–2013

Year	Globalization (trade ratio or total trade volume divided by GDP)	Decentralization (% of local government expenditure)	Marketization (% of employment from state-owned enterprises)
1952	9.51	25.90	98.57
1960	8.81	56.71	84.50
1965	6.89	23.48	75.29
1970	4.99	41.12	77.09
1975	10.18	50.13	78.38
1980	12.54	45.74	76.78
1985	22.92	60.32	72.75
1990	29.78	67.43	73.59
1995	38.66	70.76	73.48
2000	39.58	65.25	69.97
2005	63.82	74.14	57.44
2010	49.33	82.21	49.93
2013	43.90	85.40	35.15

Our models are to test the association between regional inequality (at both provincial and regional levels) and the triple-process economic transition in China over the 60 years of 1952–2013. We used one-period lagged values of the independent variables as regressors to reduce potential endogeneity problems, while all independent variables are in logarithms. We have found that the log-level models give a better fit on R^2. One important issue in the long-run time series analysis is the structural break. We located the break at the start of the reform in the late 1970s and added specific interaction terms to depict the influences of reform on these associations. The correlation analyses reveal potential multicollinearity problems due to strong correlations between the three independent variables, with a correlation coefficient greater than 0.75.

To test the significance of the three underlying mechanisms, the proxies of the triple-process of economic transition are introduced separately into the models. Several findings emerge based on our modeling results. First, models focusing on interregional inequality can better capture the influences of economic transition on regional inequality, with a higher value of R^2. The Chow tests indicate a significant break in 1979. Second, the variables representing decentralization, marketization, and globalization are significant drivers of regional inequalities at both provincial and regional levels (Table 4.4 and Table 4.5), with expected coefficient signs. Third, results suggest that there has been a possible association between globalization and regional inequality at both provincial and regional levels. In particular, the results of the interaction terms demonstrate that this relationship has been strengthened during the reform period.

Therefore, when China implemented its opening-up policies, the coastal region had found itself with a comparative advantage in exporting sectors and the faster growth in the coastal region contributed to a widening gap between regions and provinces. Coefficients for marketization also tell the same story and these findings are consistent with previous works (Fujita and Hu 2001). With respect to the effect of decentralization, regression results suggest a positive and significant association between regional inequality and local governments' fiscal capacity, while we do not find that the association was more evident during the reform era.

Beta convergence and spatial-regime analysis

The previous analyses indicate that patterns of regional development in China are a spatially heterogeneous and spatial dependent process, and there have been similarities and dissimilarities in the space–time paths of provinces in the same or different regions. Built on the multi-mechanism framework (Wei 1999, 2000), results of time-series regression have confirmed the impacts of the triple-process economic transition on regional development in general and regional inequality in particular. This section further investigates the spatial regimes of underlying driving forces of regional economic growth in China, with a focus on the reform era. By applying both non-spatial and spatial regression techniques, we quantified the impacts of globalization,

Table 4.4 Correlates of interprovincial inequalities and economic transition, 1952–2013

Variables	Model 1	Model 2	Model 3	Model 4	Model 5	Model 6
Marketization	0.283***	0.171***				
		(0.053)				
Globalization			0.209***	−0.224		
			(0.035)	(0.152)		
Decentralization					0.647***	0.754***
					(0.058)	(0.111)
Reform*marketization		0.225*				
		(0.135)				
Reform*globalization				0.431**		
				(0.165)		
Reform*decentralization						−0.261
						(0.207)
						1.036
						(0.860)
Reform (after 1979=1)		0.471***		−0.855**		
		(0.183)		(0.436)		
Constant	−1.55***	−1.84***	−2.56***	−1.69***	−4.54***	−4.93***
	(0.063)	(0.104)	(0.104)	(0.360)	(0.230)	(0.479)
Chow-test (*F statistics*)		7.85***		4.25**		7.75***
Adjusted *R* square	0.451	0.555	0.407	0.466	0.675	0.676
Number of observations	61	61	61	61	61	61

Table 4.5 Correlates of interregional inequality and economic transition, 1952–2013

Variables	Model 1	Model 2	Model 3	Model 4	Model 5	Model 6
Marketization	0.852*** (0.139)	0.253** (0.115)				
Globalization			0.881*** (0.077)	−0.702** (0.315)		
Decentralization					2.199*** (0.174)	1.158*** (0.275)
Reform*marketization		0.673** (0.296)				
Reform*globalization				1.388*** (0.795)		
Reform*decentralization						0.599
Reform (after 1979=1)		2.042*** (0.399)		−2.391*** (0.795)		−1.672 (1.768)
Constant	−2.100*** (0.220)	−3.692*** (0.228)	−5.856*** (0.229)	−2.704*** (0.656)	−12.076*** (0.694)	−8.426*** (1.017)
Chow-test (F statistics)		42.03***		15.86***		13.06***
Adjusted R square	0.378	0.753	0.682	0.789	0.726	0.806
Number of observations	61	61	61	61	61	61

decentralization, and marketization processes on the convergence or divergence of provinces, following a beta convergence framework (Zhang, Xu,
and Wang 2019).

The annual GDP per capita growth rate is selected as the dependent variable,
which is calculated by the constant price GDP and resident population in each
province. The initial GDP per capita (y_0), the ratio of fixed asset investment in
GDP (K), the ratio of higher education student enrollment in total population
(H), and the composite variable of population growth, technology advancement,
and capital depreciation rate ($n+g+\delta$) are selected to test the conditional
β-convergence using the neoclassical growth model (Barro *et al.* 1991; Mankiw,
Romer, and Weil 1992; Cravo and Resende 2013; Li and Fang 2016).

The triple processes of globalization, decentralization, and marketization are
represented by the ratio of export in GDP (EXP), the ratio of SOEs in fixed-asset
investment (SOE), and the ratio of local expenditure in GDP (LEXP), respectively (Yu and Wei 2003; Li and Wei 2010; Liao and Wei 2016). The pooled
OLS model and the spatial regime model (SRM) expansion based on the
regional division of the eastern, central, western, and north-eastern China could
be expressed as follows:

$$\ln\left(\frac{y_{i,t}}{y_{i,0}}\right) = \beta_0 \ln\left(y_{i,0}\right) + \beta X_{i,t} + \mu_{i,t}$$

$$
\begin{bmatrix}
\ln\left(\dfrac{y_{i,t}}{y_{i,0}}\right), e \\[2mm]
\ln\left(\dfrac{y_{i,t}}{y_{i,0}}\right), c \\[2mm]
\ln\left(\dfrac{y_{i,t}}{y_{i,0}}\right), w \\[2mm]
\ln\left(\dfrac{y_{i,t}}{y_{i,0}}\right), n
\end{bmatrix}
=
\begin{bmatrix}
\ln(y_{i,0}), e & X_{i,t}, e & \cdots & \\
& \vdots & & \ddots & \vdots \\
& & \cdots & \ln(y_{i,0}), n & X_{i,t}, n
\end{bmatrix}
\begin{bmatrix}
\beta_0, e \\
\beta, e \\
\vdots \\
\beta_0, n \\
\beta, n
\end{bmatrix}
+
\begin{bmatrix}
\mu_{i,t}, e \\
\vdots \\
\mu_{i,t}, n
\end{bmatrix}
$$

where $\ln\left(\dfrac{y_{i,t}}{y_{i,0}}\right)$ is the logarithm form of GDP per capita growth for province *i*
from the initial year to the next year *t*, β_0 is the convergence coefficient to be
tested. If $\beta<0$, it implies a convergence trend that the poor provinces develop
faster than the rich provinces, and the convergence rate, λ, equals $-\ln(\beta+1)$. $X_{i,t}$
is $N \times X$ matrices of observations on other explanatory variables and the constant
term. $\mu_{i,t}$ is the error term. The subscripts, *e*, *c*, *w*, and *n*, indicate the spatial
regimes in China.

Table 4.6 reports the Pearson correlation coefficients of the dependent variable and the independent variables. It is not surprising that fixed-asset investment and educated labor are positively correlated to economic growth. The ratio
of SOEs in fixed-asset investment is negatively correlated to the growth rate.

Table 4.6 Correlation coefficients among dependent and independent variables

	1	2	3	4	5	6	7	8
1. y	1							
2. y0	-0.05	1						
3. K	0.12***	0.37***	1					
4. H	0.08**	0.80***	0.58***	1				
5. $n+g+\delta$	-0.44***	0.07**	-0.15***	0.01	1			
6. SOE	-0.24***	-0.57***	-0.44***	-0.65***	0.19***	1		
7. EXP	0.05	0.52***	-0.10***	0.34***	0.26***	-0.23***	1	
8. LEXP	-0.04	0.06*	0.53***	0.09***	0.02	0.16***	-0.18***	1

However, the initial GDP per capita, the proxy of globalization, and the proxy of decentralization are insignificantly correlated to the growth of GDP per capita, and the composite variable, $n+g+\delta$, is negatively correlated to the dependent variable. Furthermore, the correlation between the initial economic status and human capital is as large as 0.8 and significant, indicating the existence of potential multicollinearity problems. In the following pooled OLS regression and SRM, the human capital variable, H, is not included.

Table 4.7 presents the results based on the pooled OLS regression and SRM. After excluding the human capital variable, the multicollinearity problem is controlled as the VIF values are less than 5.0 for all explanatory variables. The ANOVA test and Chow test are both significant at the 0.01 level, indicating that the SRM improves the modeling performance comparing with the pooled OLS regression. While the pooled OLS regression only explains 19% of the variance in economic growth, the SRM reaches as high as 27%. The pooled OLS regression implies that provinces in China have slowly converged during the period of 1978–2016, with a convergence rate of less than 1%. The fixed-asset investment has a significant positive impact on economic growth. As a developmental state, China uses the allocation of fixed-asset investment as a key instrument to promote industrialization and regional development (Ma and Wei 1997; Yu and Wei 2008; Li and Wei 2010). However, the independent variable regarding population growth has a negative impact on economic growth, which is in line with previous convergence test empirics on China (Lau 2010). While the high population growth provides more potential labor and a larger consumer market for economic development, it also limits income per capita and leads to agglomeration diseconomy. Under the industrial restructuring and transformation, economic growth in China relies less and less on cheap labor (Li and Fang 2016). Among the triple processes of decentralization, globalization, and marketization, the ratio of export in GDP is significant in explaining economic growth in provinces, but the ratio of SOE in fixed-asset investment is insignificant and the ratio of local expenditure in GDP has negative impacts on regional development.

The SRM results reveal more interesting findings that are not covered by the pooled OLS regression. First, the national trend has masked the different convergence and divergence trends within spatial regimes, similar to the findings in Chapter 3. The convergence among the eastern provinces matches with the consensus that coastal China has formed a convergence club since the reform (Tian *et al.* 2016; Wei 2017; Zhang, Xu, and Wang 2019). Moreover, north-eastern China has experienced strong β-convergence. It is argued that the gap in north-eastern China has been narrowed significantly and the poor regions have converged rapidly since the implement of the revitalization of north-eastern old industrial bases program (Huang *et al.* 2018). In comparison, central and western China showed a divergence trend during the post-reform period.

Second, the insignificant coefficient with respect to the proxy of the marketization force, proxied by the ratio of SOE in fixed-asset investment, becomes significantly related to economic growth rates in north-eastern provinces. It indicates that the heavy burden of SOEs may impede the economic development,

Table 4.7 Results of the spatial regime model (SRM) and pooled OLS regression

Variables	Pooled OLS		Spatial regime model (SRM)			
	coefficients	*VIF*	*Eastern*	*Central*	*Western*	*North-eastern*
ln(y0)	−0.0082***	4.44	−0.0158***	0.0139*	0.0143***	−0.0426***
ln(K)	0.0356***	3.39	0.0204**	0.0188	−0.0037	0.0195
ln(H)	—	—	—	—	—	—
ln(n+g+δ)	−0.0376***	1.06	−0.0705***	−0.0649***	−0.0246***	−0.0901***
ln(SOE)	−0.0017	2.58	−0.0098*	0.0172	−0.0096	−0.0620**
ln(EXP)	0.0078***	2.08	0.0194***	0.0170**	0.0057**	0.0127**
ln (LEXP)	−0.0165***	2.12	−0.0310***	−0.0430***	−0.0040	−0.0052
Convergence rate	0.8%		1.6%	−1.4%	−1.4%	4.4%
Adjusted R^2	0.1853		0.269			
Observations	899		279	186	341	93

Note
*** *p*-value<0.01;
** *p*-value<0.05;
* *p*-value<0.1.

and on the contrary, if a province implements marketization policies and reinforces the non-SOE sector, it will experience higher economic growth if the other conditions are identical, which is particularly applicable to the northern region.

Third, the proxy of globalization is also significantly related to economic growth rates, regardless of the regions. However, the effects are dependent on the geographical location of the provinces. The positive impact of globalization is strong within the eastern provinces, followed by central and north-eastern China, and the effect in the western provinces is the weakest. It is discussed that the coastal provinces have locational advantages to the global market and foreign investors from Taiwan, Hong Kong, and western countries (Yu and Wei 2003). The opening-up of coastal cities at the beginning of the reform and the deepening integration to the global market since China' entry to the WTO has further benefited the eastern provinces by attracting FDI, developing export-oriented industries, and cultivating specific local development models as discussed above (Wei and Ye 2009; Li and Wei 2010; Wei, Yu, and Chen 2011; Liao and Wei 2012).

4.4 Conclusion

This chapter deepens our understanding of regional inequality in China by looking into individual provincial dynamics in different regions and the underlying multi-mechanism process. First, we utilize both LQs and an ESTDA technique, namely space–time paths, to trace the provincial-level development trajectories. Specifically, the space–time path trajectories help to identify spatial heterogeneous development patterns and relate them to the local contexts. Second, the chapter employs both time-series regression and spatial-econometric regression to quantify the impact of underlying mechanisms, i.e., the triple processes of globalization, decentralization, and marketization, on regional inequality at the provincial and regional levels and economic growth rates at the provincial level. By utilizing the spatial-regime models, we have been able to consider spatially heterogeneous impacts on local economic growth.

By applying ESTDA techniques, we have also found a strong spillover effect of local economic development in China, while we also found that these effects are different across different economic regions. For example, the spillovers from the strong economic performance of the rich region such as Shanghai in the YRD and Guangdong in the southern part have been more evident. By scrutinizing individual province's growth trajectory, we also find that these spillover effects are intertwined with the institutional forces and inequality alleviation programs such as the target of either the Western Development program or the Rise of Central China program. Our results corroborate previous studies that emphasize the role played by the state in China's regional development. During the reform era, the major political goal of the central government in the 1980s and 1990s follows a "getting rich first" philosophy, with Guangdong Province being the exemplary case, the political administration since 2000 has transitioned to and emphasized the "common prosperity," "a harmonious socialist society," and "war on poverty" (Fan 2006; Fan, Kanbur, and Zhang 2011; Graeme 2018). Our results have shown individual provinces have interacted with these top–down policies in very different manners and a bottom–up approach is more powerful in making connections between the micro-scale process and the multiscalar pattern of regional inequality in China.

With respect to driving forces or mechanisms, our modeling efforts challenge the neoclassical account for uneven development or regional convergence. The neoclassical model is mostly based upon assumptions of economic rationality, perfect mobility, and information and competition and is drawing upon the thinking of equilibrium (Chen 2010). However, a set of important policy variables have also been found significantly related to local economic growth in the case of Chinese provinces. Furthermore, our regression analyses have highlighted the three key variables of globalization, decentralization, and marketization, and the importance of bringing economic transition as a fundamental mechanism when examining the underlying causes of changes in regional inequality. Further investigation of the underlying driving forces in the spatiotemporal dynamics validates the importance of spatial regimes in regional development and uncovers spatially heterogeneous mechanisms within regimes. The comparison shows that the spatial regime model (SRM) outperforms the pooled OLS regression, indicating the existence of spatial heterogeneity in the economic growth of provinces. While a weak but significant β-convergence trend is observed for all the provinces, both convergence and divergence trends are identified in different regions.

A strong and significant convergence trend is found for the eastern and north-eastern provinces due to the rising of originally less developed regions (Wei 2017; Huang *et al.* 2018). However, a moderate divergence trend is observed in both central and western China. Though the pooled OLS regression result shows that economic growth in China is heavily driven by fixed-asset investments, this developmental instrument is only significant within eastern China as indicated by the SRM results. For the triple processes of marketization, globalization, and decentralization, only the models focusing on eastern and north-eastern provinces confirm the significant impacts from the emergence of the private and other ownerships and the diminishing of the SOEs sector. Similarly, the globalization effect gradually fades from coastal China to central, north-eastern, and western China in promoting regional development. To summarize, the application of spatial modeling technique helps achieve a more nuanced understanding of the spatial variation of the association between China's economic transition and regional economic growth dynamics. Given the size of the Chinese economy and its scale and complexity, more in-depth case studies of two contrasting provinces, including Guangdong and Zhejiang Provinces, will be presented in the next three chapters.

References

Barro, R. J., X. Sala-i-Martin, O. J. Blanchard, and R. E. Hall. 1991. Convergence across states and regions. *Brookings Papers on Economic Activity* 1991 (1): 107.

Chen, A. 2010. Reducing China's regional disparities: Is there a growth cost? *China Economic Review* 21 (1): 2–13.

Cravo, T., and G. Resende. 2013. Economic growth in Brazil: A spatial filtering approach. *Annals of Regional Science* 50 (2): 555–575.

Dai, Q., X. Ye, Y. H. D. Wei, Y. Ning, and S. Dai. 2017. Geography, ethnicity and regional inequality in Guangxi Zhuang Autonomous Region, China. *Applied Spatial Analysis and Policy*: 1–24.

Fan, C. 2006. China's Eleventh Five-Year Plan (2006–2010): from "getting rich first" to "common prosperity". *Eurasian Geography and Economics* 47 (6): 708–723.

Fan, S., R. Kanbur, and X. Zhang. 2011. China's regional disparities: Experience and policy. *Review of Development Finance* 1 (1): 47–56.

Fujita, M., and D. Hu. 2001. Regional disparity in China 1985–1994: The effects of globalization and economic liberalization. *The Annals of Regional Science* 35 (1): 3–37.

Graeme, S. 2018. The campaign rolls on: Rural governance in China under Xi Jinping and the war on poverty. *China: An International Journal* 16 (3): 163–178.

Gu, J., S. Zhou, and X. Ye. 2016. Uneven regional development under balanced development strategies: Space–time paths of regional development in Guangdong, China. *Tijdschrift voor economische en sociale geografie* 107 (5): 596–610.

Hao, R., and Z. Wei. 2010. Fundamental causes of inland-coastal income inequality in post-reform China. *Annals of Regional Science* 45 (1): 181–206.

He, S., M. M. Bayrak, and H. Lin. 2017. A comparative analysis of multi-scalar regional inequality in China. *Geoforum* 78: 1–11.

He, S., C. Fang, and W. Zhang. 2017. A geospatial analysis of multi-scalar regional inequality in China and in metropolitan regions. *Applied Geography* 88: 199–212.

Hu, F. Z. Y. 2005. Deconstructing state-owned enterprises in socialist China under reform: A scalar examination. *Environment and Planning A: Economy and Space* 37 (4): 703–722.

Hu, F. Z. Y., and G. C. S. Lin. 2013. Placing the transformation of state-owned enterprises in north-east China: The state, region and firm in a transitional economy. *Regional Studies* 47 (4): 563–579.

Hu, Z. 2007. *Placing China's state-owned enterprises: Firm, region and the geography of production.* Hong Kong: University of Hong Kong Theses Online (HKUTO).

Huang, Y., Y. Fang, G. Gu, and J. Liu. 2018. The evolution and differentiation of economic convergence of resource-based cities in northeast China. *Chinese Geographical Science* 28 (3): 495–504.

Kanbur, R., and X. B. Zhang. 2005. Fifty years of regional inequality in China: A journey through central planning, reform, and openness. *Review of Development Economics* 9 (1): 87–106.

Kim, J. Y., and L.-Y. Zhang. 2008. Formation of FDI clustering: A new path to local economic development? The case of electronics cluster in Qingdao City. *Regional Studies* 42 (2): 265–280.

Lau, C. K. M. 2010. New evidence about regional income divergence in China. *China Economic Review* 21 (2): 293–309.

Li, G., and C. Fang. 2016. Spatial econometric analysis of urban and county-level economic growth convergence in China. *International Regional Science Review* 41 (4): 410–447.

Li, Y., and Y. H. D. Wei. 2010. The spatial-temporal hierarchy of regional inequality of China. *Applied Geography* 30 (3): 303–316.

Li, Y., and Y. H. D. Wei. 2014. Multidimensional inequalities in health care distribution in provincial China: A case study of Henan Province. *Tijdschrift Voor Economische En Sociale Geografie* 105 (1): 91–106.

Liao, F. H. F., and Y. H. D. Wei. 2012. Dynamics, space, and regional inequality in provincial China: A case study of Guangdong Province. *Applied Geography* 35 (1): 71–83.

Liao, F. H. F., and Y. H. D. Wei. 2016. *Sixty years of regional inequality in China: Trends, scales and mechanisms*. Working Paper Series N° 202. Rimisp, Santiago, Chile.

Ma, L. J., and Y. Wei. 1997. Determinants of state investment in China, 1953–1990. *Tijdschrift voor economische en sociale geografie* 88 (3): 211–225.

Mankiw, N. G., D. Romer, and D. N. Weil. 1992. A contribution to the empirics of economic growth. *Quarterly Journal of Economics* 107 (2): 407–437.

Rey, S. J., and M. V. Janikas. 2005. Regional convergence, inequality, and space. *Journal of Economic Geography* 5 (2): 155–176.

Shi, H., and S. Huang. 2014. How much infrastructure is too much? A new approach and evidence from China. *World Development* 56: 272–286.

Sun, P., Y. Xu, Z. Yu, Q. Liu, B. Xie, and J. Liu. 2016. Scenario simulation and landscape pattern dynamic changes of land use in the Poverty Belt around Beijing and Tianjin: A case study of Zhangjiakou city, Hebei Province. *Journal of Geographical Sciences* 26 (3): 272–296.

Sun, W., X. Lin, Y. Liang, and L. Li. 2016. Regional inequality in underdeveloped areas: A case study of Guizhou Province in China. *Sustainability* 8 (11): 1141.

Tian, X., X. Zhang, Y. Zhou, and X. Yu. 2016. Regional income inequality in China revisited: A perspective from club convergence. *Economic Modelling* 56 (Supplement C): 50–58.

Wei, Y. 2002. Beyond the Sunan model: Trajectory and underlying factors of development in Kunshan, China. *Environment and Planning A* 34 (10): 1725–1747.

Wei, Y. D., and C. Fang. 2006. Geographical and structural constraints of regional development in western China: A study of Gansu Province. *Issues and Studies* 42 (2): 131–170.

Wei, Y. D., and D. Yu. 2006. State policy and the globalization of Beijing: emerging themes. *Habitat International* 30 (3): 377–395.

Wei, Y. H. D. 1999. Regional inequality in China. *Progress in Human Geography* 23 (1): 49–59.

Wei, Y. H. D. 2000. *Regional development in China: States, globalization and inequality*. London and New York: Routledge.

Wei, Y. H. D. 2017. Geography of inequality in Asia. *Geographical Review* 107 (2): 263–275.

Wei, Y. H. D., and X. Ye. 2009. Beyond convergence: Space, scale, and regional inequality in China. *Tijdschrift Voor Economische En Sociale Geografie* 100 (1): 59–80.

Wei, Y. H. D., D. Yu, and X. Chen. 2011. Scale, agglomeration, and regional inequality in provincial China. *Tijdschrift Voor Economische En Sociale Geografie* 102 (4): 406–425.

Ye, X., and S. Rey. 2013. A framework for exploratory space–time analysis of economic data. *The Annals of Regional Science* 50 (1): 315–339.

Yu, D. 2006. Spatially varying development mechanisms in the Greater Beijing Area: A geographically weighted regression investigation. *The Annals of Regional Science* 40 (1): 173–190.

Yu, D. 2014. Understanding regional development mechanisms in Greater Beijing Area, China, 1995–2001, from a spatial–temporal perspective. *GeoJournal* 79 (2): 195–207.

Yu, D. L., and Y. H. D. Wei. 2003. Analyzing regional inequality in post-Mao China in a GIS environment. *Eurasian Geography and Economics* 44 (7): 514–534.

Yu, D. L., and Y. H. D. Wei. 2008. Spatial data analysis of regional development in Greater Beijing, China, in a GIS environment. *Papers in Regional Science* 87 (1): 97–117.

Yuan, Y., and Y. Wang. 2014. Multidimensional evaluation of county poverty degree in Hebei Province. *Progress in Geography* 33 (1): 124–133 [in Chinese].

Zhang, W., W. Xu, and X. Wang. 2019. Regional convergence clubs in China: Identification and conditioning factors. *The Annals of Regional Science* 62 (2): 327–350.

5 Patterns of regional inequality in Guangdong Province

As China is characterized by vast size and diversity, regional inequality not only exists among provinces or groups of provinces but are even more evident within provinces, triggering the research front of China's regional inequality to "scale down" to the intra-provincial level (Gu *et al.* 2001; Wei and Fan 2000; Wei, Yu, and Chen 2011). With the aid of more advanced GIS and spatial analysis methods, this strand of literature has found rich and diverse details of the dynamics, patterns, and mechanisms of the uneven economic landscape in Chinese provinces (Wei and Ye 2009; Dai *et al.* 2017).

In this and next chapters, we address the space–time complexity of regional inequality in provincial China through the case study of Guangdong. This chapter mainly examines the multi-scalar patterns of regional inequality in Guangdong. Following a distribution dynamics model proposed by Quah (1993a, 1993b, 1996a) and the spatial Markov chains developed by Rey (2001), we also move beyond the traditional convergence analyses to recognize the temporal and spatial dimensions of regional inequality. In the next chapter, we will analyze multiple mechanisms and factors underlying uneven regional development in Guangdong.

5.1 The case of Guangdong and the making of the core–periphery divide

Being China's leading powerhouse and a pioneer in the reform for the past several decades, Guangdong Province is a representative of regional inequality in provincial China (Lu and Wei 2007; Liao and Wei 2012, 2015). With a population of 111.69 million at the end of 2017, the province covers 179,800 square kilometers, occupying 1.9% of China's territory. In 2017, Guangdong produced 3,948 billion yuan of GDP, ranking first in China's 31 provinces (CSB 2018). Its GDP per capita increased from 410 yuan (65 US$) in 1979 to 80,316 yuan (11,640 US$) in 2017, with an annual growth rate of 15.1% (GSB 2018). In 2017, the size of Guangdong's economy measured by GDP surpassed that of Australia and Spain, ranking 13th in the world.

In general, economic development in Guangdong follows a core–periphery gradient with the Pearl River Delta (PRD) being the most developed area (Table 5.1). With the rise of the PRD, the peripheral areas have lagged far behind, which

Table 5.1 Development indicators of Guangdong Province, 2017

	GD	% of China	PRD	% of GD	Periphery	% of GD
Population (million)	111.69	7.2	61.5	55.1	44.93	44.9
Land area (sq. km)	179,643	1.9	54,733	30.4	125,067	69.6
GDP (billion yuan)	9,447.5	10.6	7,571	80.1	733.6	19.9
Investment in fixed assets (billion yuan)	3,747.8	5.9	2,546.4	67.9	1,201.4	32.1
Exports (US$ billion)	622.9	27.5	590.2	94.8	326.32	5.2
FDI (US$ billion)	22.9	17.5	371.0	95.2	11.0	4.8
Local fiscal expenditure (billion yuan)	17,345.1	8.7	1,033.0	74.8	145.2	25.2
Local fiscal revenue (billion yuan)	9,144.8	12.4	745.6	87.6	112.8	87.6

Source: Adapted from GSB (2018).

Note
GD = Guangdong.

intensified regional inequality in the province. The ratio of GDP per capita in the PRD compared with that in the rest of Guangdong (periphery) doubled from 2.2 : 1.0 in 1979 to 5.0 : 1.0 in 2017 (GSB 2018).

In the recent decade Guangdong, especially the PRD, is facing new challenges including the increase of labor cost, shortage of labor, the upsurge of raw materials, and environmental degradation (Liao and Chan 2011; Shen, Wei, and Yang 2017), plus recent trade disputes between the US and China. Scholars have paid attention to the transformation of the development model in the PRD, in which knowledge-based development has been replacing the orthodox exogenous growth fueled by the inflow of Hong Kong and Taiwanese investments (Lin 1997; Lu and Wei 2007). New efforts have been made to strengthen regional integration such as constructing intercity highways and transit systems. In 2017, the Guangdong–Hong Kong and Macao Greater Bay Area (GBA) initiative, which consists of the nine cities in the PRD and Hong Kong and Macao, was approved by the central government of China. Under this initiative, the PRD, along with Hong Kong and Macao, will become a world-class megapolis and a key area in China's ambitious "Belt and Road" program. As debates on regional development in Guangdong emphasize the economic restructuring in the PRD and the GBA, with few exceptions (Lu and Wei 2007), little is known about how economic restructuring in the PRD could have an impact on the core–periphery divide.

In response to problems of economic polarization, since the late 1990s, the provincial government of Guangdong has promoted regional integration between the PRD and the periphery, coined as "the Mountain Area Development Program" in the late 1990s and the "Anti-Poverty Development for Rural Guangdong" in the early 2000s. The provincial government also invested heavily in the construction of the intercity highways connecting the PRD and the peripheral areas (Lu and Wei 2007). Since 2005, under the administration of the new governors in Guangdong, the provincial government has initiated a "dual-track transformation" policy and built up a number of "industrial relocation parks" in the periphery to foster the upgrading of the PRD and promote more equitable development through the relocation of low-end manufacturing from the PRD to the peripheral areas (Liao and Chan 2011; Yang 2012; Lim 2016). The substantial efforts towards inequality reduction in Guangdong have also attracted attention from the World Bank, which believed that Guangdong Province has the potential to lead the nation again for more balanced and sustainable development in China (World Bank 2011).

5.2 Data and methods

As shown in Figure 5.1, Guangdong Province is located in southern China and neighbors Hong Kong. In terms of the administrative structure, in the 2010s, there were 21 municipalities and 82 county-level spatial units including 21 urban districts (city) and 61 counties (including county-level cities) in the province. Geographically, Guangdong is divided into two distinct regions, including the core region of the PRD and the peripheral region, including North Guangdong (or mountain area), East Guangdong, and West Guangdong (Figure 5.1).

In this chapter, the major indicator of the regional development status in Guangdong remains the most commonly used per capita GDP (GDPPC). The municipality-level (21 municipalities) GDPPC data from 1979 to 2016 and county-level GDPPC data from 1988 to 2016 are obtained from a report entitled "GDP Data in Guangdong, 1952–2005" and the statistical yearbooks of Guangdong (various issues from 1988 to 2018) by the Guangdong Statistical Bureau.

In terms of the calculation of GDP per capita, due to the unique *hukou* (household registration) system in China, the population data in coastal provinces tend to be underestimated since the temporal migrant population without *hukou* is often excluded in the population statistics (Chan and Wang 2008). In Guangdong, this problem is more challenging due to the massive inflow of migrant workers in specific cities such as Shenzhen and Dongguan. In order to get more accurate population data, we used a report entitled "Guangdong's Development in the Reform Era" published by the Guangdong Statistical Bureau in 2010, which released the municipality-level migrant population from 1979 to 2009. Since the county-level de facto population (population including migrants without *hukou*) is still unavailable, according to the municipality-level data, we adjusted the numbers of total population in the county-level units within specific municipalities, including Shenzhen, Dongguan, Zhongshan, Foshan, Zhuhai, and Guangzhou, where the total population is more likely to be underestimated. Then, we computed the ratios of de jure population (population not including migrants without *hukou*) to de facto population (population including temporal migrants) for the other 15 municipalities. We found that the resulting ratios ranged from 0.85 to 1.1, indicating that the biases in the total population of the counties within these 15 municipalities can be acceptable for our analyses, given

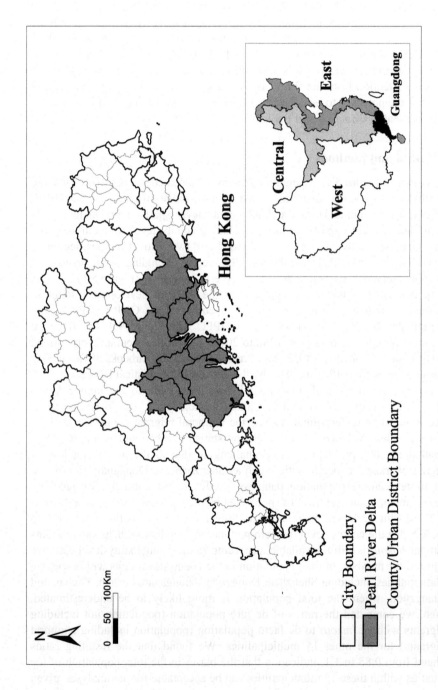

Figure 5.1 Location of Guangdong and regional divisions.

the data limitation. The GDP data were converted into a constant price in 1980 based on the provincial implicit GDP deflator. The GIS maps (shapefiles), referring to boundary files of Guangdong Province down to the county level, were downloaded from the China Data Center in the U.S.

In comparison with other indexes such as CV and Gini coefficient, a major advantage of the entropy indexes such as the Theil index (mean logarithmic deviation) is that they are readily decomposable.[1] In this analysis of regional inequality patterns in Guangdong Province, the Theil index is used to investigate the evolution and the sources of regional inequality in Guangdong. This study also adopts a distribution dynamics model to identify the dynamics of regional inequality among counties in Guangdong (Quah 1993a, 1993b, 1996b; Fotopoulos 2008).

Kernel density estimation is applied to estimate the changes in the distributions of relative GDPPC (the ratio of GDPPC in each county compared with the mean value in the province). In comparison with the traditional histogram, kernel density estimation can smooth the data but retain the overall structure.[2] However, although the kernel density estimation allows characterizing the evolution of the distribution shape, it does not offer any information about the movements of the counties within the distribution. A possible way to remedy this inadequacy is to track the evolution of each county's position in the distribution shapes and examine the transition probability matrices in a Markov-chain-like process (Le Gallo 2004).

The specific advantages of the Markov-chain method are twofold. First, the Markov transition matrix enables us to characterize such spatial-economic asymmetries and highlights the performance of each region, as well as the nature of its mobility (both upward and downward) in detecting the trend of convergence, divergence, and polarization (Fingleton 1997; Carluer 2005). Second, the Markov-chain method is also realistic since it can identify the long-run properties towards some form of poverty-trap or convergence club (Fingleton 1997, pp. 399–400), which cannot be deciphered by the β convergence analysis that relies on smooth time-trends approximation and suffers from Galton's fallacy of regression toward mean (Fingleton, 1997; Quah, 1993a, 1993b).

The basic approach of the Markov chains is to classify different spatial units (counties) into various subcategories based on the relative GDPPC and examine their transition probabilities for a given period (Quah, 1993a, 1993b, 1996a). First, a matrix F_t is constructed to store the cross-sectional distribution of county-level relative GDPPC at time point t. A set of K different GDPPC classes are defined. Therefore, a transition probability matrix M can be established, which has a dimension of K by K, where K is the number of subcategories. A typical element of a transition probability matrix $m_{(i,j,t)}$ indicates the probability that a county that is in class i at time t ends up in class j in the following period. Formally, the $(K, 1)$ vector R_t indicates the frequency of the counties in each class j at time t, following the equation below:

$$R_{t+1} = M * R_t$$

where M is the (K, K) transition probability matrix representing the transitions between the two distributions. If transition probabilities are stationary, that is, if the probabilities between the two classes are time-invariant, then

$$R_{t+P} = M^P * R_t$$

Under the assumption of the time-invariant matrix $(t \to \infty)$, the properties of this matrix can be further examined to determine the ergodic distribution (or the long-term distribution) of R_t to indicate if the regional system is converging or diverging.

By adopting the Markov chains, researchers also attempt to incorporate the spatial dependence or autocorrelation in determining the transition probability matrices. Quah (1996b) used spatial conditioning, and Rey (2001) proposed a more explicit spatial Markov chain to examine the magnitude of spatial dependence in the Markov-chain framework. The transition matrix is expanded, and the transition probabilities of a region are conditioned on the GDPPC class of its spatial lag for the beginning of the year. In doing so, we can obtain a spatial transition matrix and expand the traditional K by K matrix into K conditional matrices of dimension (K, K). In other words, we categorized the spatial lags into the same number of groups as GDPPC. Therefore, a K by K by K three-dimensional transitional matrix is constructed. The element of such a matrix, $m_{ij}(k)$, represents the probability that a region in category i at the time point t will converge to category j at the next time point if the region's spatial lag falls in category k at time point t $(k = 1, ..., K; t = 1, ..., T)$.

In this chapter, the GDPPC data are categorized into four groups (rich, developed, less developed, and poor) using the quartile method, and the cutoff values are selected so that the overall distribution in the entire sample of the relative GDPPC prove to be close to being uniform. This discretion based on the gridlines in uniform distribution generally follows the previous empirical studies using Markov chains (Sakamoto and Islam 2008). This approach has been adopted in other studies of convergence across Chinese provinces. In particular, it uses the Markov transition matrix methodology to capture the dynamics embodied in the data and to produce corresponding ergodic distributions. The results indicate that the distribution of per capita income across Chinese provinces has become bi-modal in 2003. However, a closer examination shows that the dynamics contained in the pre- and post-reform periods are different, producing very different types of ergodic distribution. While the ergodic distribution based on the pre-reform dynamics proves to be positively skewed, the one based on the post-reform period's dynamics proves to be negatively skewed. On balance, whether per capita income level of the Chinese provinces will converge soon still remains an open question, and it also better corresponds to the core–periphery structure in Guangdong in line with the geographical notions of the core, semi-core, semi-periphery, and periphery (Wei, Yu, and Chen 2011). The time interval of the Markov-chain transition matrix is one year, and the spatial lags are defined by the queen contiguity matrix. The Markov chain-based analysis was carried out in a software called PySAL (Open-Source Python Library for Spatial Analytical Functions) developed by the GeoDa Center at Arizona State University (Rey and Anselin 2010).

Besides spatial Markov chains, we employ Griffith's spatial filtering approach to eliminate spatial autocorrelation and then quantify the relationship between the spatial association and regional inequality (Getis and Griffith 2002). The main advantage of these filtering procedures is that the studied variables (which are initially spatially correlated) are divided into spatial and non-spatial components. This approach is also preferred because it can be easily incorporated in other regression model specifications, such as panel data framework (Patuelli *et al.* 2011), and can also be used to furnish a space–time model while controlling for spatial autocorrelation in residuals (Griffith 2008).

The selection of spatial filters is based on the computational formula of Moran's *I* (*MI*) statistic. This methodology uses eigenvector decomposition techniques, which extract the orthogonal and uncorrelated numerical components from a $N \times N$ modified spatial weight matrix:

$$w = \left(\mathbf{I} - \frac{II^T}{n}\right) C (\mathbf{I} - \frac{II^T}{n})$$

where C is an identity matrix of dimension $n \times n$ binary 0–1 geographic connectivity matrix, and I is an $n \times 1$ vector containing 1s. The eigenvectors of the modified matrix are calculated to maximize the sequential *MI* values. The first computed eigenvector, E1, is the one that results in the largest *MI* value among all eigenvectors of the modified matrix. This is followed by the second eigenvector, E2, which is a set of numbers that aimed to maximize the *MI* value while being orthogonal and uncorrelated with E1. The process continues until N eigenvectors have been computed. The final set of these eigenvectors includes all possible mutually orthogonal and uncorrelated map patterns (Getis and Griffith 2002; Thayn and Simanis 2013). When employed as regressors, these eigenvectors could be treated as proxies for missing explanatory variables that capture the underlying geographical structure (Patuelli *et al.* 2011). It should be noted that employing all N eigenvectors in a regression framework is not desirable due to issues related to model parsimony and statistical significance and is often impossible to add to other covariates. Therefore, a smaller subset of candidate eigenvectors can be selected from the N eigenvectors on the basis of their *MI* values. In this analysis, we follow the spatial filtering method suggested by (Griffith *et al.* 2013). The spatial weight matrix is based on the rook's contiguity definition (i.e., on border-sharing schemes) and coded according to the C-coding scheme, which yields a symmetric matrix W (Tiefelsdorf and Griffith 2007).

5.3 Multi-scalar regional inequality in Guangdong

In this section, a multi-scale decomposition analysis is undertaken to portray a holistic scenario about the evolution of regional inequality in Guangdong over the past three decades. Figure 5.2 shows that the evolution of regional inequality is sensitive to the geographical scales. Both of intercity and inter-county inequalities showed an inverted-U shape pattern after 1994. By contrast, interregional inequality displays a more consistently upward trend until the 2010s despite a slight decrease in the early 1990s. Notably, the levels of regional inequality at multiple scales have decreased since the late 2000s, despite slight upticks in 2009.

Regional inequality in Guangdong has not shown persistent divergence or convergence trajectories and these changes are responding to the different stages of reforms. First, a more dramatic rising trend of regional inequality in the early 1990s can be observed, which is consistent with Fan's (1995) study using the per capita gross value of industrial and agricultural output (PCGVIAO). The rise of regional inequality in this period was driven by the development of Shenzhen and Zhuhai, two special economic zones (SEZ) located at the border between Guangdong and Hong Kong or Macao (Figure 5.2).

Second, in the early 1990s, Deng Xiaoping's South China tour in Guangdong had stimulated a new round of "Socialist Marketization" reform in the province that was ceased after the 1989 Tiananmen incident. Since then, the implementation of open-door policies and market reform had been expanded to the whole province while the influence of the SEZ policies in the 1980s gradually faded, which narrowed the gap between other municipalities in the province and the SEZ municipalities. In particular, since the early 1990s, the municipality of Zhuhai, an SEZ municipality located in the western part of the PRD, has been lagging behind in development. In comparison with other municipalities in the eastern part of the PRD (Figure 5.2), the municipality of Zhuhai is relatively far from Hong Kong, which is the motor of the economic development in the PRD. Its development was also constrained by the heavy burden of debt as a result of

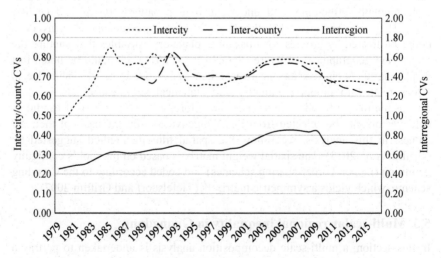

Figure 5.2 Regional inequalities at different scales in Guangdong, 1979–2016.

massive infrastructure investments such as the airport construction in the early 1990s (Yang 2006).

Third, since the early 2000s, regional development in Guangdong has been driven by a new round of inflowing FDI after China's entry into the World Trade Organization (WTO). At the same time, the development of a knowledge-based economy in the PRD has also been accelerated (Lu and Wei 2007). Such a transformation has provided more resources in favor of the municipalities in the PRD and intensified regional inequality in the province.

Last, there has been slightly declining inequality since 2006. The finding is consistent with Zhang *et al.*'s (2018) work on regional inequality in Guangdong. However, Zhang *et al.* (2018) pay more attention to the population flows within Guangdong. Researchers also found that labor and low-cost industries in the PRD have begun migrating to the rest of Guangdong (Yang 2012), partly due to the increasingly stringent environmental regulation in the PRD (Liao and Chan 2011; Shen, Wei, and Yang 2017). Hence, besides population flows, the recent trend of convergence is greatly attributed to more investments made to the periphery areas (Liao and Chan 2011).

In order to unfold the relationship between multi-scalar inequalities in Guangdong, we decompose the overall inter-county inequality into the inequality between the PRD and the rest of the province (the periphery) and the inequalities within the PRD and within the peripheral region respectively, which resembles the core–periphery structure in Guangdong (Figures 5.3). As illustrated in Figure 5.3, the core–periphery divide between the PRD and the rest of Guangdong accounts for more than 50% of the inter-county inequality in Guangdong, being the largest source of regional inequality.

Another important source of regional inequality in Guangdong is the urban–rural disparity. Figure 5.4 shows that the urban–rural disparity has consistently accounted for over 50% of the overall inter-county inequality in Guangdong. The

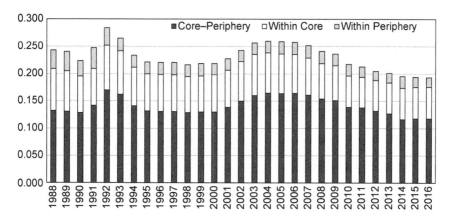

Figure 5.3 Theil decomposition of overall inter-county inequality in Guangdong, 1988–2016 (core–periphery).

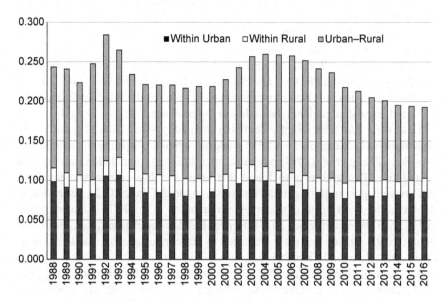

Figure 5.4 Theil decomposition of overall inter-county inequality in Guangdong, 1988–2016 (urban–rural).

persistent urban–rural disparity is also related to the core–periphery inequality since most of the rural counties in Guangdong (46 out of 61, or 75%) are located in the periphery, while nearly half of the urban districts are in the PRD.

In short, uneven economic development in Guangdong is sensitive to the time dimension and geographical scales. It is also related to changing policies such as the SEZ policies in the 1980s and the early 1990s, China's entry into the WTO in the early 2000s, and the most recent policies relaxing migration control in China. However, the provincial-level inequality-reducing policies initiated since the late 1990s could barely achieve their goal. Convergence in recent years deserves more attention in the context of further globalization and economic restructuring.

5.4 Distributional and spatial dynamics of regional inequality

In this section, the dynamics that underline regional inequality or the "long-run" properties of convergence or divergence across 82 counties and cities in Guangdong are analyzed with a distribution dynamics model and in particular the kernel density estimation and Markov chains (Quah, 1993a, 1993b, 1996a, 1996b).

As illustrated in Figure 5.5, the shape of the distribution for the county-level GDPPC has changed considerably over time. The density plots clearly suggest a

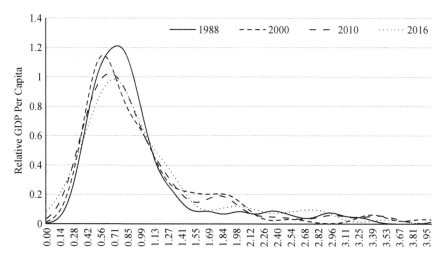

Figure 5.5 Kernel densities of relative per capita GDP at the county level, 1988, 2000, 2010, 2016.

skewed distribution shape of the relative GDPPC in Guangdong. In comparison with the years of 1988 and 2000, more counties reported below half of the average GDPPC in 2016, and only a small subset of counties transited towards above average. This result may reflect that a substantial proportion of counties near the average GDPPC have become relatively poorer during the reform era.

The results of the Markov-chain analyses more clearly point out the system dynamics in Guangdong's regional development, which are sensitive to the different stages in the course of the reform. In general, the transition probabilities along the dialog are high. In other words, if a county falls into the specific class (rich, developed, less developed, and poor), the probability of its being in the same group is at least 83.2%. The transition frequency between different groups is low, and the highest transition frequency is only 10.9% (Table 5.2). The results also show that it is very difficult for a county to leapfrog from poor to rich or from less developed to rich and vice versa, indicating the stable structure in Guangdong's regional development and the persistence of core–periphery inequality. Furthermore, the results of ergodic distribution also indicate a trend of divergence or polarization in the 1990s because there would be more counties falling into the poorest and richest group over the long run. In contrast, per distributional dynamics in the 2000s, convergence could be inferred. Hence, there is no clear evidence of either divergence or convergence and the evolution of regional inequality is contingent upon the time period chosen for the analysis.

The analysis of the evolving spatial patterns of regional development and spatial Markov chains provides more details for the economic geography of inequality dynamics in Guangdong. Figure 5.6 shows that the core–periphery pattern of regional development based on the divide between the PRD and the

Table 5.2 Markov-chain transitional matrices for county-level GDP per capita, 1988–2016

	P [<=0.558]	L [0.558–0.781]	D [0.781–1.120]	R [>=1.120]
1988–2016				
P (582)	0.919	0.081	0.000	0.000
L (570)	0.077	0.832	0.091	0.000
D (570)	0.000	0.084	0.874	0.042
R (574)	0.000	0.003	0.031	0.965
Ergodic distribution	0.226	0.236	0.244	0.294
1988–2000				
P (240)	0.900	0.100	0.000	0.000
L (267)	0.105	0.813	0.082	0.000
D (233)	0.000	0.107	0.841	0.052
R (244)	0.000	0.004	0.033	0.963
Ergodic distribution	0.276	0.263	0.192	0.268
2001–2016				
P (342)	0.933	0.067	0.000	0.000
L (303)	0.053	0.848	0.099	0.000
D (337)	0.000	0.068	0.896	0.036
R (330)	0.000	0.003	0.030	0.967
Ergodic distribution	0.169	0.215	0.298	0.318

rest of Guangdong is salient: most of the counties in the rich category are the counties in the PRD; as the distance to the PRD increases, counties are more likely to become poor. In comparison with the map in 1988, the 2016 map has shown that the statuses of many counties in the periphery remained the same.

Moreover, the boundary of the richest counties has changed slightly: the originally less developed counties near the PRD, such as the counties in Huizhou municipality, moved upward, as did the counties in the Guangzhou municipality (i.e., Conghua and Zengcheng counties). The revealing fact that the eastern PRD located closer to Hong Kong develops faster implies that the core–periphery structure of development in Guangdong is also attributed to the globalization forces channeled through the external core of Hong Kong (Weng 1998; Ng and Tuan 2003). With respect to the periphery area, our results echo Gu *et al.*'s (2001) study that many counties in the originally developed industrial municipalities driven by state-owned sectors in the peripheral regions, such as the counties in Shaoguan in North Guangdong and Zhanjiang in West Guangdong, have declined in the post-reform period (Figure 5.6). In contrast, as found in a recent report from the World Bank (2011), a small subset of counties or districts in the periphery area, particularly in the Qingyuan and Yangjiang municipalities neighboring the northern part of the PRD (Figures 5.1 and 5.6), have moved upward.

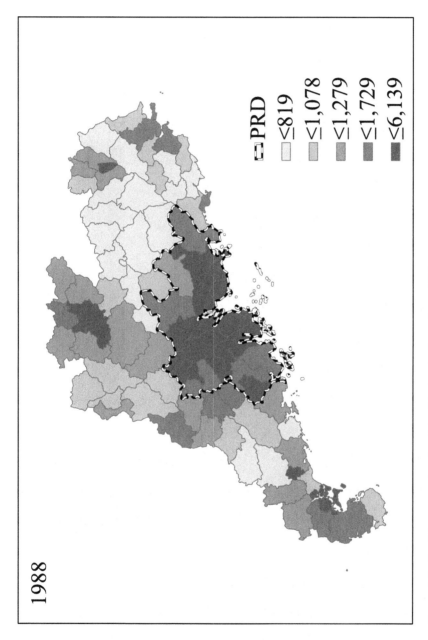

Figure 5.6a Spatial patterns of regional development in Guangdong: 1988.

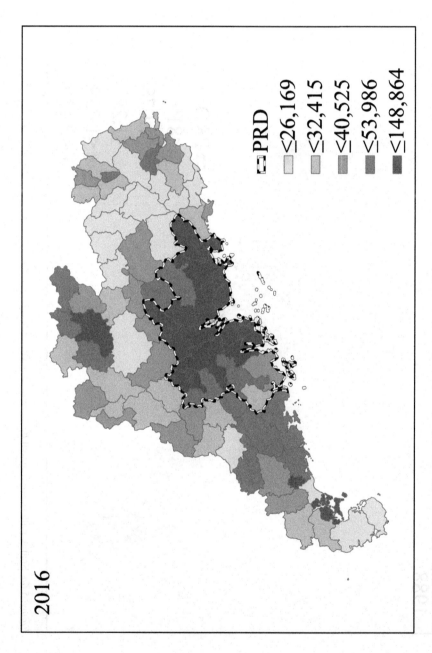

Figure 5.6b Spatial patterns of regional development in Guangdong: 2000.

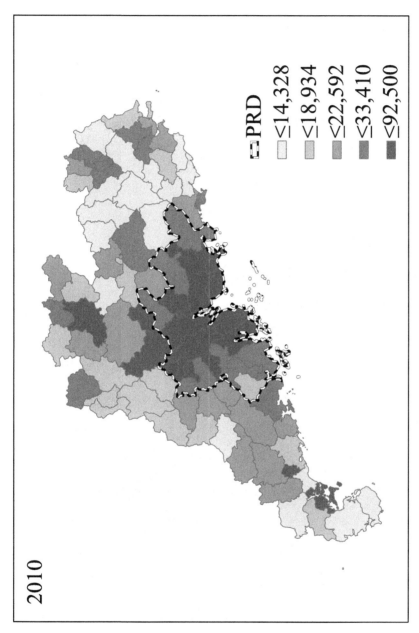

Figure 5.6c Spatial patterns of regional development in Guangdong: 2010.

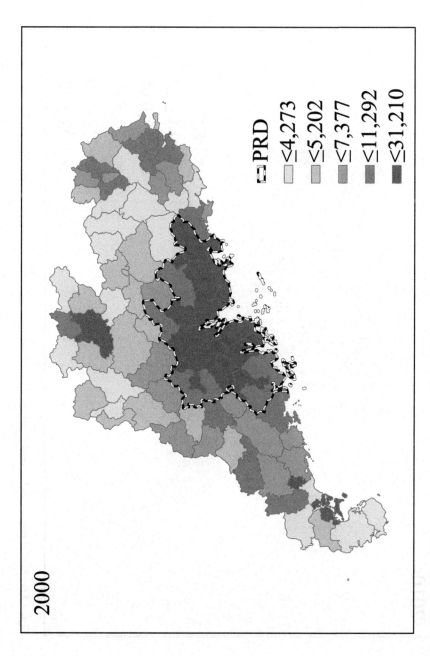

Figure 5.6d Spatial patterns of regional development in Guangdong: 2016.

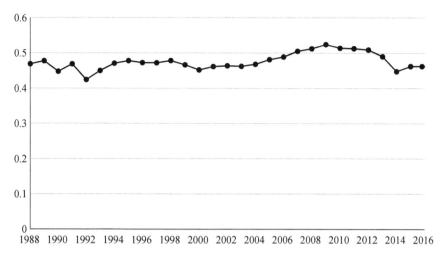

Figure 5.7 Global Moran's *I* of county-level GDP per capita in Guangdong, 1988–2016.

The development in these specific counties is greatly fueled by their abundant land resource and lower cost of labor as well as the recently surging cost of production in the PRD.

We also computed the global Moran's *I* to capture the overall tendency of geographical concentration of regional development in Guangdong (Figure 5.7). Different from the evident inverted-U shape trajectory of the inter-county inequality measured by the Theil index, the resulting global Moran's *I* increased from 0.469 in 1988 to 0.524 in 2009 and decreased from 0.514 to 0.462 in 2010–2016, and all are significant at the 0.01 level. This result implies that when the spatial dependence is taken into account, the inequality measured by Moran's *I* is slightly less sensitive to the fluctuations at specific time points and provides a holistic picture of the increased regional inequality in Guangdong.

The results of the spatial Markov-chain analysis are shown in Table 5.3. They provide more details about the possible association between the direction and probability of transitions and the neighborhood context. For example, for the richest counties, the probability of a downward transition is affected by the economic development of nearby counties. As shown in Table 5.2, the richest counties, in general, have a 3.1% tendency of moving downward. However, if a rich county is surrounded by other richest counties, the tendency of moving downward drops to 2.9%. Meanwhile, if the neighbors are relatively poorer counties, such as the developed counties, the tendency of moving downward increases to 4.7% (Table 5.3). This neighborhood effect is also evident for the upward transitions of poor counties. The chance of a poor county moving out of the bottom averages 8.1% (Table 5.2). However, if its neighbor is richer, such as the developed county, it has a higher probability of moving upward (11%). We also

Table 5.3 Spatial Markov-chain transition matrix for county-level GDP per capita in Guangdong, 1988–2016

| Spatial lag | 1988 | N | 2016 | | | |
			P	L	D	R
P	P	124	0.906	0.094	0.000	0.000
	L	38	0.112	0.789	0.099	0.000
	D	11	0.000	0.125	0.858	0.017
	R	10	0.000	0.000	0.017	0.983
L	P	162	0.948	0.052	0.000	0.000
	L	127	0.071	0.847	0.082	0.000
	D	96	0.000	0.075	0.896	0.030
	R	45	0.000	0.011	0.032	0.958
D	P	123	0.890	0.110	0.000	0.000
	L	245	0.073	0.842	0.085	0.000
	D	195	0.000	0.108	0.862	0.030
	R	72	0.000	0.009	0.047	0.943
R	P	13	0.959	0.041	0.000	0.000
	L	24	0.016	0.871	0.113	0.000
	D	134	0.000	0.034	0.879	0.087
	R	303	0.000	0.000	0.029	0.971

find that the transitions in the intermediate groups are also influenced by the neighborhood context. For instance, for a developed county, the probability of moving upward towards a rich county is 4.2%. But if its neighbor is a rich county, it has a higher chance (8.7%) of becoming a rich economy. At the same time, if a less developed county is surrounded by poor counties, the tendency of moving downward ascends from 7.7% regardless of its neighborhood status (Table 5.2) to 11.2% (Table 5.3).

5.5 Spatial dependence of inequality dynamics

This section further applies the spatial filtering approach to gauge the spatial effects on regional inequality dynamics. The first step in the construction of a spatial filter to be applied to the county-level GDP per capita is the eigenvectors of the spatial weight matrix, followed by the choice of a subset of "candidate" eigenvectors from which the selection is made. Candidate eigenvectors are selected based on their *MI* values and their correlations with the geo-referenced GDP per capita data, using a minimum threshold of 0.5 for the statistic *MI*/max (*MI*). Once a set of "candidate" eigenvectors has been selected, its statistical significance as explanatory variables for Guangdong's GDP per capita data has to be established.

The application of spatial filtering results in two sample series, one with actual data and the other with filtered data. We then examine the multi-scalar characteristics and distribution dynamics of regional inequality with two sample series; therefore, the only differences between them are attributed to spatial effects.

Starting with Figure 5.8, we estimate regional inequalities in Guangdong using a population-weighted coefficient of variation (WCV) and compare trends of regional inequality at multiple geographical scales. Figure 5.8 leads to some interesting findings: first, the regional inequality is sensitive to spatial scales as mentioned earlier. We have also found that regional inequality at three scales tended to increase in the early 1990s and then became stable until the end of 1990. The inequality rose again in the early 2000s and declined afterwards, although the decrease of inter-county inequalities occurred later in the study period. In other words, the evolution of regional inequality can hardly be simplified into convergence and divergence. Third, Figure 5.8 also shows that at more disaggregated geographical scales, there are more intensive disparities. Notably, this finding holds when taking into account spatial effects. Last, the impact of spatial agglomeration on regional inequality is significant, whereas the relationship is contingent upon geographical scales.

Table 5.4 further illustrates that spatial dependence accounts for over 90% of the inequality at the regional level, while the influence declines to around 60% at the municipality level and approximately 40% at the county level. Therefore, by using a spatial filtering approach, we have been able to quantify these relationships.

In order to shed further light on the regional inequalities across counties in Guangdong, we apply two methods, including a cross-profile dynamics and stochastic kernel approach, to depict the distribution dynamics of regional inequality and intra-distribution mobility of spatial units in greater detail. We start with Figure 5.9 showing cross-profile dynamics. The vertical axis is the relative per capita income. Two curves in the figure point to the situations in 1988 and 2012. The most striking feature of Figure 5.9 is not this comparative stability through time. It is the change in choppiness through time in the cross-profile plots indicated by local peaks. The curve of 2012 suggests that the relative declines are more likely to occur in counties in the periphery region.

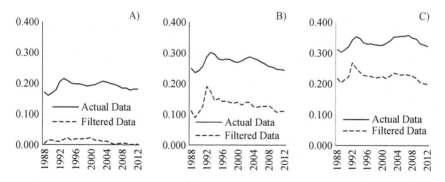

Figure 5.8 Multi-scale inequalities with/without spatial filters in Guangdong: (A) inter-regional inequalities; (B) inter-municipality inequalities; (C) inter-county inequalities.

Table 5.4 Spatial inequality with and without spatial filters

Year	Theil			GINI		
	Non-filtered	Filtered	% of spatial dependence	Non-filtered	Filtered	% of spatial dependence
Interregional						
1988	0.064	0.000	99.95	0.170	0.004	97.93
1995	0.087	0.000	99.94	0.199	0.014	92.85
2000	0.082	0.001	98.52	0.193	0.023	88.28
2005	0.087	0.001	99.92	0.199	0.006	97.22
2010	0.070	0.000	99.99	0.178	0.001	99.27
Intercity						
1988	0.124	0.034	72.88	0.249	0.112	55.19
1995	0.158	0.056	64.45	0.280	0.151	45.85
2000	0.138	0.046	66.94	0.269	0.139	48.22
2005	0.159	0.037	76.62	0.277	0.123	55.47
2010	0.125	0.027	78.61	0.246	0.107	56.50
Inter-county						
1988	0.176	0.088	49.99	0.311	0.217	30.24
1995	0.199	0.098	50.54	0.334	0.228	31.66
2000	0.184	0.089	51.52	0.326	0.223	31.59
2005	0.222	0.094	57.82	0.355	0.229	36.05
2010	0.187	0.070	62.53	0.331	0.205	38.01

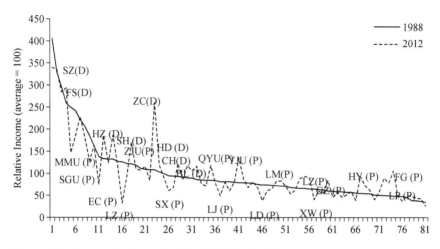

Figure 5.9 Cross-profile dynamics (D = PRD, P = Periphery).

However, the upward mobility of counties in the periphery region is also evident, partly explaining the recent decline of regional inequality in Guangdong.

Figure 5.9 also shows that a set of counties or cities in the PRD, including Foshan, Guangzhou, Zhongshan, and Zhuhai, have moved upward in the distribution, while a number of counties in the periphery area converged towards the average at the same time.

Consistent with the cross-profile dynamics shown in Figure 5.9, many counties that are distant to the PRD in the periphery area have been diverging from below (Figure 5.10). Counties moving upward are those areas geographically closer to the PRD. In addition, the spatial effect on the cross-profile dynamics is evident (Figure 5.11). Figure 5.11 highlights that if the spatial effect is removed, the gap between the richest and poorest is narrowed. There are more counties moving upward in the poor region while more counties are declining in the rich region.

Although the cross-profile dynamics are informative, they do not identify underlying dynamic regularities in the data. We thus turn to the stochastic kernel representation of intra-distribution dynamics. Similar to a Markov chain, stochastic kernel densities are the continuous version of the model of distribution dynamics. Let F_t denote the cross-section distribution of GDP per capita at time t, then the distribution evolves according to:

$$F_{t+1} = MF_t$$

where M denotes the distribution from time t to time $t+1$, and tracks where points in F_t end up in F_{t+1}, and it can also be viewed as a stochastic kernel or

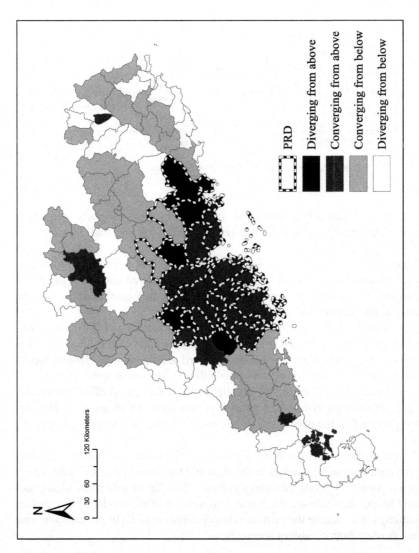

Figure 5.10 Changing GDP per capita in Guangdong, 1988–2016.

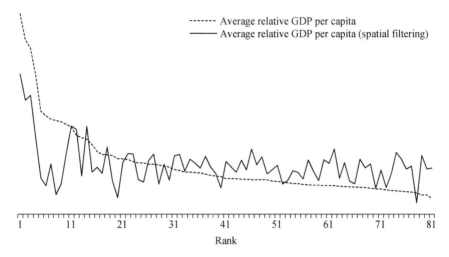

Figure 5.11 Intra-distribution mobility in Guangdong, 1988–2012.

transition function that describes the (time-invariant) evolution of the cross-section distribution in time. We employ the stochastic kernel approach and estimate the highest density plots using a five-year transition period. The highest density plot is defined as "the smallest region of the sample space containing a given probability" (Maza and Villaverde 2009). Thus, each vertical strip in Figure 5.12 denotes the conditional density of a per capita income level in time t. For any point y on the period t axis, looking in the direction parallel to the $t+5$-time axis traces out a conditional probability density. In particular, Figure 5.12 shows the highest density regions for probabilities of 25%, 50%, 75%, and 99% (as it passes from a darker to a less dark area). In addition, it illustrates, like a bullet, the mode (value of per capita GDP in time $t+5$ where the density function takes on its maximum value) for each conditional density for each per capita GDP in time t. Just as a transition matrix based on Markov-chain approaches, the 45-degree diagonal in the graph indicates persistence properties. Therefore, most of the densities are concentrated along this diagonal, and the elements in the cross-section distribution remain where they started.

As evident from Figure 5.12a, a large proportion of the probability mass tends to remain agglomerated along the main diagonal over the five-year horizon, and it is clear that the poorest counties have been facing more challenges to move upward. On the other hand, we find that some counties well-above-average decline in the intra-distribution shape, which is consistent with the recent decline in regional inequalities among counties. The plot based on spatial filter data reveals an evident spatial effect on regional mobility in Guangdong (Figure 5.12b). It mainly suggests that if spatial autocorrelation is eliminated,

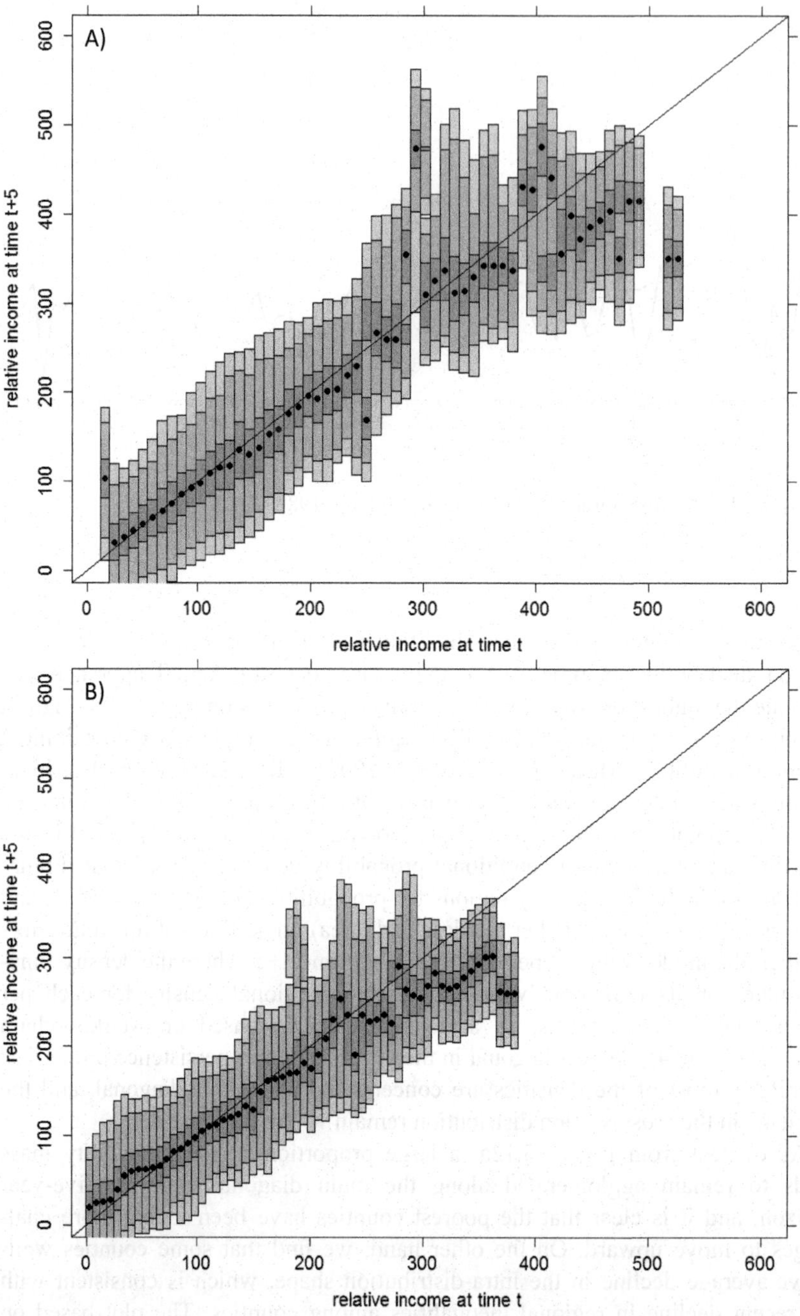

Figure 5.12 Stochastic kernel density of per capita GDP in Guangdong, 1988–2012: (A) actual data (average = 100); (B) filtered data (average = 100).

the upward mobility of these most affluent counties is constrained, and the gap between the rich and poor tends to shrink. In short, our results indicate that spatial effects have been more influential on the mobility of the wealthiest counties within the distribution of county-level GDP per capita.

5.6 Conclusion

Guangdong has led provincial China in the reform and open-door process and has also become an economic powerhouse of China. We find that regional inequality in Guangdong does not follow either a convergence or divergence trend but increased at the early stage of reform, fluctuated, and declined somewhat since the global financial crisis. It is sensitive to geographical scales and such structural changes in the post-reform period as China's accession into the WTO and the socialist market reform. Our case study of Guangdong has also demonstrated the strengthening process of the core–periphery divide between the PRD and the rest of the province. By emphasizing the distinctive distributional dynamics in different stages of economic reform, the chapter also corresponds to the increasing interests of economic geographers in the transformation of the economic landscape from an evolutionary perspective (Martin and Sunley 2012).

Overall, the spatial pattern of regional development in Guangdong follows a core–periphery gradient, and only a subset of counties or cities neighboring the PRD in the periphery might have benefited from the spillover from the PRD. However, a large number of the counties or cities in the semi-core and semi-periphery areas, such as counties in the Zhanjiang and Shaoguan municipalities, have experienced a progressive bias towards a "poverty trap" in the 2000s. With global Moran's *I* and spatial Markov chains, we have demonstrated the significance of spatial dependence and self-reinforcing agglomeration in Guangdong's regional development, which is consistent with the findings in the recent studies of regional development in Zhejiang (Ye and Wei 2005) and Jiangsu (Liu *et al.* 2019). Agglomeration in the core regions seems a common process among provinces in China. Geography or spatiality also matters for the mobility of regions within the distribution of county-level GDP per capita. We have found that spatial effects have constrained the upward mobility of the poorest counties, while they tend to better explain the mobility of the wealthiest counties in the GDP per capita distribution. This polarization effect has contributed to the emerging "poverty trap" in the periphery region distant to the core region of the PRD.

Due to the increasing cost of labor and upgrading in the PRD, more incentives have been offered for low-end and polluting manufacturing activities to migrate from the PRD to the periphery, especially under the program called "emptying the cage, changing the bird." Our analysis of most recent economic data implies that recent declining inter-county inequality in Guangdong is more attributed to convergence among cities and counties within the PRD rather than the catching-up of poor counties in the periphery or remote areas. We hold that the relocation of manufacturing activities would have limited impacts on the core–periphery divide in Guangdong. Moreover, new institutional change, such as the GBA initiative, and recent infrastructure development (e.g., high-speed bullet train between Guangzhou and Hong Kong, and the Hong Kong–Macao–Zhuhai bridge) would help goods and services move more freely and efficiently within the PRD and reinforce the effect of agglomeration economies as mentioned earlier. Therefore, how to grow and upgrade the economy of the PRD and at the same time narrow the gap between the core region and the periphery is an important issue but also a challenging task.

In this chapter, we quantify the effects of geographical and structural constraints of regional development on multi-scalar patterns of regional inequality in Guangdong and find that the core–periphery divide still plays a significant role in shaping the landscape of uneven regional development. The socialist market reform has made the market rather than the state or the government the main motivator for regional economic growth in Guangdong. The strategic intervention and regional policies aimed at a more balanced growth have had very limited success in the imbalanced growth of the core and periphery regions. Finally, based on our analysis, there is no clear evidence to support either the theories of convergence or divergence and a more detailed investigation of forces underlying regional development in Guangdong is presented in the next chapter.

Notes

1 The Theil index is defined as

$$I(y:x) = \sum_{i=1}^{N} y_i \log(y_i/x_i)$$

where x_i is the share of population of county i in the province and y_i is the share of GDP of county i in the province. $I(y:x)$ can be decomposed into

$$I(y:x) = I_0(y:x) + \sum_{g=1}^{G} Y_g I_g(y:x)$$

where the first term on the right $I_0(y:x)$ measures interregional inequality, and the second term is a weighted sum of intraregional inequalities within G groups, where $I_g(y:x)$ measures the inequality within the gth region.

2 Similar to Le Gallo (2004), the densities are calculated non-parametrically using a Gaussian kernel, and the bandwidth is selected as suggested by Silverman (1986, section 3.4.2).

References

Carluer, F. 2005. Dynamics of Russian regional clubs: The time of divergence. *Regional Studies* 39 (6): 713–726.

Chan, K. W., and M. Wang. 2008. Remapping China's regional inequalities, 1990–2006: A new assessment of de facto population data. *Eurasian Geography and Economics* 49 (1): 21–55.

CSB (China Statistical Bureau). 2018. *Zhongguo Tongji Nianjian (China Statistical Yearbook)*. Beijing: China Statistical Press.

Dai, Q., X. Ye, Y. D. Wei, Y. Ning, and S. Dai. 2017. Geography, ethnicity and regional inequality in Guangxi Zhuang Autonomous Region, China. *Applied Spatial Analysis and Policy*: 1–24.

Fan, C. C. 1995. Of belts and ladders: State policy and uneven regional development in post-Mao China. *Annals of the Association of American Geographers* 85 (3): 421–449.

Fingleton, B. 1997. Specification and testing of Markov chain models: An application to convergence in the European Union. *Oxford Bulletin of Economics and Statistics* 59 (3): 385–403.

Fotopoulos, G. 2008. European Union regional productivity dynamics: A "distributional" approach. *Journal of Regional Science* 48 (2): 419–454.

Getis, A., and D. A. Griffith. 2002. Comparative spatial filtering in regression analysis. *Geographical Analysis* 34 (2): 130–140.

Griffith, D. A. 2008. A comparison of four model specifications for describing small heterogeneous space–time datasets: Sugar cane production in Puerto Rico, 1958/59–1973/74. *Papers in Regional Science* 87 (3): 341–355.

Griffith, D. A., Y. Chun, M. E. O'Kelly, B. J. Berry, R. P. Haining, and M. Kwan. 2013. Geographical analysis: Its first 40 years. *Geographical Analysis* 45 (1): 1–27.

GSB (Guangdong Statistical Bureau). 2018. *Guangdong Tongji Nianjian (Guangdong Statistical Yearbook)*. Beijing: China Statistical Press.

Gu, C., J. Shen, K. Wong, and F. Zhen. 2001. Regional polarization under the socialist-market system since 1978: A case study of Guangdong Province in south China. *Environment and Planning A* 33 (1): 97–119.

Le Gallo, J. 2004. Space–time analysis of GDP disparities among European regions: A Markov chains approach. *International Regional Science Review* 27 (2): 138–163.

Liao, F. H. F., and Y. D. Wei. 2012. Dynamics, space, and regional inequality in provincial China: A case study of Guangdong Province. *Applied Geography* 35 (1–2): 71–83.

Liao, F. H., and Y. D. Wei. 2015. Space, scale, and regional inequality in provincial China: A spatial filtering approach. *Applied Geography* 61: 94–104.

Liao, H. F., and R. C. K. Chan. 2011. Industrial relocation of Hong Kong manufacturing firms: towards an expanding industrial space beyond the Pearl River Delta. *GeoJournal* 76 (6): 623–639.

Lim, K. F. 2016. 'Emptying the cage, changing the birds': State rescaling, path-dependency and the politics of economic restructuring in post-crisis Guangdong. *New Political Economy* 21 (4): 414–435.

Lin, G. C. S. 1997. *Red capitalism in south China: Growth and development of the Pearl River Delta*. Vancouver: UBC Press.

Liu, B., M. Xu, J. Wang, L. Zhao, and S. Xie. 2019. Spatio-temporal evolution of regional inequality and contribution decomposition of economic growth: A case study of Jiangsu Province, China. *Papers in Regional Science* 98 (3): 1485–1498.

Lu, L., and Y. D. Wei. 2007. Domesticating globalisation, new economic spaces and regional polarisation in Guangdong Province, China. *Tijdschrift voor economische en sociale geografie* 98 (2): 225–244.

Martin, R., and P. Sunley. 2012. The place of path dependence in an evolutionary perspective on the economic landscape. *Geography* 6 (4): 395–438.

Maza, A., and J. Villaverde. 2009. Spatial effects on provincial convergence and income distribution in Spain: 1985–2003. *Tijdschrift voor economische en sociale geografie* 100 (3): 316–331.

Ng, L. F. Y., and C. Tuan. 2003. Location decisions of manufacturing FDI in China: Implications of China's WTO accession. *Journal of Asian Economics* 14 (1): 51–72.

Patuelli, R., D. A. Griffith, M. Tiefelsdorf, and P. Nijkamp. 2011. Spatial filtering and eigenvector stability: Space–time models for German unemployment data. *International Regional Science Review* 34 (2): 253–280.

Quah, D. 1993a. Empirical cross-section dynamics in economic growth. *European Economic Review* 37 (2–3): 426–434.

Quah, D. 1993b. Galton's fallacy and tests of the convergence hypothesis. *Scandinavian Journal of Economics*: 427–443.

Quah, D. 1996a. Regional convergence clusters across Europe. *European Economic Review* 40 (3): 951–958.

Quah, D. 1996b. Twin peaks: Growth and convergence in models of distribution dynamics. *The Economic Journal*: 1045–1055.

Rey, S. 2001. *Spatial dependence in the evolution of regional income distributions: spatial econometrics and spatial statistics*. Basingstoke: Palgrave, 194–213.

Rey, S. J., and L. Anselin. 2010. PySAL: A Python library of spatial analytical methods. In M. M. Fischer and A. Getis (eds.) *Handbook of applied spatial analysis*, 175–196. Berlin: Springer-Verlag.

Sakamoto, H., and N. Islam. 2008. Convergence across Chinese provinces: An analysis using Markov transition matrix. *China Economic Review* 19 (1): 66–79.

Shen, J., Y. D. Wei, and Z. Yang. 2017. The impact of environmental regulations on the location of pollution-intensive industries in China. *Journal of Cleaner Production* 148: 785–794.

Silverman, B. W. 1986. *Density estimation for statistics and data analysis monographs on statistics and applied probability*. London: Chapman and Hall.

Thayn, J. B., and J. M. Simanis. 2013. Accounting for spatial autocorrelation in linear regression models using spatial filtering with eigenvectors. *Annals of the Association of American Geographers* 103 (1): 47–66.

Tiefelsdorf, M., and D. A. Griffith. 2007. Semiparametric filtering of spatial autocorrelation: The eigenvector approach. *Environment and Planning A: Economy and Space* 39 (5): 1193–1221.

Wei, Y. H. D., and C. C. Fan. 2000. Regional inequality in China: A case study of Jiangsu Province. *Professional Geographer* 52 (3): 455–469.

Wei, Y. H. D., and X. Ye. 2009. Beyond convergence: Space, scale, and regional inequality in China. *Tijdschrift voor economische en sociale geografie* 100 (1): 59–80.

Wei, Y. H. D., D. Yu, and X. Chen. 2011. Scale, agglomeration, and regional inequality in provincial China. *Tijdschrift Voor Economische En Sociale Geografie* 102 (4): 406–425.

Weng, Q. 1998. Local impacts of the post-Mao development strategy: The case of the Zhujiang Delta, Southern China. *International Journal of Urban and Regional Research* 22 (3): 425–442.

World Bank. 2011. *Reducing inequality for shared growth in China: Strategy and policy options for Guangdong province*. Washington, DC: World Bank.

Yang, C. 2006. The geopolitics of cross-boundary governance in the Greater Pearl River Delta, China: A case study of the proposed Hong Kong–Zhuhai–Macao Bridge. *Political Geography* 25 (7): 817–835.

Yang, C. 2012. Restructuring the export-oriented industrialization in the Pearl River Delta, China: Institutional evolution and emerging tension. *Applied Geography* 32 (1): 143–157.

Ye, X., and Y. D. Wei. 2005. Geospatial analysis of regional development in China: The case of Zhejiang Province and the Wenzhou Model. *Eurasian Geography and Economics* 46 (6): 445–464.

Zhang, Y., D. Tong, and X. Liang. 2018. New perspective on regional inequality: Theory and evidence from Guangdong, China. *Journal of Urban Planning and Development* 144 (1): 04018002.

6 Mechanisms of uneven development in Guangdong Province

In the last chapter, we have shown the changing patterns of regional development and inequality in Guangdong. This chapter deepens our understanding of the major drivers behind the mosaic of uneven development in Guangdong to better understand sources or mechanisms of regional inequality. As we elaborated in Chapter 2, our analysis follows the multi-mechanism framework emphasizing the trip process of globalization, decentralization, and marketization, and the importance of foreign direct investment (FDI), local states, and the market power.

Furthermore, to better understand the multi-scalar patterns of regional inequality and the process of spatial polarization, we apply a multi-level modeling regression technique and incorporate spatial filters in a set of panel and space–time model specifications, aiming to achieve a more reliable estimation of multiple mechanisms over space and time. We also review the recent transformation of the Pearl River Delta (PRD) model to better understand changing regional development in Guangdong. The conclusion section summarizes the findings and discusses methodological and policy implications.

6.1 Opening-up, globalization, and FDI development

Since the late 1970s, globalization and the implementation of the open-door policy have increased the importance of global forces in economic and regional development in China (Wei 2000). Among the four special economic zones (SEZs) opened in China in 1979, three of them (Shenzhen, Zhuhai, Shantou) are located in Guangdong. Guangdong has benefited the most from the preferential open-door policies. Reasons why Guangdong was chosen by the central government as the bridgehead of the socialist market reform and China's opening-up process merit special attention (Lin 1997; Gu *et al.* 2001; Lu and Wei 2007).

First, the PRD has served as the traditional gateway for foreign trade and sea transportation in China. As one of the most important agricultural bases of China, the PRD is also known for having an intensive farming system of silk cocoons and pond fish (Lu and Wei 2007). Led by the port city of Guangzhou, the PRD region was one of the earliest trade outlets in Chinese history, which can be traced back to the well-known "Maritime Silk Road" opened to overseas traders in the Han Dynasty (220–206 bc) (Lin 1997; Lu and Wei 2007). Despite the banning of maritime trade in 1757, Guangzhou remained the only national trading port in China. The long history of foreign trade and connections with the Western economies can be further manifested by the establishment of a number of factories, including rubber, soap, and machinery, etc., after the Opium War in the middle of the 19th century (Lu and Wei 2007). After 1978, the PRD region has played a very special role in China's reform. Zhuhai and Shenzhen, two cities located on the border between mainland China and Macao and Hong Kong, were designated as two special economic zones in the 1980s. The central government further designated Guangzhou as an open and coastal city in 1984 and the whole delta as an open economic region in 1985 (Lu and Wei 2007).

Second, ethnic and kinship ties between Hong Kong and Guangdong were considered a major draw. The census statistics published by Hong Kong SAR government in 1961 indicated that more than half of Hong Kong people were born in mainland China at that time and 94% of the population in Hong Kong spoke Cantonese, which is the Chinese dialect popular in areas centered on Guangzhou (Shen 2003). More importantly, during the 1950s–1970s, Hong Kong, a former British colony, had become an industrialized economy and an important business center, making this island one of the four *dragon economies* in Asia. In the 1970s–1990s, the rise of labor cost and limited land resources in Hong Kong drove Hong Kong firms to expand their operations into other low-cost regions, such as south-east Asia and mainland China. It was believed that the reform started in the southern coast could assist attracting foreign capital and help China integrate into the world economy through Hong Kong.

Last, Guangdong is located far from Beijing and its economy was not among the most developed in China in the late 1970s. The core of the national economy in the late 1970s was industrial bases in the north, east, and north-east (Lin 1997). The economy in the PRD, which is the core region of the Guangdong Province, was historically more focused on the light industry based on local agricultural materials. Before the reform, Guangdong was largely ignored by the central government in resource allocation because of its coastal location in the defensive First Front (Lu and Wei 2007). From 1952 to 1978, the growth rate of per capita national income in Guangdong was only 3.1%, below the national average of 3.9% (Wei 2000; Lu and Wei 2007). Moreover, Guangdong Provincial Party Secretary Xi Zhongxun was a senior member of the Chinese Communist Party and among the first generation of Chinese leadership. Hence, it is appropriate to infer that the experiment in Guangdong would not affect the whole country economically and politically even if it fails (Lin 1997).

During the reform era, Guangdong had indeed succeeded in attracting FDI, especially that from overseas Chinese economies including Hong Kong and Taiwan. The total amount of utilized FDI skyrocketed from less than US$2 billion in the 1980s to around US$25 billion in the 2010s (Figure 6.1). Over 20% of the total FDI in China chose Guangdong as the destination during the period of 2000–2016 (CSB, GSB 2001–2017).

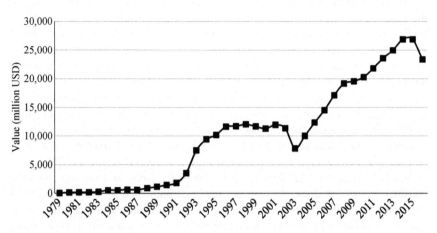

Figure 6.1 The growth of FDI in Guangdong, 1979–2016.

In terms of the forms of FDI, equity joint ventures and other forms of FDI such as processing with supplied materials (or PSM, *lailiaojiagong*) took the majority of FDI in Guangdong (or approximately 70%) in the 1980s and the 1990s. During the same period, manufacturing firms engaged in *sanlaiyibu*, which is a mode of FDI specializing in processing supplied materials, samples, and parts, occupied the lion's share (Yang 2012). Among different sources of FDI, Hong Kong was the largest origin of external capital, followed by Taiwan, Japan, North America, and Europe (Xu and Yeh 2013). After 2000, the share of wholly foreign-owned enterprises (WFOEs) increased from 29.7% in 2000 to 68.5% in 2015. The sources of FDI in Guangdong have also been diversified. Capital from Taiwan, Singapore, and Western countries has increased in proportion in recent years (Xu and Yeh 2013). The changing characteristics of FDI in Guangdong are consistent with national-level FDI policies and the intensifying globalization triggered by China's accession into the WTO.

Geographically, FDI in Guangdong is concentrated in the PRD, which accounted for over 80% of the total FDI in the province (Figure 6.2). In terms of industrial allocation, the manufacturing industry took in much of FDI in Guangdong (more than 60% in the early 2000s). However, more FDI has recently been flowing into the services industries, including information and computer services and software, leasing and business services, and real estate (Table 6.1). For example, the share of information transmission, computer services, and software has increased from less than 5% in 2010 to nearly 15% in 2015. Possibly due to rising production cost and the sluggish demand in advanced economies in the aftermath of the global financial crisis, the share of manufacturing dropped drastically from over 75% in 2005 to less than 25% in 2015.

Besides FDI, foreign trade in Guangdong has also grown rapidly during the reform era. The total trade volume soared by 400-fold during 1980–2016, reaching US$1,022 billion in 2016. In the 1990s and the 2000s, Guangdong's exports

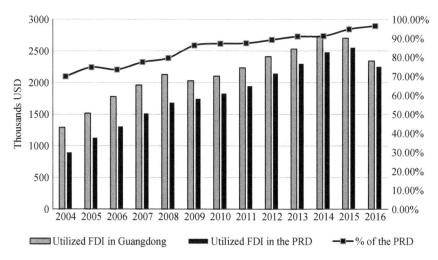

Figure 6.2 The PRD's shares of FDI in Guangdong, 2004–2016.

Table 6.1 Sectoral patterns of FDI in Guangdong, 2000–2015

Sector	2000	2005	2010	2015
Farming, forestry, animal husbandry and fishery	1.18	0.62	0.71	0.48
Mining	0.19	0.70	0.10	0.05
Manufacture	64.87	75.98	56.08	24.74
Production and supply of electric power, gas and water	3.27	1.57	3.25	3.52
Construction	2.83	0.32	0.53	2.31
Transport, storage and postal services	2.19	3.03	2.78	2.26
Information transmission, computer services and software	n/a	1.70	2.08	14.61
Wholesale and retail trades	1.97	1.58	9.82	7.94
Hotels and catering services	n/a	0.67	0.76	0.27
Finance	0.13	0.29	0.34	8.41
Real estate	16.58	6.83	16.24	15.52
Leasing and business services	4.20	4.26	4.50	17.34
Scientific research, technical services and geologic prospecting	n/a	0.97	2.10	1.83
Management of water conservancy, environment and public facilities	n/a	0.07	0.14	0.24
Services to households and other services	n/a	1.02	0.16	0.13
Education	0.09	0.01	0.00	0.06
Health, social security and social welfare	0.64	0.02	0.01	0.01
Culture, sports and recreation	n/a	0.36	0.42	0.28

accounted for nearly a third of the total exports in China, with Hong Kong being the largest trading partner (Lin 1997; Xu and Yeh 2013; Ye *et al.* 2019). Although facing competition from other regions such as the Yangtze River Delta, exports derived from Guangdong still accounted for over 25% of the national total in recent years. Specifically, being "the workshop of the world," export-oriented processing plays a key role in the foreign trade of Guangdong. According to the statistics released by the Department of Foreign Trade and Economic Cooperation of Guangdong Province, export-oriented processing contributes approximately 50–70% of total exports in Guangdong. Like FDI, foreign trade measured by the total volume of exports is heavily concentrated in the PRD, which comprised 80–90% of the provincial total (GSB, 1990–2017).

6.2 Market reform, ownership transformation, and fiscal decentralization

Along with FDI, the socialist market reform launched in the mid-1980s and accelerated in the early 1990s created a climate that encouraged non-state sectors to grow. Ownership restructuring, in particular, is considered an important aspect of China's economic transition (Wei 2004). As illustrated in Table 6.2, the shares of fixed investments from state-owned enterprises (SOEs) and collectively owned enterprises (COEs) in 1995 were as high as 48% and 15.6% respectively. This implies the importance of domestic investment for regional development in Guangdong. Even in the 1980s, the establishment of SEZs led to hundreds of offices and branches of the central and local governments from the inland provinces (Lu and Wei 2007). Since the 2000s, funds from privately owned enterprises have surpassed those from foreign enterprises; the investments made by these private enterprises further surpassed that of SOEs in 2015 (Table 6.2).

From 1978 to 2016, total fixed investments in Guangdong increased from 2.72 billion yuan to 3,300 billion yuan, with an annual growth rate of 20.5%, much higher than that of GDP. The growth of fixed investments in Guangdong was closely related to the decentralization of decision-making power during the reform era. Like other coastal provinces, fiscal and investment reforms have provided greater incentives for the growth of local economies, and local officials are encouraged to be actively involved in economic development. At the same time,

Table 6.2 Fixed investment allocation in Guangdong by ownership, 1995–2015 (%)

	1995	2000	2005	2010	2015
SOEs	48.3	39.8	28.8	32.0	21.2
COEs	15.6	13.9	5.5	4.6	4.3
Private	10.7	13.1	19.6	14.6	22.6
Funds from Hong Kong, Macao, Taiwan, and other foreign regions	19.5	17.2	25.1	13.7	11.6

administrative reforms allowed many SOEs for local management and their investment decisions were more likely to be made by local governments and enterprises (Wei 2000).

Under the market reform, private and foreign-owned enterprises are considered as an integral part of the economic system that used to be dominated by SOEs. As shown in Figure 6.3, the three economic censuses clearly show the process of ownership transformation in Guangdong during 2004–2013, in which private enterprises have become another major agent of regional development (Lin and Hu 2011), and their shares in total employment increased from less than 25% in 2004 to more than 30% in 2013. In contrast, the shares of employment from SOEs and COEs dropped most significantly, followed by those of Hong Kong and Taiwanese firms (Figure 6.3).

As discussed in Wei (2004), the spatial ramification of ownership transformation is closely tied to uneven regional development. In Guangdong, the geography of ownership restructuring is also associated with the core–periphery divide in the province. The employment of SOEs was relatively more concentrated in Shaoguan, Zhanjiang, or other cities out of the PRD, accounting for nearly half of the provincial total. In contrast, over 80% of jobs created by the private enterprises were located within the delta region. Foreign enterprises tend to agglomerate in the PRD too, which accounted for over 90% of the total employment of those enterprises in Guangdong (Table 6.3). Similar patterns of spatial inequality are observed in the case of Hong Kong and Taiwanese firms. The share of PRD in the employment of Hong Kong and Taiwanese enterprises dropped slightly from 92% to less than 90% during 2004–2013. In short, marketization and ownership transformation are key components of the economic transition in Guangdong. Partly due to its more

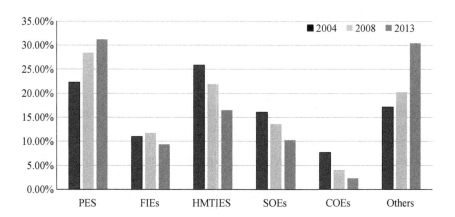

Figure 6.3 Changing shares of employment by ownership in Guangdong, 2004–2013.

Notes
PES = private enterprises; FIES = foreign-invested enterprises; HMTIES = Hong Kong Macau Taiwan invested enterprises; SOEs = state-owned enterprises; COEs = collectively owned enterprises

Table 6.3 Changing shares (%) of employment by ownership and regions, 2004–2013

Regions/municipalities	2004	2008	2013
SOEs			
The Pearl River Delta	52.78	57.77	57.77
Eastern Region	14.44	12.78	12.70
Western Region	16.71	14.78	14.67
Northern Region	16.07	14.66	14.86
COEs			
The Pearl River Delta	71.60	71.82	64.54
Eastern Region	7.15	10.24	13.80
Western Region	6.66	9.55	12.41
Northern Region	14.59	8.39	9.24
Private enterprises			
The Pearl River Delta	68.24	80.10	83.50
Eastern Region	13.74	9.42	8.36
Western Region	8.77	6.01	4.57
Northern Region	9.25	4.46	3.57
Foreign-invested enterprises			
The Pearl River Delta	93.77	93.93	94.17
Eastern Region	4.29	3.01	2.67
Western Region	1.19	0.83	0.89
Northern Region	0.75	2.23	2.27
Hong Kong Macau Taiwan invested enterprises			
The Pearl River Delta	92.24	90.47	89.74
Eastern Region	3.60	3.18	4.09
Western Region	1.55	1.37	1.13
Northern Region	2.60	4.97	5.05

favorable environment and superior location and infrastructure systems, most of these jobs created by foreign and privately owned enterprises were located in the PRD.

In addition to marketization and globalization, decentralization is considered as the third process of the triple process of China's economic transition (Wei 2002). Before the reform, the Chinese fiscal system was highly centralized, characterized by the notion of "eating from one big pot" (*chi daguofan*). The system provided very little incentives for local governments to collect and generate revenues (Wang 2010). In 1978, on the eve of economic reforms, Guangdong's revenue reached 4.2 billion yuan, but the total expenditure was only 2.9 billion. This implies that, in the pre-reform period, Guangdong might have transferred a

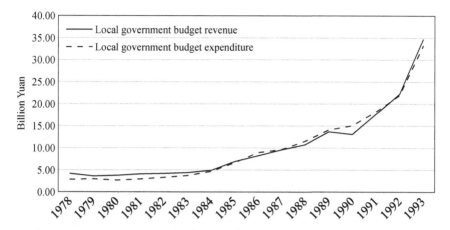

Figure 6.4 Revenue and expenditure in Guangdong, 1978–1993.
Source: GSB (2000).

substantial proportion of its revenues to the central government. During the reform era, local governments have been granted more spending expenditure and were allowed to retain some of their revenues for local investments. Consequently, as shown in Figure 6.4, in the 1980s and the early 1990s, Guangdong's budgetary expenditure increased and was very close to its budgetary revenues.

As the fiscal contract system in the 1980s created serious fiscal challenges for the central government due to declining fiscal capacity, a new fiscal system was established in 1994. The 1994 reform not only simplified the tax structure but, more importantly, established a national tax administration in favor of the interests of the central government. Hence, local governments were deprived of the power to keep their local revenues, as compared with the situation in the 1980s (Wang 2010). However, local governments still have more resources generated from other sources such as land finance and greater spending power. For example, local spending expenditure in Guangdong increased from 52 billion yuan in 1995 to 1,345 billion yuan in 2016, with an annual growth rate of 34.27%.

Fiscal revenue and expenditure within Guangdong are geographically more concentrated in the PRD, which contributed over 65% of the total fiscal revenue and expenditure. Fiscal revenue per capita was 1,442 yuan in 2000, which increased to 11,664 yuan in 2016, a rise of 800% (Figure 6.5). The absolute difference between the PRD and the periphery, referring to the difference between the highest and lowest fiscal revenue per capita, also rose from 1,255 yuan in 2000 to 9,191 yuan in 2016, which was more than seven times larger than that in 2000. As shown in Figure 6.5, the gap increased slightly from 2000 to 2004, but it grew rapidly in recent years.

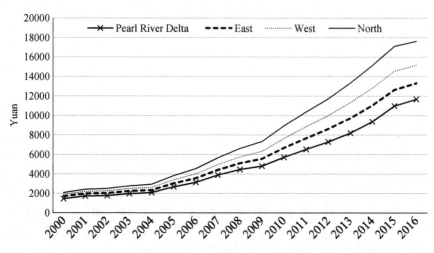

Figure 6.5 Fiscal revenue per capita in the PRD, east, west, and north of Guangdong, 2000–2016.

6.3 Modeling of multi-mechanism of regional inequality

The proceeding section further applies multi-level and spatial modeling to gauge the effects of the triple process of economic transition on uneven development in Guangdong using more rigorous spatial regression analysis methods.

Results of multi-level regression analyses

As argued by Li and Wei (2010), despite the wide usage of multi-level modeling in the fields of public health, demographic, and transportation geography, the application of multi-level modeling in the study of regional inequality is still limited (Li and Wei 2010). In this research, we apply multi-level modeling to test the spatial-temporal hierarchy of development mechanisms down to the county level in Guangdong. In doing so, we attempted to better understand the relative importance of the triple process in Guangdong's regional development. Our model has three levels. The one-level model is a pooled regression using county-level data regardless of the core–periphery and temporal hierarchies. The two-level model adds the core–periphery continuum as suggested in the Markov chains, which allows us to control for the geographical and structural effects within the four groups (core, semi-core, semi-periphery, and periphery). The three-level model further controls for the time points (1988, 1993, 1998, 2003, 2008), which takes the between-year variations into account. Such time points were selected based on data availability.

$$y_{ijt} = \beta_0 + \beta_1 x_{ijt} + v_{0t} + \mu_{0jt} + e_{ijt}$$

As shown in equation (6.1), the y_{ijt} refers to the dependent variable (GDPPC) in county i that belongs to the core–periphery continuum j defined by the Markov chains at year t, and x_{ijt} is the independent variables in county j at year t; v_{0t} is the error term at year t; μ_{0jt} is the error term of core–periphery continuum j at year t; e_{ijt} is the error term of i county in core–periphery continuum j at year t.

We selected a number of exploratory variables based on the multi-mechanism that conceptualizes Guangdong's regional development as an aforementioned triple process of globalization, marketization, and decentralization.

1   Globalization (FDIPC): Guangdong's development over the past three decades has been fueled by the export-oriented economy and inflow of FDI. So the per capita FDI (FDIPC) is the most commonly used indicator to measure the extent of globalization (Gu *et al.* 2001).
2   Marketization (NSOE): Guangdong's development is also based on the establishment of the socialist market system and the retreat of the state-owned enterprises (SOE) in the economy (Gu *et al.* 2001). The share of non-SOE in the total employment (NSOE) is employed to describe the influence of marketization.
3   Decentralization (DECEN): The decentralization process is captured by the ratio of local budgetary spending per capita to the provincial government's budgetary spending per capita. It mainly reflects the degree of fiscal decentralization and the shift of power from upper-level governments to local governments (Hao and Wei 2010; Wang 2010).
4   Investment (FIXPC): It has been widely acknowledged that socialist economies are traditionally investment driven, and the per capita fixed-asset investment (FIXPC) is selected to represent whether the development is driven by the investments particularly from the central government (Yu and Wei 2008).
5   Urban–rural divide (URBAN): China's regional development policy is also biased toward the urban area, which has intensified the urban–rural inequality (Long *et al.* 2011). A dummy variable URBAN is employed to reflect the impact of urban-biased development. If the spatial unit at the county level is an urban district, it is coded by 1; otherwise, it is a 0.
6   Topography (MOUNTAIN): In Guangdong, most of the plain area is located in the PRD, while mountain counties are mostly located in the periphery. A dummy variable (MOUNTAIN) is used to investigate the impact of physical topographical conditions on the economic development in Guangdong.

The results of one-level, two-level, and three-level regression models are reported in Table 6.4 and discussed as follows. First, based on the results of likelihood ratio tests, the one-level model can explain 82.9% of the total variances of the county-level GDPPC, and there is a significant reduction in deviances from both the one-level model to the two-level model ($p<0.001$) and from the two-level model to the three-level model ($p<0.001$; Table 6.4). This result indicates that the core–periphery hierarchy of regional inequality as suggested by the Markov chains exists and regional inequality is also sensitive to different time points.

Table 6.4 Results of the multi-level regressions

	One-level (county)		Two-level (county & core–periphery)		Three-level (county & core–periphery & time)	
	Coefficient	P-value	Coefficient	P-value	Coefficient	P-value
FDIPC	8.472	0.0253	8.106	0.0053	7.305	0.0113
DECEN	213.062	0.6687	1,678.574	0.0001	1,716.451	0.0001
NSOE	13,425.501	0.0001	4,548.353	0.1170	5,646.382	0.0593
FIXPC	1.725	0.0001	0.380	0.0001	0.370	0.0001
URBAN	1,640.425	0.1065	1,934.463	0.0062	2,097.407	0.0027
MOUNTAIN	−655.637	0.4149	−555.074	0.3290	−330.837	0.5569
−2loglikelihood	8,361.751		8,110.889		8,096.617	
R square	0.829		Likelihood ratio test	<0.001	Likelihood ratio test	<0.001

Second, the results differ from Li and Wei (2010), who also used multi-level modeling and found that the FDI is a singular factor that causes regional disparities at the provincial level in China. The model shows that local governments, foreign investors, and the state collectively affect the local economic development in Guangdong. Many development agents in China's regional development are actually operating at the lower levels (city or county) under provinces, and their roles are likely masked by the analysis of large spatial entities such as provinces (Wei and Fan 2000).

Third, the influence of marketization is significant in the one-level model but insignificant and marginally significant ($p=0.12$ and $p=0.06$) in the two-level and three-level models. In other words, the multi-level modeling avoids exaggerating the effect of marketization on the regional inequality in Guangdong. It implies that, among the triple processes, globalization coupled with decentralization has become the most important mechanism that causes regional disparities between counties and between the core and the peripheral areas as well as between different time points in Guangdong (Table 6.4). However, our results contradict Gu, Shen, Wong, and Zhen's (2001) study based on the data before the mid-1990s, which suggested that the FDI was an auxiliary factor underlying the regional inequality in Guangdong. In fact, as an indicator of globalization, FDI has been increasingly important in the economic development in Guangdong, especially after China's accession into the WTO in the early 2000s. Notably, FDI has strong policy and geographical preferences and is characterized by path dependence (Ng and Tuan 2003). As mentioned earlier in the chapter, the peripheral area only accounted for a tiny share of the FDI in Guangdong, while most of the FDI was concentrated in the PRD. The uneven distribution of FDI has become an important, rather than auxiliary, factor causing the regional disparities in Guangdong.

On the other hand, our findings confirm the positive relationship between fiscal decentralization and the uneven development in Guangdong. The fiscal decentralization in the reform era has encouraged local governments in Guangdong to actively engage in local economic development. With the changes in fiscal capacity, local governments can finance infrastructure development and public goods to promote economic growth and attract investors. This process, however, often results in the greater development in the already affluent regions and the detriment in the poor areas. Fiscal decentralization also reinforces the local governments' reliance on local revenue, which encourages the local protectionism and has weakened the capability of the regional-level government to redistribute resources for an equity objective. Therefore, fiscal decentralization, despite its effectiveness in creating a growth-oriented environment in Guangdong, tends to have a negative impact on equitable development and indirectly aggravates regional inequality.

Multi-level modeling also deepens our understanding of the impact of marketization on regional inequality in Guangdong. In comparison with globalization and decentralization, marketization has no longer been a significant factor accounting for the uneven economic development in Guangdong, where the socialist market reform was initiated earlier than the other provinces in China. In addition, the domestic private enterprises have experienced remarkable growth in Guangdong, and their distribution tends to be more balanced in comparison with the overly concentrated foreign-invested enterprises. Therefore, the development of the non-state-owned sector or domestic private enterprises has the potential to mediate the uneven development in Guangdong driven by the unevenness of FDI.

Last, the results also show that fixed-asset investments have exerted strong influences on regional development in Guangdong, and it is consistently significant in the multi-level model (Table 6.4). These results demonstrate that the economic development in Guangdong relies greatly on investments, while the distribution of fixed-asset investments is imbalanced and focused on the PRD as mentioned earlier, exerting significant influences on the rising regional disparities. Fifth, the resulting multi-level model indicates that the urban–rural variable is marginally significant in the one-level model; however, when the core–periphery hierarchy is taken into account, the urban–rural divide significantly affects the regional inequality in Guangdong. In this sense, the application of multi-level modeling provides a more nuanced understanding that the rural industrialization in the PRD is still far from alleviating the overall economic inequality in the whole province. Lastly, the topography variable (MOUNTAIN) is insignificant in the multi-level model, and its coefficient is negative. Therefore, the economic developments in these counties are constrained by their physical and topographical conditions, which also intensify the regional inequality in the province.

Results of spatial panel regression

Besides multi-level modeling, by incorporating spatial filters in a set of panel regression and space–time modeling frameworks, we further address the space–time and core–periphery heterogeneity of multi-mechanisms in China's regional development. We first estimate both OLS and spatial filter panel regression models using county-level socioeconomic data in 1990, 1995, 2000, 2005, and 2010. Table 6.5 reports the overall pseudo-R^2 and *MI* of residuals as well as year-specific filters that can account for spatial autocorrelation in the data. The spatial filtering panel regression model removes all of the residual spatial autocorrelation and further increases pseudo-R^2 values. We also compare the spatial filter panel data model to the selected benchmark spatial panel regression models, including spatial lag panel and spatial error panel (Patuelli *et al.* 2011).

A spatial lag and error panel model are expressed as

$$y_{it} = \delta \sum_{j=1}^{N} \left(w_{ij} y_{it} \right) + x_{it} \beta + u_i + \varepsilon_{it}$$

where δ is the spatial autoregressive coefficient and w_{ij} is an element of spatial weight matrix W, describing the spatial arrangements of the units in the sample.

Table 6.5 Spatial filter regression and selected eigenvectors, 1990–2010

Year	OLS		Spatial filtering		
	Pseudo R²	MC for residuals	Selected eigenvectors	Pseudo R²	MI for residuals
1990	0.662	0.462	E1, E2, E3, E4, E7, E9, E10, E11, E12, E19, E21	0.910	–0.145
1995	0.794	0.057	E3, E4, E7, E8, E9, E10, E11, E12, E15, E16, E17	0.958	–0.183
2000	0.730	0.153	E3, E4, E5, E7, E8, E9, E10, E11, E12, E13	0.959	–0.195
2005	0.706	0.188	E3, E4, E7, E8, E9, E10, E11, E12,E13, E15	0.962	–0.046
2010	0.761	0.160	E3, E7, E8, E10, E11, E12, E13, E15, E20, E21	0.958	–0.164

u_i denotes a spatial-specific effect, and ε_{it} is an independently and identically distributed error term.

The spatial error model is computed as follows:

$$y_{it} = x_{it}\beta + u_i + \varphi_{it}$$

$$\varphi_{it} = p \sum_{j=1}^{N} \left(w_{ij}\varphi_{it}\right) + \varepsilon_{it}$$

where φ_{it} is the spatially autocorrelated error term and p is the spatial autocorrelation coefficient.

Table 6.6 presents results based on four model specifications including simple pooled OLS regression, spatial filter panel regression, spatial lag panel regression (equation 6.5), and spatial error panel regression (equation 6.6 and equation 6.7). Multicollinearity is not a problem as VIF estimates are all lower than 2.5. Based on the results (Table 6.6), four interesting findings emerge. First, measured by BIC, the three spatial panel regression model specifications report better fitting statistics in comparison with the simple pooled OLS model, which explains 77.2% of the total variance of the county-level GDPPC. Results of likelihood ratio tests also identified that there is a significant reduction in deviance. Second, consistent with Patuelli *et al.*'s (2011) study, the fitting of the spatial-filter random-effect panel model, based on BIC, is superior to the spatial-lag and error-model specifications, mostly because its random effects term is a surrogate for various model deficiencies. Third, Table 6.6 shows that variables representing decentralization, marketization, and globalization are significant drivers of regional development in Guangdong (Table 6.6). Nevertheless, in comparison with the pooled OLS model, the *t* values of coefficients for GOVPC and NSOEPT decrease.

Table 6.6 Results of spatial filter mixed effect and spatial panel models

	Pooled OLS				Spatial filter panel			Spatial lag panel			Spatial error panel		
	Coef.	Sig.	T-value	VIF	Coef.	Sig.	T-value	Coef.	Sig.	T-value	Coef.	Sig.	T-value
FDIPC	0.014		0.876	2.116	0.061	***	5.313	0.029	**	2.417	0.063	***	5.193
NSOEPT	1.103	***	7.778	1.758	0.528	***	5.616	0.039	***	4.688	0.089	***	6.565
GOVPC	0.102	***	4.010	1.518	0.078	***	3.479	0.118	***	4.432	0.095	***	3.915
FIXPC	0.147	***	11.906	2.211	0.061	***	3.924	0.716	***	6.491	0.590	***	5.854
Urban	0.996	***	6.568	2.432	0.565	***	4.423	0.616	***	5.727	0.770	***	6.298
Mountain	-0.146	***	-3.710	1.263	-0.077		-1.550	-0.291	***	-4.069	-0.238	***	-4.157
$W*y_{it}$								0.593	***	15.381			
$W*\varphi_{it}$											0.758	***	20.665
Constant	6.042	***	82.409		6.674	***	85.490	2.399	***	31.562	6.586	***	58.888
BIC	349.347				104.034			155.617			121.774		
Adjust R^2	0.772												
Log likelihood ratio test					<0.001			<0.001					

More importantly, FDIPC, reflecting globalization, is significant in explaining regional development, and its coefficients are positive in spatial regression models. However, the pooled OLS model shows that the coefficient of FDIPC is insignificant. The result that the globalization effect has been declining is contrary to the basic nature of regional development in Guangdong. Therefore, spatial panel models, while taking into consideration spatial autocorrelation, result in a more reliable estimation of the development mechanisms. In addition, urbanization is a key driver of regional development, and physical conditions matter given the fact that the coefficient of MOUNTAIN is significantly negative. The results also suggest that the effect of the provincial government's policies aiming at reducing the gap between mountainous counties and those richest ones in the PRD has been constrained by these geographical conditions.

The results of spatial panel models are mainly concerned about the time-invariant coefficients. However, as Li and Wei (2010) argued, many factors of regional development are characterized by temporal heterogeneity/hierarchy. Following Griffith's (2008) space–time model, five time dummies and time-specific terms are added in equation 6.1 to detail the temporal heterogeneity of the underlying factors while taking into account spatial autocorrelation. The space–time model is expressed as follows:

$$y_{it} = \beta_{0,t}I_{it} + \beta_{1,t}x_{it} + sf_{it} + \varepsilon_{it}$$

where y_{it} denotes the GDPPC of county i in time t; I_{it} denotes the binary 0/1 indicator variable to time t for the county i; x_{it} denotes the triple process of economic transition, including FDIPC, GOVPC and NSOEPT; and β_{0t} denotes the regression coefficients for the temporal dummies. $\beta_{1,t}$ denotes the regression coefficients for covariates of FDIPC, GOVPC, and NSOEPT in time t.

Figure 6.6 shows the time-varying coefficients of the three variables of FDIPC, GOVPC, and NSOEPT. The simple pool OLS regression reveals a conspicuous decrease in the coefficient of FDIPC through the period of 1990–2010. However, the spatial lag/error models and spatial filtering models all confirm the fact that coefficients of FDI increased especially in the early 2000s right after China's entry into the WTO. Spatial filter and spatial lag models reduce standard errors of these coefficients as compared with the results of OLS regression. Furthermore, the impact of marketization and decentralization on regional development is sensitive to different time points (Figure 6.6). Consistent with the finding from Li and Wei (2010) and Liao and Wei (2012), the influence of market reform has been declining. By contrast, the influence of government and public spending increased consistently, indicating the more important role of local governments' expenditure in Guangdong's development under decentralization.

The model based on equation 6.8 can be further expanded by taking into account the core–periphery structure in Guangdong. We borrow the idea of the spatial regime model and add two regimes in the model (equation 6.9). Core region refers to the PRD, and the periphery region is those counties in the areas out of PRD.

$$\begin{bmatrix} y_{it,c} \\ y_{it,p} \end{bmatrix} = \begin{bmatrix} x_{t,c} & y_{t,c} \\ & & x_{t,p} & y_{t,p} \end{bmatrix} \begin{bmatrix} \beta_{it,c} \\ \beta_{it,p} \end{bmatrix} + sf_{it} + \varepsilon_{it}$$

where β_{it}, denotes the specific coefficients of covariates for counties in the core/
periphery region in time t.

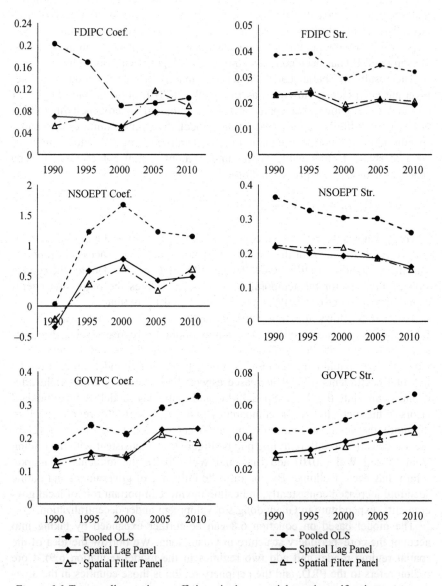

Figure 6.6 Temporally varying coefficients in three spatial panel specifications.

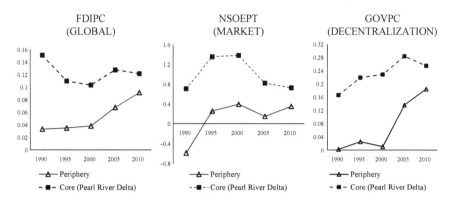

Figure 6.7 Spatially and temporally varying coefficients derived from two-regime spatial filtering mixed-effect mode.

Figure 6.7 presents spatially and temporally varying coefficients in the core and periphery regions. Clearly, the impact of the triple process of economic transition on regional development in the core region of the PRD is significantly more intensive than their counterparts in the periphery region. These results suggest that regional development in the PRD is more intensively driven by the triple process of economic transition. We also find that these coefficients differ from each other in their evolution. Coefficients of FDIPC, reflecting globalization effect, tend to decline in the PRD region recently. As Lu and Wei (2007) described, the original PRD model has been modified while other factors, such as public spending, have become another agent of the development. The coefficients reflecting the effect of marketization are declining in the PRD while increasing in the periphery. This finding suggests that market reform tends to be less influential in the PRD, where market reform has been initiated earlier than the periphery.

6.4 New economic spaces and imbalanced development

By utilizing space–time modeling techniques, the above analysis reveals the major mechanisms of regional development in Guangdong, confirming the effect of a triple process of economic transition on regional polarization with the PRD being the core region. The proceeding section aims to achieve a more thorough understanding of the PRD model and sheds further light on the mechanisms of imbalanced development in Guangdong.

The formation and transformation of the PRD model attracted considerable scholarly attention since the late 1990s. Earlier work was concerned about the role played by the influx of small- and medium-sized Hong Kong invested enterprises in the rapid industrialization of the PRD (Lin 1997). The division of labor, known as the "back factory front shop" model, highlights the importance of

Hong Kong as the headquarters of the workshop of the world and its role in the urbanization in the PRD. Different from the experience from the Western economies, these investments from overseas Chinese economies and mainly Hong Kong and Taiwan tend to specialize in the manufacture of labor-intensive products such as textiles, garments, toys, and even consumer electronics (Sit and Yang 1997). During the 1980s and the 1990s, they were attracted by local assets in the small and rural towns of the PRD, including cheaper land, rich pool of migrant workers, thick institutions or ethnic ties, and less bureaucratic but more entrepreneurial local states (Oi 1992; Lin 1997). However, as discussed in Lu and Wei (2007), the original PRD model might have been obsolete and there have been new forms of regional development (Lu and Wei 2007; Yang 2012; Zhang and Kloosterman 2016; Liu 2017).

First, although export-oriented processing or industrialization remains an important motor of economic growth, the rise of the domestic market in China and changing business environment in the PRD has had a profound impact on FDI development. Hong Kong firms, for example, have expanded their operations beyond the PRD due to the rise of land prices and increasingly stringent environmental regulation (Liao and Chan 2011). Their effects on local economic development in the delta have greatly been eroded by larger transnational corporations (TNCs), such as Foxconn, P&G, Honda, Nissan, Samsung, and Toyota, from Taiwan, Western Europe, Japan, and the U.S. In the early 2000s, through their collaboration with the Guangzhou Automotive Industrial Group (GAIG), Honda and Toyota built up their branch plants in Guangzhou. By 2012, the joint ventures with Honda and Toyota had sold more than 300,000 vehicles in the Chinese market and became two of the most profitable companies in China's automobile industry (Liu 2017). By the end of 2016, more than half of the global 500 TNCs had invested in the PRD in general and the core cities of Guangzhou and Shenzhen in particular. The provincial government also provided various preferential policies and tax incentives that encouraged the TNCs to establish their R&D centers and relocate their higher value-added activities to the PRD region. Shenzhen, for instance, has successfully lured high-tech ICT TNCs, including Apple, Cisco, Microsoft, and Qualcomm. Based on the high concentration of regional-level R&D centers of large and leading firms in the ICT industry, Shenzhen has become one of the three leading innovation hubs in China, on par with Shanghai and Beijing (Yang 2015).

Second, the upgrading of the economy in the PRD has not been purely reliant upon the external capital or TNCs but has increasingly been supported by the development of the regional innovation system (RIS). Particular attention has been paid to the development of new globally competitive Chinese firms. Both Huawei and ZTE, two major high-tech telecommunication companies, were founded in the PRD (Fan 2011). These two companies contributed more than half of the total R&D expenditures in the city of Shenzhen, and more importantly, Huawei is one of the very few leading innovators in China feared by global leading firms in the ICT industry. Moreover, since the 2000s, the back-factory and front-office model has also been reshaped by the insertion of advanced producer service (APS) activities, including finance, accounting and legal services, in the PRD. Employment in these sectors, as mentioned above, doubled from 2.41 million in 2003 to 4.65 million in 2010, and FDI actually realized in advanced services also increased from US$2.83 billion in 2006 to US$5.68 billion in 2010 (Zhang and Kloosterman 2016, p. 4). These new services activities are characterized by high geographical concentration in the core cities of Guangzhou and Shenzhen. The connections between the two cities dominate the intercity business networks in the PRD and help the region to connect to major globalizing cities in China, including Beijing and Shanghai and other global cities out of mainland China such as Hong Kong, London, New York, and Singapore (Zhang and Kloosterman 2016).

Third, in addition to changing economic spaces in the PRD, the Chinese context of regional development has differed significantly from that of the Deng era (i.e., the 1980s–1990s). Since the 1990s, Guangdong in general and the PRD in particular have faced new challenges from the YRD and other regions including the inland provinces such as Chongqing. In order to regain the status of "one step ahead" in China's regional development, Guangdong's provincial government proposed several new collaboration initiatives such as the Pan-PRD program in the early 2000s (Yeung 2005) and the GBRA mentioned in the previous chapter. Most of these programs were proposed by the Guangdong provincial government rather than the central government and aimed at strengthening the collaboration between Guangdong and other provincial entities in China. For instance, under the new GBRA initiative, the spatial network of development in the PRD will be driven by its three growth poles including Hong Kong–Shenzhen, Guangzhou–Foshan and Zhuhai–Macao, in which Hong Kong and Macao are two relatively independent and special administrative regions in China.

Within the GBRA, major economic development axes will also synergize local assets across the second-tier cities, including Foshan, Dongguan, Zhongshan, Huizhou, Zhaoqing, and Jiangmen. Indeed, besides constructing intercity railways and high-grade roads, key transport infrastructures such as the Hong Kong–Zhuhai–Macao bridge, the proposed Shenzhen–Zhongshan bridge and the Shenzhen–Maoming railway have been completed or launched in tandem to foster new development synergy between the east and west banks of the PRD. Moreover, urban and regional planning in the PRD has emphasized more on livability and green spaces or green belts, in an attempt to make "the Greater Bay Area a place with bluer skies, greener mountains, clearer water and a better environment" (Hong Kong Constitutional and Mainland Affairs Bureau 2019, p. 33). Meanwhile, due to the lack of world-class universities in Guangdong, the provincial government has collaborated with many well-known universities in China and Hong Kong, such as Peking University, the University of Hong Kong, and the Chinese University of Hong Kong. Numerous incentives have been offered to encourage these reputed universities to build up their satellite campuses in Guangdong. Several universities in cities or towns in Zhuhai, Shenzhen, Guangzhou, and other cities in Guangdong, accompanied by new economic zones, incubators, R&D centers, etc., were also built to foster collaboration between universities and local business and industries (Lu and Wei 2007; Fu, Diez, and Schiller 2012).

To summarize, the original PRD model, known as rapid industrialization driven by low-cost and export-oriented manufacturing, has to be re-evaluated. Special attention should be paid to the emergence of new economic spaces centered on the knowledge-based economy. As a result, we argue that the gap between the core and the periphery regions in Guangdong might at least persist in the near future. Furthermore, as the periphery region plays a key role in the ecological sustainability in Guangdong, how to stimulate economic growth in the lagging region while not destroying the ecological environment therein is also a pressing issue and a tough task.

6.5 Conclusion

Drawing upon Wei's (2002) conceptualization of the triple process of China's economic transition, including globalization, marketization, and decentralization, this chapter deepens our understanding of the mechanisms of regional development and inequality in Guangdong. In general, the empirical case of Guangdong confirms the applicability of a multi-mechanism framework when analyzing regional disparities in China. Specifically, taking into consideration spatial effects as well as space–time heterogeneity is valuable to achieve a deeper understanding of the relationship between space, scales, dynamics, and inequality. The results of multi-level modeling are capable of better explaining the factors underlying regional inequality in Guangdong over space and time. We have found that many development agents such as the local governments, foreign investors, and the central state are functioning at the low levels under provinces, which are likely to be concealed in the analysis of large spatial aggregates such as provinces and groups of provinces (Wei and Fan 2000).

The above findings thus contribute to the literature and suggest meaningful theoretical and policy implications. First, our modeling efforts highlight the space–time heterogeneity of these triple processes of economic transition while taking into account spatial autocorrelation and the core–periphery divide in Guangdong. The resulting multi-level model provides a basis for the regional development policy to promote the spontaneous development of domestic private enterprises, which are spatially more balanced and locally embedded and which have the potential to play a role in mediating the polarized development in Guangdong that is driven by the overly uneven distribution of the globalization forces. Second, our models using spatial filters lead to better model performance and a substantial reduction of standard errors associated with independent variables' coefficients. The spatially sensitive and temporally varying coefficients imply that the influences of globalization, marketization, and decentralization are sensitive to different stages of economic development in Guangdong and the core–periphery gradient centered on the PRD region.

Another aim of the chapter is to examine the formation and the transformation of the PRD model. We argue that the triple processes of economic transition have much stronger influences on regional development in the PRD. However, their roles and relative importance have changed since the 2000s. For example, domestic enterprises and high-tech industries have emerged as a new driver of recent economic growth rather than the original manufacturing investments from Hong Kong. We also find that recent efforts towards inequality reduction have not achieved the expected effects. As discussed in this chapter, most of these "new" economic activities in the PRD, such as high-end service sectors and high-tech industries, are more prone to agglomeration economies mentioned in the previous chapter, and then might have worsened the core–periphery divide at the provincial level. Similarly, development policies such as the new GBA initiative might enhance the competitiveness of the PRD region as the core, while it may also result in a new round of economic polarization in Guangdong. Given the results in this work, the spatial policy in Guangdong should place more emphasis on the spatial spillover from the PRD to the periphery region and more efforts should be made to foster new clusters of development in the periphery.

References

CSB (China Statistical Bureau). 2001. *Zhongguo Tongji Nianjian (China Statistical Yearbook)*. Beijing: China Statistical Press.

Fan, P. 2011. Innovation, globalization, and catch-up of latecomers: Cases of Chinese telecom firms. *Environment and Planning A: Economy and Space* 43 (4): 830–849.

Fu, W., J. R. Diez, and D. Schiller. 2012. Regional innovation systems within a transitional context: Evolutionary comparison of the electronics industry in Shenzhen and Dongguan since the opening of China. *Journal of Economic Surveys* 26 (3): 534–550.

Griffith, D. A. 2008. A comparison of four model specifications for describing small heterogeneous space-time datasets: Sugar cane production in Puerto Rico, 1958/59–1973/74. *Papers in Regional Science* 87 (3): 341–355.

GSB (Guangdong Statistical Bureau). 1990. *Guangdong Tongji Nianjian (Guangdong Statistical Yearbook)*. Beijing: China Statistical Press.

GSB (Guangdong Statistical Bureau). 2001. *Guangdong Tongji Nianjian (Guangdong Statistical Yearbook)*. Beijing: China Statistical Press.

Gu, C., J. Shen, K. Wong, and F. Zhen. 2001. Regional polarization under the socialist-market system since 1978: A case study of Guangdong province in south China. *Environment and Planning A* 33 (1): 97–119.

Hao, R., and and Z. Wei. 2010. Fundamental causes of inland-coastal income inequality in post-reform China. *Annals of Regional Science* 45 (1): 181–206.

Hong Kong Constitutional and Mainland Affairs Bureau. 2019. *Greater Bay Area Development Plan*. Hong Kong: The Steering Committee for the Development of the Greater Bay Area.

Li, Y., and Y. H. D. Wei. 2010. The spatial-temporal hierarchy of regional inequality of China. *Applied Geography* 30 (3): 303–316.

Liao, H. F., and R. C. K. Chan. 2011. Industrial relocation of Hong Kong manufacturing firms: Towards an expanding industrial space beyond the Pearl River Delta. *GeoJournal* 76 (6): 623–639.

Liao, H. F. F., and Y. H. D. Wei. 2012. Dynamics, space, and regional inequality in provincial China: A case study of Guangdong Province. *Applied Geography* 35 (1): 71–83.

Lin, G. C. S. 1997. *Red capitalism in south China: Growth and development of the Pearl River Delta*. Vancouver: UBC Press.

Lin, G. C. S., and F. Z. Y. Hu. 2011. Getting the China story right: Insights from national economic censuses. *Eurasian Geography and Economics* 52 (5): 712–746.

Liu, Y. 2017. The dynamics of local upgrading in globalizing latecomer regions: A geographical analysis. *Regional Studies* 51 (6): 880–893.

Long, H., J. Zou, J. Pykett, and Y. Li. 2011. Analysis of rural transformation development in China since the turn of the new millennium. *Applied Geography* 31 (3): 1094–1105.

Lu, L., and Y. D. Wei. 2007. Domesticating globalisation, new economic spaces and regional polarisation in Guangdong Province, China. *Tijdschrift voor economische en sociale geografie* 98 (2): 225–244.

Ng, L. F. Y., and C. Tuan. 2003. Location decisions of manufacturing FDI in China: Implications of China's WTO accession. *Journal of Asian Economics* 14 (1): 51–72.

Oi, J. C. 1992. Fiscal reform and the economic foundations of local state corporatism in China. *World Politics* 45 (1): 99–126.

Patuelli, R., D. A. Griffith, M. Tiefelsdorf, and P. Nijkamp. 2011. Spatial filtering and eigenvector stability: Space–time models for German unemployment data. *International Regional Science Review* 34 (2): 253–280.

Shen, J. 2003. Cross-border connection between Hong Kong and Mainland China under 'two systems' before and beyond 1997. *Geografiska Annaler: Series B, Human Geography* 85 (1): 1–17.

Sit, V. F. S., and C. Yang. 1997. Foreign-investment-induced exo-urbanisation in the Pearl River Delta, China. *Urban Studies* 34 (4): 647–677.

Wang, E. 2010. Fiscal decentralization and revenue/expenditure disparities in China. *Eurasian Geography and Economics* 51 (6): 744–766.

Wei, Y. H. D. 2000. *Regional development in China: States, globalization and inequality*. London: Routledge.

Wei, Y. H. D. 2002. Multiscale and multimechanisms of regional inequality in China: Implications for regional policy. *Journal of Contemporary China* 11 (30): 109–124.

Wei, Y. H. D. 2004. Trajectories of ownership transformation in China: Implications for uneven regional development. *Eurasian Geography and Economics* 45 (2): 90–113.

Wei, Y. H. D., and C. C. Fan. 2000. Regional inequality in China: A case study of Jiangsu Province. *Professional Geographer* 52 (3): 455–469.

Xu, Z., and A. Yeh. 2013. Origin effects, spatial dynamics and redistribution of FDI in Guangdong, China. *Tijdschrift voor economische en sociale geografie* 104 (4): 439–455.

Yang, C. 2012. Restructuring the export-oriented industrialization in the Pearl River Delta, China: Institutional evolution and emerging tension. *Applied Geography* 32 (1): 143–157.

Yang, C. 2015. Government policy change and evolution of regional innovation systems in China: Evidence from strategic emerging industries in Shenzhen. *Environment and Planning C: Government and Policy* 33 (3): 661–682.

Ye, Y., K. Wu, Y. Xie, G. Huang, C. Wang, and J. Chen. 2019. How firm heterogeneity affects foreign direct investment location choice: Micro-evidence from new foreign manufacturing firms in the Pearl River Delta. *Applied Geography* 106: 11–21.

Yeung, Y. 2005. Emergence of the pan-Pearl River Delta. *Geografiska Annaler: Series B, Human Geography* 87 (1): 75–79.

Yu, D., and Y. D. Wei. 2008. Spatial data analysis of regional development in Greater Beijing, China, in a GIS environment. *Papers in Regional Science* 87 (1): 97–117.

Zhang, X., and R. C. Kloosterman. 2016. Connecting the 'workshop of the world': Intra- and extra-service networks of the Pearl River Delta city-region. *Regional Studies* 50 (6): 1069–1081.

7 Regional inequality in Zhejiang Province

7.1 Introduction

This chapter investigates regional inequality in provincial China through a case study of another coastal province, namely, Zhejiang Province. Zhejiang contrasts with Guangdong regarding its patterns as well as mechanisms of uneven development. We emphasize the role of local context and bottom–up forces in the spatiotemporal evolution of regional development while acknowledging the broad economic transition in China. Like Guangdong, rising regional inequality in Zhejiang has drawn considerable attention from the provincial government and made several poverty-alleviation policies possible. In the 2000s, 25 counties were tagged as "underdeveloped region" by the provincial government and the Underdeveloped Counties Well-off (*Qianfada xiangzhen Benxiaokang*) project was launched to promote their economic development (Wang 2013). The Coast-Mountain Cooperation (*Shan-Hai Xiezuo*) project has been launched since 2003 to pair coastal municipalities like Hangzhou, Ningbo, and Wenzhou with interior municipalities like Quzhou, Lishui, and Zhoushan, and strengthen the economic cooperation and transfer of investment, jobs, and fiscal resources among counties (Ma 2012).

Drawing upon the multi-scale and multi-mechanism framework, this chapter analyzes regional development and inequality in Zhejiang Province, including analyzing the spatiotemporal transition and mobility of clusters and the Wenzhou model of development. The chapter also sheds further light on the efficacy of policies towards inequality alleviation in a province that has been faced with new challenges and policy dilemmas regarding regional economic development in the aftermath of the global financial crisis in the 2010s.

7.2 Research setting

Zhejiang is a coastal province located to the south-west of Shanghai (Figure 7.1). As one of the core provinces in the Yangtze River Delta (YRD) region, Zhejiang is the smallest coastal province, and only covers 1.1% of China's territory but carries 4.1% of the nation's population. Zhejiang has been spearheading China's economic growth and privatization since the reform. The annual growth rates of

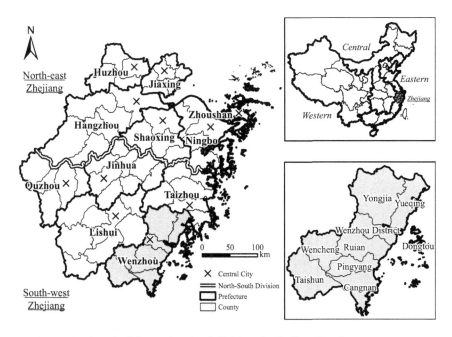

Figure 7.1 Regions in China and regional divisions in Zhejiang Province.

GDP and GDP per capita in Zhejiang are 12.2% and 11% respectively from 1978 to 2015, which are much higher than the national average (9.6% and 8.5% respectively). The industrial output of state-owned enterprises (SOEs) has dropped drastically from 61% in 1978 to 4.7% in 2015, while the share of private enterprises (PEs) and foreign-invested enterprises (FIEs) are 41.2% and 21.8% in 2015, respectively. The private sector in Zhejiang is featured as clusters of small-scale, family-owned, light industries, which are deeply integrated with the global economy (Wei 2009, 2011). In 2015, Zhejiang accounts for 13% and 14% of China's exports and foreign direct investment (FDI), respectively, of which the major investors are from Hong Kong, the United States, Singapore, and Japan (NBSC 2016; ZSB 2016).

Regional development in Zhejiang is uneven and has its unique historical legacy. Traditionally, Zhejiang was divided into the north-eastern part consisting of Hangzhou, Ningbo, Jiaxing, Huzhou, Shaoxing, and Zhoushan prefectures, and the south-western part of Wenzhou, Taizhou, Jinhua, Quzhou, and Lishui (Table 7.1). The northern Zhejiang is part of the flat plateau of the YRD and the start point of the Grand Canal connecting Beijing and Hangzhou. The prosperous trade of handcraft, tea, and silk in the Ming and Qing Dynasties made northern Zhejiang one of the most developed regions in China (Forster 1998). During Mao's era, economic development in Zhejiang was stagnated largely because

Table 7.1 Development indicators of Zhejiang Province in 2015

	Zhejiang	% of China	NE Zhejiang	% of Zhejiang	SW Zhejiang	% of Zhejiang
Land area, km^2	104,468	1.08	45,881	43.92	58,587	56.08
hukou population, million	48.74	3.55	24.64	50.55	24.1	49.45
de facto population, 2010 census, million	54.43	4.06	29.73	54.63	24.69	45.37
GDP, billion RMB	4,303.84	6.28	2,921.47	67.88	1,382.37	32.12
GDP per capita, RMB	88,302	–	118,566	–	57,360	–
Investment in fixed assets, billion RMB	2,661.91	4.74	1,769.7	66.48	892.21	33.52
Exports, billion USD	276.6	12.17	186.55	67.44	90.05	32.56
FDI, billion USD	16.96	13.43	16	94.34	0.96	5.66
Local fiscal expenditure, billion RMB	581.81	3.31	381.71	65.61	200.1	34.39
Local fiscal revenue, billion RMB	445.69	2.93	325.76	73.09	119.93	26.91

the central government had allocated investment and infrastructure into the interior provinces (Ma and Wei 1997).

Since 1978, Zhejiang as a coastal province has been favored in the reform and opening-door policies. The entrepreneurship tradition and place-based business networks developed in Zhejiang's trade history have stimulated the rapid economic growth in coastal Zhejiang by channeling the overseas capital, technology, and management into regions like Ningbo and Wenzhou (Wei and Ye 2004, 2009). The Wenzhou model of development, which is centered on family-owned small businesses embedded in thick local institutions, has flourished in rural Wenzhou (Wei, Li, and Wang 2007). As a result, the traditional north–south divide has been gradually replaced by the emerging coastal–interior divide (Ye and Wei 2005).

The majority of data in this chapter is extracted from the statistical yearbooks of Zhejiang (ZSB 2010, 2016), which covers 11 municipalities (typically prefecture levels) and 71 county-level units (e.g., counties, city districts, and county-level cities) in Zhejiang. GDP per capita in constant price is used as the indicator of regional development. The de facto population data are estimated by interpolating the ratio between the *hukou* (household registration) and residential (or de facto) population in 1982, 1990, 2000, and 2010 census, which is used to compare with the de jure population in the result (Liao and Wei 2012).

7.3 Multi-scale patterns of regional inequality

The temporal trend of inter-county inequalities measured by CV, Gini, and Theil provide a holistic picture of the evolution of regional inequality in Zhejiang since the reform, which has several implications (Figure 7.2). In general, regional inequality in Zhejiang is at a lower level than other coastal provinces, including our case of Guangdong. Such changing patterns of regional inequality can be better understood through an analysis of reform and development processes in Zhejiang. The comprehensive reform in urban industrial sectors from 1978 to the mid-1980s led to rising inequality at the county scale until the 1990s. The most radical marketization reforms were implemented since Deng Xiaoping's Southern Tour in 1992. Benefiting from the opening-up and proximity to the global market, the coastal prefectures and counties in Zhejiang have experienced more rapid economic growth, which has left the interior region behind (Wei and Ye 2004). Known for its Wenzhou model of development centered on private enterprises, the catch-up of the coastal Wenzhou-Taizhou region has altered the traditional north–south divide with the emerging coastal–interior divide (Wei and Ye 2009).

Furthermore, as shown in Figure 7.3, regional inequality in Zhejiang is sensitive to scales, which is consistent with previous findings in China and Zhejiang (Yue *et al.* 2014; He, Bayrak, and Lin 2017). Following the decline from the mid-1980s to the early 1990s, the inequality at the prefecture and county level increased again, while regional-level inequality further decreased.

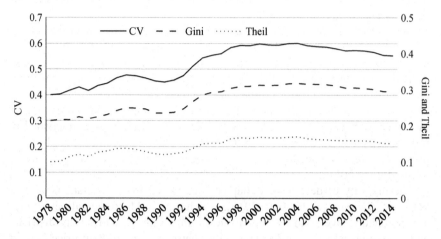

Figure 7.2 Inter-county inequality in per capita GDP.

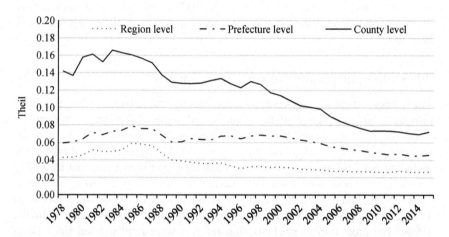

Figure 7.3 Temporal trend of multi-scale regional inequality in Zhejiang Province.

A steady decline of inequality at the prefecture and county level is observed since the early 2000s, which is characterized by, to some extent, regional convergence. Like other coastal provinces, China's entry to the WTO in 2001 has led to a new round of inflowing FDI and flourishing export-oriented economies in prefectures and counties in Zhejiang. As mentioned in the previous chapter, fiscal decentralization has linked local expenditure more tightly to local revenue and provided a strong stimulus for the local government to improve public services and investment conditions in order to promote economic growth (Brehm 2013). The development and spatial restructuring of

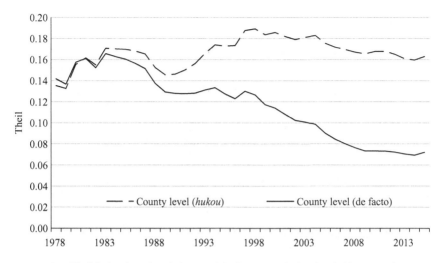

Figure 7.4 Theil index based on hukou and de facto population in Zhejiang Province.

private enterprises and foreign-invested enterprises, as well as the greatly loosened *hukou* system, have benefited more prefectures and counties in Zhejiang. In recent years, the regional-level spatial inequality has begun to stabilize.

The impact of population mobility on regional inequality in Zhejiang is evident (Figure 7.4). Since the 1980s, economic growth in coastal Zhejiang has drawn considerable rural migration into the urban regions seeking higher wages as manufacturing workers (Lin and Gaubatz 2015). As a result, the gap between the *hukou* and resident measures has become wider, implying that regional inequality measured by the *hukou* population is distorted and overestimated (Li and Gibson 2013). It is argued that the greatly loosened *hukou* registration system has helped to achieve more even regional development in China by spatially balancing the capital and human resource among the developed and underdeveloped regions (Chan and Wang 2008). After 2008, the difference between the two measures has stabilized, which is attributed to the slowdown of economic engine and correspondingly declining migration of low-income earners (Chan 2010).

7.4 Distributional dynamics of regional inequality or convergence

To investigate the disparity and the "long-run" convergence properties among counties in Zhejiang, the distributional dynamics and spatial Markov-chain methods are used in this section (Quah 1993). As shown in Figure 7.5, the shape of the distribution has changed considerably over time. The normal distribution

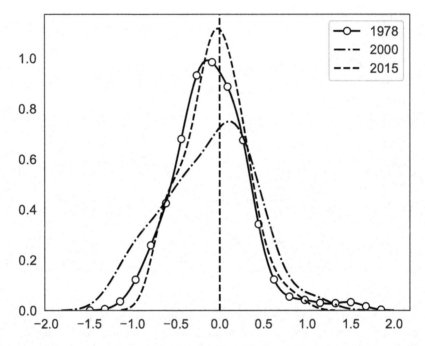

Figure 7.5 Distributional dynamics of GDP per capita in Zhejiang.

in 1978 has converted to a distribution skewing towards the poor side in 2000, while fewer counties are concentrated around the average level, indicating a complex diverging process during the period of 1978–2000. From 2000 to 2015, convergence is observed as more counties are close to the provincial average, which is in line with the declining Theil index after the early 2000s.

Table 7.2 contains the transition probability matrices and corresponding ergodic distribution for the whole period of 1978 to 2015 and two sub-periods of 1978 to 2000 and 2000 to 2015. The GDP per capita data is discretized by grid values that split the entire sample uniformly (Sakamoto and Islam 2008). Four category groups of poor (P), less developed (L), developed (D), and rich (R) are used to better represent the geographical notion of core, semi-core, semi-periphery, and periphery (Wei, Yu, and Chen 2011). The upper bound of each group is given by the value in parentheses. The ergodic distribution indicates the steady distribution after infinite times of transition if the current process continues to hold.

There are also several findings derived from Table 7.2. First, all the diagonal probabilities in three periods are higher than the non-diagonal ones, indicating that it is more likely for counties to remain in their current status. Within the diagonal probabilities, the two ends of the distribution are higher than the middle ones for the periods of 1978 to 2015 and 1978 to 2000, which means that

Table 7.2 Markov transition matrix based on one-year transition, 1978–2015

Samples	Grid line [upper bound]			
	P [0.668]	L [0.909]	D [1.225]	R [4.409]
1978–2015				
P (671)	0.937	0.063	0.000	0.000
L (666)	0.062	0.884	0.054	0.000
D (658)	0.000	0.04	0.897	0.064
R (669)	0.000	0.000	0.061	0.939
Ergodic	0.206	0.209	0.286	0.298
1978–2000				
P (401)	0.928	0.072	0	0
L (436)	0.085	0.849	0.067	0
D (364)	0	0.063	0.843	0.093
R (383)	0	0	0.076	0.924
Ergodic	0.259	0.221	0.233	0.287
2000–2015				
P (270)	0.952	0.048	0	0
L (230)	0.017	0.952	0.03	0
D (294)	0	0.01	0.963	0.027
R (286)	0	0	0.042	0.958
Ergodic	0.058	0.159	0.475	0.308

the core and periphery regions are more likely to stay as core or periphery. Second, the non-diagonal probabilities are much lower than the diagonal ones, indicating a relatively stable regional development system with gradual change. Furthermore, the possibility for counties to leapfrog two levels upward or downward is zero.

Last, the first sub-period is characterized by a more even ergodic distribution, while the ones of the second sub-period and the whole period are biased towards the rich and developed side. It is because the upward movement possibilities are in general higher than the downward ones in the second sub-period and the whole period, which implies a long-run convergence that echoes with the trend of Theil index. However, the traditional Markov method treats regions as independent of each other and ignores the spatial effects between regions (Rey 2001; Le Gallo 2004). Spatial Markov transition matrices are adopted to reveal the transition probability conditioned on the status of neighbors.

As illustrated in Table 7.3, the spatial effects are found to be salient on the transition matrices. First, as the spatial lag changes from poor to rich, the possibility to remain as a poor county declines, and the possibility to stay in other status increases. Second, the same type of upward movement, e.g., from poor to less developed, will increase as the development level of a county's neighbor

Table 7.3 Spatial Markov transition matrix based on one-year transition, 1978–2015

Spatial lag			Grid line [highest point]			
		N	*P [0.668]*	*L [0.909]*	*D [1.225]*	*R [4.409]*
P	P	470	0.962	0.038	0	0
	L	168	0.113	0.863	0.024	0
	D	17	0	0.176	0.765	0.059
	R	18	0	0	0	1
	Ergodic		0	0	0	1
L	P	174	0.902	0.098	0	0
	L	268	0.049	0.896	0.056	0
	D	160	0	0.05	0.913	0.038
	R	61	0	0	0.098	0.902
	Ergodic		0.163	0.329	0.368	0.140
D	P	22	0.727	0.273	0	0
	L	177	0.051	0.887	0.062	0
	D	306	0	0.033	0.925	0.042
	R	154	0	0	0.084	0.916
	Ergodic		0.046	0.247	0.470	0.237
R	P	5	0.8	0.2	0	0
	L	53	0	0.887	0.113	0
	D	175	0	0.029	0.846	0.126
	R	436	0	0	0.05	0.95
	Ergodic		0.000	0.067	0.267	0.665

improves. Third, the ergodic distribution becomes more biased towards the rich and developed side as the spatial lag condition switches from less developed to developed and rich. The finding confirms the strong spatial effects of neighboring counties in promoting or hampering the local economy.

Since there is no leapfrog of the two-step movement in the spatial Markov transition matrices, the major trend of movements could be summarized as Table 7.4 after comparing the symmetric possibilities. For example, when surrounded by poor (P) counties, the possibility of moving from less developed (L) to poor (P) is 11.3%, which is much higher than the possibility from P to L as 3.8%. Thus, the movement trend between P and L is downward if it is conditioned by poor spatial lag. When surrounded by less developed (L) counties, the possibility from P to L, 9.8%, is larger than the possibility from L to P, 4.9%, then the movement trend is upward. As illustrated by Table 7.4, the spillover effects from more developed counties to underdeveloped counties are obvious since rich, developed, and less developed counties have a positive impact on the catching-up of their poorer neighboring counties. However, the backwash effects are also non-negligible. When a less developed or developed county is surrounded by poor counties or a rich county is surrounded by less developed counties or developed counties, it is more possible for them to move downward than upward.

Table 7.4 Major trends in spatial Markov matrices conditioned on neighbor's state-space

Neighbor county	$P \leftrightarrow -L$	$L \leftrightarrow D$	$D \leftrightarrow R$
P	←	←	→
L	→	~	←
D	→	→	←
R	→	→	→

Note

when conditioned on k and state i is lower than j, if the transition probability $p^k_{i \rightarrow j}$ is smaller than $p^k_{i \leftarrow j}$, then the dominating trend is backward movement, or ←; if $p^k_{i \rightarrow j} > p^k_{i \leftarrow j}$, then it is →; if $p^k_{i \rightarrow j}$ and $p^k_{i \leftarrow j}$ are within 1%, it is ~.

Uneven development is observed at the county level using GDP per capita maps. In 1978, city districts in the prefectures of Hangzhou and Ningbo were identified as the rich areas in Zhejiang (Figure 7.6). Some counties or districts in the interior areas near Quanzhou and Jinhua were also wealthier, which can be attributed to Mao's policy of national defense. As shown in Figure 7.6, from 1978 to 1992, counties in the northern and south-eastern Zhejiang experienced more rapid growth, while counties in south-western Zhejiang lagged behind. The pattern remained similar in the 2000s and spill-over effects were evident for counties outside the south-western part of Zhejiang.

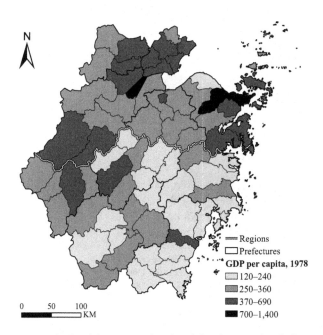

Figure 7.6a Spatial patterns of regional development in Zhejiang, 1978.

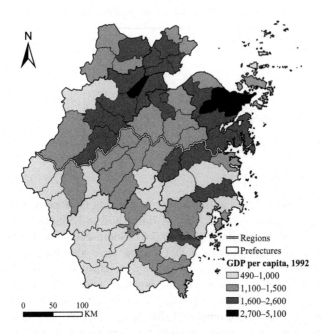

Figure 7.6b Spatial patterns of regional development in Zhejiang, 1992.

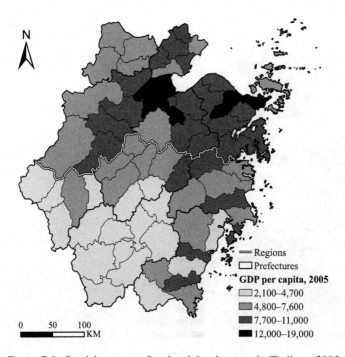

Figure 7.6c Spatial patterns of regional development in Zhejiang, 2005.

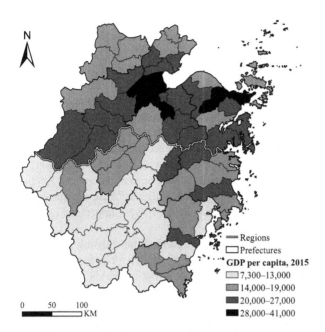

Figure 7.6d Spatial patterns of regional development in Zhejiang, 2015.

7.5 ESDA-based analysis of regional development

The spatial effects are not reflected in the conventional inequality measures like Theil index, in particular, which may even lead to a biased or misleading understanding of regional inequality. Global Moran's I is calculated to measure the magnitude of spatial agglomeration during the period (Getis and Ord 1992). As shown in Figure 7.7, the spatial autocorrelation of GDP per capita remained at a relatively low level around 0.2 before the mid-1980s, and rapidly increased and stayed at a higher level above 0.3 from 1985 to 1996. A sudden drop of concentration is observed in 1997, possibly due to the Asian Financial Crisis. After then, the spatial agglomeration continued to increase from 1998 and reached the highest level above 0.5 from 2007 to 2015.

The comprehensive urban industrial reform from 1978 to the mid-1980s has benefited the city districts of prefectures that are sparsely distributed in Zhejiang Province. As a result, the spatial concentration is not intensified during the period. But the radical marketization reform since 1992 has geographically disproportional impacts towards the coastal Zhejiang and leads to the rise of both inequality and concentration (Figure 7.7). The rapid spatial concentration, together with the emerging coastal–interior divide, has not been alleviated with the narrowing gap among counties since the 2000s, which implies that regions are converging in attribute but becoming more uneven in space. The trend of spatial polarization has only slowed down and slightly declined since the global financial crisis in 2007–2008 when the decrease of regional inequality has been stabilized, indicating the occurrence of spatial restructuring during the period (Wei, Li, and Wang 2007; Wei 2012).

Local indicator of spatial autocorrelation (LISA) method is used to reveal significant local clusters and outliers that are embedded in the globally intensifying spatial agglomeration in Zhejiang Province (Figure 7.8). At the beginning of the reform in 1978, the high-high clusters of economic development were mainly concentrated in the developed city districts in northern Zhejiang or the surrounding areas, such as Xiaoshan and Yuhang around the Hangzhou city district, Yinzhou around Ningbo city district, and the city districts of Shaoxing and Zhoushan, while the low-low clusters were mostly located in southern Zhejiang. Wenzhou city district stands out as a high-low outlier because the surrounding counties were poor and their economic development was suppressed before the reform (Wei and Ye 2004).

In 1992, the northern high-high clusters expanded into Fuyang in Hangzhou and Cixi in Ningbo that was low-high outlier previously. The low-low clusters shifted into the interior mountainous Zhejiang, most of which were in Lishui prefecture. The city district of Taizhou also stands out as a new high-low outlier. As shown in Figure 7.8, spatial clustering of counties in northern Zhejiang has been more evident since 2005, centered on the axis of Hangzhou–Shaoxing–Ningbo. Counties in south-western Zhejiang stood out as a typical "poverty trap" expanding to more interior counties in Jinhua and Quzhou prefectures from 1992 to 2015. The transition and mobility of spatial clusters is attributed to different development processes and fortunes between northern and southern Zhejiang, as well as coastal and interior Zhejiang. In contrast, the surrounding counties near Shanghai, Hangzhou, and Ningbo greatly benefited from globalization, state investments, and local institutional forces promoting industrialization and

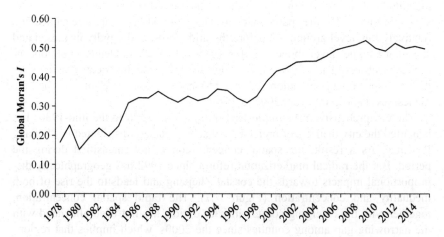

Figure 7.7 Global Moran's *I* of GDP per capita in Zhejiang Province, 1978–2015.

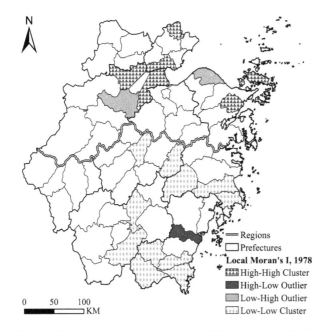

Figure 7.8a LISA map of county-level GDP per capita in Zhejiang, 1978.

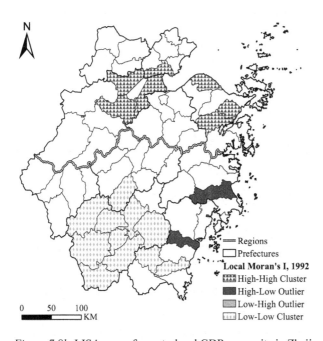

Figure 7.8b LISA map of county-level GDP per capita in Zhejiang, 1992.

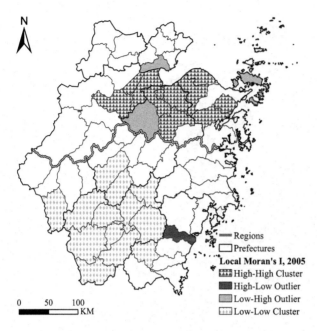

Figure 7.8c LISA map of county-level GDP per capita in Zhejiang, 2005.

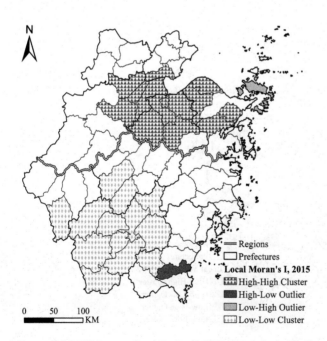

Figure 7.8d LISA map of county-level GDP per capita in Zhejiang, 2015.

urbanization. Specifically, in recent regional development, Hangzhou has emerged as a center of high-technology and high-end service industries, and Ningbo benefitted as a core harbor for chemical industries and logistic services relying on its deep-water ports (Zhu 2006) (Figure 7.6).

The emerging coastal counties in southern Zhejiang is mainly due to the rise of non-state sectors and the importance of entrepreneurship. The Wenzhou model of development, centered on small-scale, private enterprises, and trading networks, has spread beyond Wenzhou to Taizhou and Jinhua and cultivated agglomerations of specialized light industries (Ye and Leipnik 2013). Consequently, the rapid economic growth in Wenzhou, Taizhou, and Jinhua has transformed counties from the low-low clusters to insignificant spatial clusters and maintained the high-low outlier of Wenzhou city district. Because of the mountainous location, outdated infrastructure, and lack of investment from the state and the global market, the interior, south-western Zhejiang like Lishui and Quzhou prefectures are lagging behind and show a local concentration of poor economies (Wei and Ye 2009; Yue *et al.* 2014).

To quantify the dynamics of spatial agglomeration, LISA Markov is used to explain the transitions of "pockets of local non-stationarity" (Gallo and Ertur 2003). As shown in Table 7.5, the possibility for counties to stay or convert to the high-high or low-low cluster is generally higher than staying or converting to

Table 7.5 LISA Markov-chain transition matrices for county-level GDP per capita, 1990–2015

	HH	*LH*	*LL*	*HL*
1990–2007				
HH	0.973	0.017	0.002	0.007
LH	0.085	0.881	0.025	0.008
LL	0.002	0.009	0.972	0.017
HL	0.056	0.000	0.077	0.866
Ergodic distribution	0.488	0.097	0.340	0.075
2008–2015				
HH	0.955	0.028	0.000	0.017
LH	0.042	0.896	0.063	0.000
LL	0.000	0.009	0.978	0.013
HL	0.021	0.000	0.043	0.936
Ergodic distribution	0.164	0.094	0.578	0.164
1990–2015				
HH	0.969	0.020	0.002	0.010
LH	0.075	0.884	0.035	0.006
LL	0.001	0.009	0.975	0.015
HL	0.046	0.000	0.067	0.887
Ergodic distribution	0.396	0.098	0.411	0.094

the low-high or high-low outlier. It means the concentration of counties with similar economic level and the effect of spatial clustering on regional income mobility.

When comparing the results before and after 2008 or the most recent global economic recession, some interesting findings could be derived. On the one hand, from 2008 to 2015, the transition possibility from other types to a low-low cluster is higher than other transitions, which explains the radical change in LISA maps in Figure 7.6. The Wenzhou city district has even lost its advantageous status as a growth pole in southern Zhejiang. More interior counties in northern Zhejiang moved toward rich clusters because they are more favored in economic development due to their advantageous location in proximity to Hangzhou and Ningbo and new infrastructure development. As a result, the north–south divide in Zhejiang has become evident again.

7.6 Local analysis of spatially varying mechanisms

Geographically weighted regression (GWR) is used in comparison with the ordinary least squared (OLS) method to understand the mechanisms and their spatial heterogeneity. Built on Casetti (1972), GWR tackles the spatial non-stationarity by allowing spatially varying coefficient for each data point based on spatially weighted neighboring observations (Brunsdon, Fotheringham, and Charlton 1996; Fotheringham, Brunsdon, and Charlton 2002):

$$y_i = \beta_0\left(u_i, v_i\right) + \sum_k \beta_k\left(u_i, v_i\right)x_{ik} + \epsilon_i$$

where y_i is the dependent variable for the ith observation, x_{ik} is the kth explanatory variable for observations, (u_i, v_i) is the coordinates of the ith point in space and $\beta_k(u_i, v_i)$ is a realization of the continuous function $\beta_k(u, v)$ at point i, and ε_i is a normally distributed disturbance term.

Drawing upon the multi-mechanism framework, the dependent variable is proxied by the GDP per capita in constant price and five independent variables are selected based on the review of transitional processes in Zhejiang and empirics in provincial China:

1   Fixed assets investment per capita (FIX) is selected to represent the overall extent of investment during China's shifting to a market economy. The regional allocation of fixed assessment is viewed as an important instrument for China's government to coordinate regional development and regional policy. It is hypothesized that this variable is positively related to regional development.
2   Ratio of a county's secondary sector output value in the provincial total (AGM) to proxy the agglomeration level. The study by Cheong and Wu (2014) suggests that the secondary industry sector contributes half of the regional inequality in China. Ke (2010) also finds that industrial agglomeration is an

important factor for productivity in China. It is hypothesized that this variable is positively related to regional development.

3 The decentralization process is represented by the local fiscal expenditure per capita (LEX). Since the fiscal decentralization in the 1980s and 1990s, the local governments have been granted with greater power and stimulus to support the local development. It is hypothesized that this variable is positively related to regional development.

4 The marketization process is proxied by the ratio of SOEs in gross output value of industrial enterprises above designated size (SOE). There is a consensus that the SOEs represent economic entities with relatively rigid institutional structure, lagging technological innovation, and aging equipment. It is hypothesized that this variable is negatively related to regional development.

5 The globalization process is represented by the per capita foreign capital actually used (FDI). Previous empirics find that FDI contributes significantly to the economic growth of coastal provinces characterized by the export-oriented economy. It is hypothesized that this variable is positively related to regional development.

The regression result suggests that GWR is a better option than OLS, as suggested by the comparison in adjusted R^2, AICc, and F-test in ANOVA (Table 7.6). The spatial heterogeneity is significant for several variables in most of the years, like the investment, marketization, and globalization variables. But there are also several variables that are spatially stationary, suggesting the use of mixed GWR.

The comparison between mixed GWR and OLS are listed in Table 7.7. Based on the adjusted R^2 and AICc value, the mixed GWR not only outperforms OLS, but also slightly improves the GWR model. The result suggests that the decentralization mechanism, proxied by local fiscal expenditure per capita, is not significant in both years, which echoes the findings in the previous study (Wei and Ye 2009). The impacts of marketization are validated by the significantly negative impact of SOE in 1995. As the government's agent in economy, SOEs have negative influences on regional development due to the bureaucratic institutional structure, backward technology and equipment, and uncompetitive productivity and commodities (Yu and Wei 2003). The SOE variable becomes insignificant for the model in 2015 because the economy in Zhejiang is already dominated by the non-state sector like other coastal provinces. The globalization variable is significant and positively related to regional development in 2015 but is only insignificantly positive in 1995. The reason might be that FDI per capita in the 1990s was low and highly uneven among counties, so it does not necessarily mean that the effect of globalization is not evident in the regional development of Zhejiang.

The fixed-asset investment and industrial agglomeration are also important factors, which indicates that regional development in Zhejiang is investment-driven and industrial agglomeration plays an important role in economic growth. Maps of local coefficient estimates further reveal several interesting findings (Figure 7.7 and Figure 7.8). First, though there is little difference in the investment coefficients in 1995 and 2015 by OLS, the mixed GWR result shows

Table 7.6 Regression results of OLS and GWR, 1990–2015

	1990	1995	2000	2005	2010	2015
FIX	**1.04E+00**	**4.77E-01**	**5.22E-01**	**5.02E-01**	**6.27E-01**	**4.52E-01**
AGM	**1.89E+04**	**4.86E+04**	**6.77E+04**	**9.98E+04**	**2.20E+05**	**1.06E+05**
LEX	8.10E-01	9.20E-01	1.08E+00	9.43E-01	-2.47E-01	-6.09E-01
SOE	-1.59E+02	**-8.93E+02**	-3.90E+03	-1.25E+04	-4.27E+03	-1.52E+04
FDI	**-9.34E+00**	**1.73E+00**	**5.46E+00**	**2.34E+00**	**-1.80E+00**	**6.32E+00**
R^2	0.84/0.87	0.85/0.90	0.82/0.89	0.82/0.90	0.79/0.87	0.70/0.84
AICc	966/955	1,093/1,072	1,171/1,148	1,234/1,205	1,298/1,280	1,362/1,329
F of ANOVA (GWR vs. OLS)	**2.92**	**3.73**	**3.82**	**4.35**	**3.30**	**4.77**

Table 7.7 Comparison of the results from OLS and mixed GWR

1995

	OLS	*mixed GWR*		
		mean coef.	*min coef.*	*max. coef.*
FIX	4.77E-01	4.13E-01	−2.31E-01	1.53E+00
AGM	4.86E+04	4.46E+04	1.98E+04	6.18E+04
LEX	9.20E-01	2.13E+00	–	–
SOE	−8.93E+02	−1.14E+03	−2.95E+03	2.36E+02
FDI	1.73E+00	3.32E+00	−7.86E+00	1.51E+01
R^2	0.85	0.91		
AICc	1,093	1,070		

2015

	OLS	*mixed GWR*		
		mean coef.	*min coef.*	*max. coef.*
FIX	4.52E−01	4.89E−01	−8.12E−02	9.53E−01
AGM	1.06E+05	1.50E+05	6.25E+04	3.15E+05
LEX	−6.09E−01	−1.72E−02	−1.04E+00	1.88E+00
SOE	−1.52E+04	−1.26E+04	−4.18E+04	6.47E+04
FDI	6.32E+00	2.26E+00	–	–
R^2	0.70	0.85		
AICc	1,362	1,325		

evident spatial heterogeneity with regard to the local impacts (Figure 7.9). In 1995, the investment factor mainly takes effects in southern Zhejiang, especially the coastal Wenzhou–Taizhou region, by providing reliable infrastructure for the booming private enterprises. But in 2015, a coastal–interior gradient is observed. The investment instrument could maximize its impacts in the interior of Zhejiang because of historical debt in construction and the government's push for inequality alleviation, while for coastal Zhejiang it only has marginal effects.

Second, the influence of industrial agglomeration has been strengthened in recent years and its spatial pattern has been reversed (Figure 7.10). The impact of industrial agglomeration is profound in northern and coastal Zhejiang in 1995. But in 2015, the interior, southern Zhejiang could benefit the most from developing agglomeration economies, highlighting the importance of economic restructuring in promoting poor regions. Last, the spatial pattern of variable estimates also helps to understand the mechanisms under the changing regional division in Zhejiang. In the mid-1990s, the emerging coastal–inland divide is mainly driven by the concentration of fixed-asset investment in the coastal Wenzhou–Taizhou region and high industrial output in the coastal Hangzhou–Ningbo region. As a commonly used governmental instrument, fixed-asset investment was used by the locally embedded institutions in Wenzhou to

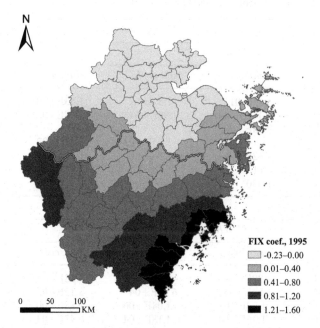

Figure 7.9a GWR results for fixed-asset investment per capita in 1995.

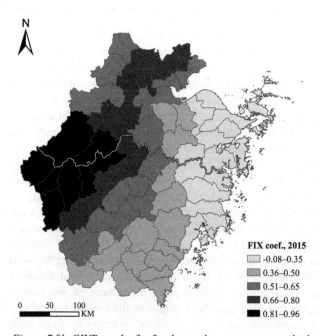

Figure 7.9b GWR results for fixed-asset investment per capita in 2015.

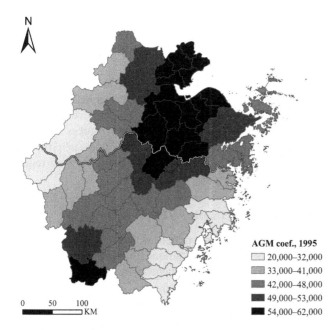

AGM coef., 1995

- 20,000–32,000
- 33,000–41,000
- 42,000–48,000
- 49,000–53,000
- 54,000–62,000

Figure 7.10a GWR results for industrial agglomeration in 1995.

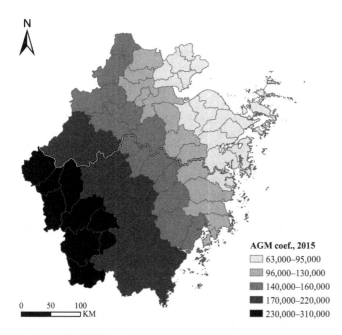

AGM coef., 2015

- 63,000–95,000
- 96,000–130,000
- 140,000–160,000
- 170,000–220,000
- 230,000–310,000

Figure 7.10b GWR results for industrial agglomeration in 2015.

improve the business environment and paved the way for flourishing private enterprises. Together with the traditional industrial agglomerations in Hangzhou and Ningbo, coastal Zhejiang has become more developed than interior Zhejiang, which leads to the transition from the north–south divide to the coastal–interior divide.

Since the 2000s, the provincial government has placed more resources to develop a more balanced economy and alleviate poverty and regional inequality (Ye, Li, and Cheng 2014). The fixed-asset investment is used to solve the uneven regional development and the transfer of industries and fiscal resources to interior Zhejiang is encouraged. Together with the shock of the global financial crisis and the persistent slowdown of the economic engine, the Wenzhou–Taizhou region has lagged behind again and a new north–south divide has emerged.

7.7 Analyzing the Wenzhou model with ESTDA

Following the bottom–up strategy, in conjunction with a set of exploratory spatial and temporal data analysis (ESTDA) technique, this section carries out a more detailed investigation of regional development in the Wenzhou–Taizhou region, with a comparison to Hangzhou and Ningbo. The location quotient method is used to evaluate the trend of regional status in terms of economic development and socioeconomic factors:

$$LQ = \frac{X_i / \sum X_i}{Y_i / \sum Y_i}$$

Where X_i and $\sum X_i$ are the regional and total value of the indicator, like GDP, export, fixed-asset investment, local fiscal expenditure, and industrial output, and Y_i and $\sum Y_i$ are the regional and total population base. Therefore, LQ over unity means that a region's status is above the average level in Zhejiang, while LQ less than unity indicates the opposite.

As shown in Figure 7.11, the gap between two clusters, the traditional one of Hangzhou and Ningbo and the emerging one of Wenzhou and Taizhou, has been narrowing from 1990 to the early 2000s. It is in line with the literature and previous discussion that the north–south divide of the economic landscape has become fragmented and more complex with a sign of coastal–inland divide (Wei and Ye 2004). However, the status of Wenzhou has remained the same since the early 2000s, as has the Taizhou municipality. Meanwhile, Hangzhou and Ningbo were converging to the average, which indicates the gap among prefectures within the coastal region would have narrowed due to the catching-up of other prefectures. As shown in Figure 7.12, the success of the Wenzhou model in the 1990s is closely related to the exponentially increasing exports. With the place-based relationship (*guanxi*) network, Wenzhou has benefited from the globalization process by channeling foreign investment, market information, new equipment, and global culture back to Wenzhou (Wei and Ye 2004; Wei 2009).

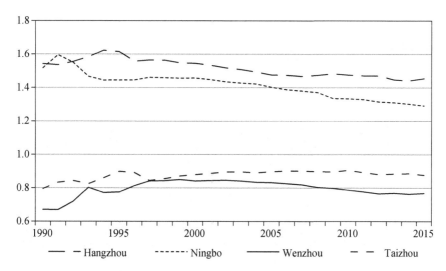

Figure 7.11 Location quotients of GDP per capita in selected prefectures.

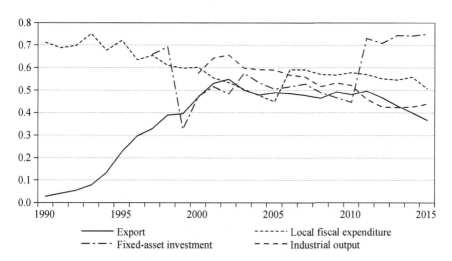

Figure 7.12 LQs of various socioeconomic indicators in Wenzhou municipality.

However, the advantageous status of Wenzhou's export has faded since the early 2000s. Ningbo and Taizhou, with favored location and high quality of infrastructure like deep-water ports, have become the major harbors in Zhejiang. Wenzhou is also known for spearheading the marketization in China. The "thick," locally embedded pro-business government in Wenzhou has taken one step ahead towards privatization and implemented development policies to improve the business environment for the non-state sector. The share of SOEs in industrial output has declined to 21.3% in Wenzhou while the provincial level is 42.7% in 1990 (ZSB 1991). But with the deepening privatization in Zhejiang, Wenzhou has gradually lost its leading role in ownership restructuring. The share of SOEs in Wenzhou is similar to the level of Zhejiang Province, of which it is 8.21% and 8.15% for Wenzhou and Zhejiang in 2000, and 4.62% and 4.75% in 2015, respectively (ZSB 2001, 2016). The weakening capacity of the local government is also reflected by Wenzhou's declining status in terms of local fiscal expenditure and fixed-asset investment (Figure 7.12).

The space–time path method, as mentioned in Chapter 3, is employed to explore the detailed spatiotemporal dynamics of individual counties. In Figure 7.13, economic development trajectories of nine counties in the Wenzhou–Taizhou region are illustrated. The points are labeled from dark tone in the early years to light tone in more recent years. Most of the trajectories could be classified as Type I pattern (see the discussion on the space–time path technique in Chapter 4 for details), meaning that both the local and the adjacent county's economies are developing at the same time. The spatial effects of the city districts of Wenzhou and Taizhou are evident, as the nearby counties experienced more rapid economic growth in the 1980s and 1990s. Several counties, like Wenling and Yuhuan in Taizhou, and Ruian and Yueqing in Wenzhou, have once moved beyond the provincial average in the period. As the prototype of the Wenzhou model, Ruian and Yueqing are also known for their specialized light industries and extensive and external network linkages with global markets (Wei and Ye 2009). At its peak, the local economic development level of Ruian and Yueqing was as high as 1.2 and 1.3 times of the provincial average in 1997. However, the counties influenced by the Wenzhou model of development and the spillovers of Wenzhou city district have encountered persistent recession in the 2000s and 2010s. All the selected counties in Wenzhou and Yuhuan in Taizhou have entered the Type II pattern of trajectory, with both the local and adjacent counties declining in their relatively advanced position among counties in Zhejiang.

To get a more accurate measure of the development trajectory, the Euclidean distance, ΔRS^t_i, in the space–time path space is calculated (Table 7.8). Comparing with the beginning of reform in 1978, most counties achieved Type I pattern of development in 2015 except the city district of Wenzhou. Among the counties, Yueqing has experienced a profound improvement in terms of the position in economic space among counties in Wenzhou, followed by Yongjia and Ruian. Yuhuan and Wenling are the two highest ones in Taizhou, followed by the city district. For the first sub-period, seven out of nine counties are in Type I pattern and show spontaneous development of the local and adjacent counties, which underlies the rise of the coastal Wenzhou–Taizhou region. But in the second sub-period, the trend has been slowed as the distance change in economic space becomes smaller than the previous sub-period. Type II and Type IV pattern of development appear, indicating the diminishing sustainability of economic development for the Wenzhou–Taizhou cluster. The backward spinning trend is observed for most trajectories

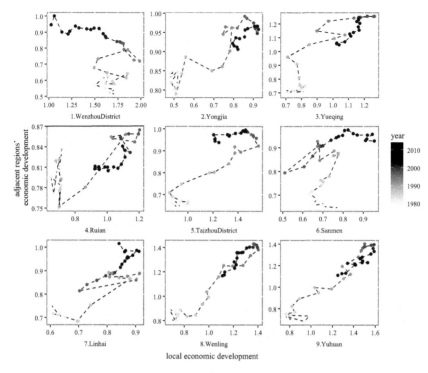

Figure 7.13 Space-time paths of economic development of nine interested counties.

Table 7.8 The Euclidean distance change ΔRS_i in the economic space

County	1978–2015		1978–1991		1992–2015	
	ΔRS_i	Pattern	ΔRS_i	Pattern	ΔRS_i	Pattern
Wenzhou						
city district	0.82	III	0.28	III	0.55	III
Ruian	0.21	I	0.08	I	0.07	I
Yueqing	0.48	I	0.38	I	0.05	IV
Yongjia	0.33	I	0.25	II	0.04	I
Taizhou						
city district	0.45	I	0.48	I	0.17	III
Wenling	0.55	I	0.52	III	0.08	I
Linhai	0.35	I	0.24	I	0.13	I
Yuhuan	0.60	I	0.62	I	0.12	II
Sanmen	0.33	I	0.23	I	0.20	II

in Figure 7.11 after the late-1990s, which implies that the southern cluster in Zhejiang has been lagging behind the northern region.

In contrast to the neighboring counties, the city district of Wenzhou shows Type III pattern mode for the whole period. The relative income level has dropped from two times in the early 1990s to merely the same as the provincial average in the 2010s. There are two reasons for the declining local status of Wenzhou city district. First, the spatial scaling-up of enterprises outside Wenzhou has hampered the regional competitiveness. As Wei *et al.* (2007) pointed out, the relocation of Wenzhou enterprises has intensified since the late 1990s as a maneuver to avoid regional lock-ins. The relocation of mature and big-sized enterprises leads to poorer productivity and declining regional development. Wenzhou firms have also diversified their investment in services, especially real estate, while the manufacturing sector lacks capital and talents to upgrade. Second, the rapid growth of inflow migrants has a "diluting" effect. In 2010, the de facto to *hukou* population ratio in Wenzhou city district was as high as 2.09, ranking the first among counties in Zhejiang. The majority of the migrants in Wenzhou are manufacturing workers with low education levels, long working hours, and low-income wages, which supports the local development but contributes less in industrial upgrading and improving the average income level. From 2000 to 2015, the GDP growth rate in Wenzhou city district was 10.8%, which is almost the same as the provincial average of 11% (Lin and Gaubatz 2015).

The Wenzhou model is featured as spatial agglomerations of small-scale private enterprises in labor-intensive and low-tech light industries. Industrialization centered on manufacturing and the massive migration of cheap labor from the rural areas have underlaid the rapid economic growth and altered the spatial configuration of regional development in Wenzhou (Lin and Gaubatz 2015). Meanwhile, with the overcapacity of the manufacturing sector and the slow process of industrial upgrading, the marginal benefits from the Wenzhou model have declined constantly. Measured by industrial output per capita, the competitiveness of the Wenzhou model has been diminishing in recent years (Figure 7.9). The productivity of workers is not improved, which urgently calls for upgrades in economic structure and technology profile (Wei, Li, and Wang 2007).

7.8 Conclusion

Drawing upon a multi-scale and multi-mechanism framework, this chapter investigates the multi-scalar patterns and spatial-temporal dynamics of regional development in provincial China through a case study of Zhejiang Province. Following the increasing inequality since the reform and opening-up and after the radical marketization reform, the inequality among regions, prefectures, and counties in Zhejiang has declined since the early 2000s. The long-run property detected by the Markov-chain method further confirms the convergence of regional development in Zhejiang.

In contrast to the narrowing gap among counties, spatial analysis indicates an intensifying spatial concentration of economies and highlights the spatial effects in regional development. The level of spatial agglomeration has increased rapidly even with the declining inequality since the 2000s. Clusters of rich counties have gradually expanded in northern Zhejiang in the Hangzhou–Ningbo region, while southern interior Zhejiang has lagged behind as the clusters of poor counties. The distributional dynamics detected by the spatial Markov-chain method reveals that spillover effects from the developed region are evident in promoting the neighboring counties.

By utilizing spatiotemporal analysis methods, this chapter helps to reach a more nuanced understanding of regional dynamics in provincial China. With the rise of the Wenzhou model of development centered on small-scale, private enterprises, the traditional north–south divide in the regional development of Zhejiang is replaced with the emerging coastal–interior divide (Wei and Ye 2004, 2009). But since the global financial crisis and slowdown of China's economic growth after 2008, the southern part of coastal Zhejiang, mainly in Wenzhou and Taizhou prefectures, has fallen behind in economic growth and a new north–south divide has emerged, which is rooted in the context of diminishing foreign demand and investment, industrial restructuring and upgrading in China, regional lock-ins in the relational, interregional, and structural terms of the Wenzhou model (Wei, Li, and Wang 2007).

The application of mixed GWR enables us to incorporate spatial heterogeneity into the driving forces of regional development. Investment, agglomeration economies, decentralization, and globalization are found to be the important variables in understanding regional inequality. The spatial non-stationarity of fixed-asset investment and industrial agglomeration implies that the emerging coastal–interior divide in the 1990s is closely related to heavy investment in the Wenzhou–Taizhou region to pave the way for a better business environment and more externality for booming private enterprises, of which the impacts are limited and diminishing in the 2010s.

The analysis of bottom–up forces in Wenzhou and its comparison with Hangzhou, Ningbo, and Taizhou reveals more details about the evolution of regional inequality and the mechanisms. The spatiotemporal trajectory in economic space implies that Wenzhou and counties in Wenzhou have experienced rapid and profound economic growth in the 1990s, but most of them have recessed from early 2000. The factors that support the Wenzhou model of development, e.g., foreign trade and investment, the pro-business and developmental capability of local institutions, ownership and economic structure advantages, and labor-intensive and low-tech light industries, have faded away or faced challenges under the new context, which questions the sustainability of the Wenzhou model.

References

Brehm, S. 2013. Fiscal incentives, public spending, and productivity: County-level evidence from a Chinese province. *World Development* 46: 92–103.

Brunsdon, C., A. S. Fotheringham, and M. E. Charlton. 1996. Geographically weighted regression: A method for exploring spatial nonstationarity. *Geographical Analysis* 28 (4): 281–298.

Casetti, E. 1972. Generating models by the expansion method: Applications to geographical research. *Geographical Analysis* 4 (1): 81–91.

Chan, K. W. 2010. A China paradox: Migrant labor shortage amidst rural labor supply abundance. *Eurasian Geography and Economics* 51 (4): 513–530.

Chan, K. W., and M. Wang. 2008. Remapping China's regional inequalities, 1990–2006: A new assessment of de facto and de jure population data. *Eurasian Geography and Economics* 49 (1): 21–55.

Cheong, T. S., and Y. Wu. 2014. The impacts of structural transformation and industrial upgrading on regional inequality in China. *China Economic Review* 31 (Supplement C): 339–350.

Forster, K. 1998. *Zhejiang in reform.* Sydney: Wild Peony Pty Limited.

Fotheringham, A., C. Brunsdon, and M. Charlton. 2002. *Geographically weighted regression: The analysis of spatially varying relationships.* London: John Wiley & Sons.

Gallo, J., and C. Ertur. 2003. Exploratory spatial data analysis of the distribution of regional per capita GDP in Europe, 1980–1995. *Papers in Regional Science* 82 (2): 175–201.

Getis, A., and J. K. Ord. 1992. The analysis of spatial association by use of distance statistics. *Geographical Analysis* 24 (3).

He, S., M. M. Bayrak, and H. Lin. 2017. A comparative analysis of multi-scalar regional inequality in China. *Geoforum* 78: 1–11.

Ke, S. 2010. Agglomeration, productivity, and spatial spillovers across Chinese cities. *The Annals of Regional Science* 45 (1): 157–179.

Le Gallo, J. 2004. Space–time analysis of GDP disparities among European regions: A Markov chains approach. *International Regional Science Review* 27 (2): 138–163.

Li, C., and J. Gibson. 2013. Rising regional inequality in China: Fact or artifact? *World Development* 47: 16–29.

Liao, F. H. F., and Y. D. Wei. 2012. Dynamics, space, and regional inequality in provincial China: A case study of Guangdong Province. *Applied Geography* 35 (1): 71–83.

Lin, S. N., and P. Gaubatz. 2015. New Wenzhou: Migration, metropolitan spatial development and modernity in a third-tier Chinese model city. *Habitat International* 50: 214–225.

Ma, L. J., and Y. Wei. 1997. Determinants of state investment in China, 1953–1990. *Tijdschrift voor economische en sociale geografie* 88 (3): 211–225.

Ma, Y. 2012. A review of the Shan-Hai cooperation project at the ten-year anniversary. *Zhejiang Today* (6): 18–21.

National Bureau of Statistics of China (NBSC). 2016. *China statistical yearbook.* Beijing: China Statistics Press.

Quah, D. 1993. Galton's fallacy and tests of the convergence hypothesis. *Scandinavian Journal of Economics*: 427–443.

Rey, S. 2001. Spatial dependence in the evolution of regional income distributions. In *Spatial econometrics and spatial statistics*, 194–213. Basingstoke: Palgrave.

Sakamoto, H., and N. Islam. 2008. Convergence across Chinese provinces: An analysis using Markov transition matrix. *China Economic Review* 19 (1): 66–79.

Wang, L. 2013. Changing policies that aim to assist development in underdeveloped regions in Zhejiang. *Development* (in Chinese) (277): 109–111.

Wei, Y. H. D. 2009. China's shoe manufacturing and the Wenzhou model: Perspectives on the world's leading producer and exporter of footwear. *Eurasian Geography and Economics* 50 (6): 720–739.

Wei, Y. H. D. 2011. Beyond the GPN: New regionalism divide in China: Restructuring the clothing industry, remaking the Wenzhou model. *Geografiska Annaler: Series B, Human Geography* 93 (3): 237–251.

Wei, Y. H. D. 2012. Restructuring for growth in urban China: Transitional institutions, urban development, and spatial transformation. *Habitat International* 36 (3): 396–405.

Wei, Y. H. D., W. Li, and C. Wang. 2007. Restructuring industrial districts, scaling up regional development: A study of the Wenzhou model, China. *Economic Geography* 83 (4): 421–444.

Wei, Y. H. D., and X. Y. Ye. 2004. Regional inequality in China: A case study of Zhejiang Province. *Tijdschrift Voor Economische En Sociale Geografie* 95 (1): 44–60.

Wei, Y. H. D., and X. Y. Ye. 2009. Beyond convergence: Space, scale, and regional inequality in China. *Tijdschrift Voor Economische En Sociale Geografie* 100 (1): 59–80.

Wei, Y. H. D., D. Yu, and X. Chen. 2011. Scale, agglomeration, and regional inequality in provincial China. *Tijdschrift Voor Economische En Sociale Geografie* 102 (4): 406–425.

Ye, X., and M. Leipnik. 2013. Beyond small business and private enterprises in China: Global and spatial perspectives. *Entrepreneurship and Economic Growth in China*: 289–316.

Ye, X., J. Li, and Y. Cheng. 2014. Multi-scale and multi-mechanism analysis of the spatial pattern and temporal change of regional economic development disparities in Zhejiang Province. *Progress in Geography* (in Chinese) 33 (9): 1177–1186.

Ye, X., and Y. D. Wei. 2005. Geospatial analysis of regional development in China: The case of Zhejiang Province and the Wenzhou model. *Eurasian Geography and Economics* 46 (6): 445–464.

Yu, D. L., and Y. H. D. Wei. 2003. Analyzing regional inequality in post-Mao China in a GIS environment. *Eurasian Geography and Economics* 44 (7): 514–534.

Yue, W., Y. Zhang, X. Ye, Y. Cheng, and M. R. Leipnik. 2014. Dynamics of multi-scale intra-provincial regional inequality in Zhejiang, China. *Sustainability* 6 (9): 5763–5784.

Zhejiang Statistical Bureau (ZSB). 1991. *Zhejiang statistical yearbook*. Beijing: China Statistics Press.

Zhejiang Statistical Bureau (ZSB). 2001. *Zhejiang statistical yearbook*. Beijing: China Statistics Press.

Zhejiang Statistical Bureau (ZSB). 2010. *Zhejiang compendium of statistics 1949–2008*. Beijing: China Statistics Press.

Zhejiang Statistical Bureau (ZSB). 2016. *Zhejiang statistical yearbook*. Beijing: China Statistics Press.

Zhu, L. 2006. Review and prospect on spatial development structure of Zhejiang Province. *Economic Geography* (in Chinese) 26 (5): 767–770.

8　Conclusion

China's rapid economic growth since the reform has been accompanied by a substantial uneven regional distribution of income, which requires a careful assessment. In this book, built upon a multi-scale and multi-mechanism framework and a geographical perspective, we have comprehensively examined patterns and mechanisms of regional development and inequality in China with an emphasis on the effects of economic transition. This book has studied the multi-scalar patterns of regional inequality in China, especially during the reform era. By presenting two in-depth case studies of Guangdong and Zhejiang Provinces, we have also shown the importance of local contexts and the complexity of China's uneven regional development. In this chapter, we summarize the major findings of this research and discuss their theoretical and policy implications, while pointing out directions for future studies.

8.1　Major findings

Our studies have provided clear evidence that the degree of spatial inequality is sensitive to geographical scales, and spatiality matters in the study of regional inequality. During the reform period from the 1980s to the 2010s, although interprovincial inequality fluctuated, interregional inequality has risen despite a noticeable drop since 2005. The recent slowdown of China's economic growth, known as the "New Normal," has had profound impacts on regional economic growth in the coastal regions, and possibly results in the reduction in regional disparities. We also find that between-region and intra-prefecture-level inequalities drop more quickly as compared with the contributions made by between-prefecture and intra-prefecture inequalities. Hence, some signals of "new" convergence and the effect of urbanization on spatial inequality at the intra-urban scale should warrant attention (Kanbur, Wang, and Zhang 2017; Li, Wei, and Wu 2019). Locations of individual provinces and geographical contexts also matter. Prefectures and provinces within north-eastern and eastern regions demonstrate economic convergence trajectories, while prefectures and provinces within western and central China have experienced divergence.

When considering the spatial effects, which constitute another important spatial aspect of regional inequality, the spillover effects at the provincial level vary among different regions. In the Yangtze River Delta, the spillover from Shanghai on its neighboring provinces including Jiangsu and Zhejiang are more evident as compared with the case of the Beijing–Tianjin–Hebei region, which is characterized by weak spillover or even backwash effects. The cases of Guangdong and Zhejiang Provinces reveal that there has been a "poverty trap" in the remote areas such as northern Guangdong and south-western Zhejiang. The persistence of the core–periphery divide in Guangdong is greatly driven by the self-reinforcing agglomeration centered on the PRD. Patterns of uneven regional development in Zhejiang, however, are greatly attributed to the emergence of new clusters.

Regarding the mechanisms of regional development and inequality, the change of regional inequality in China corresponds to the triple process of transition: globalization, decentralization, and marketization. The transformation of the economic system during the reform period has triggered the articulation of states, foreign investors, and local institutions and geographies in China's regional development. Our case studies or bottom–up analyses have confirmed that the core–periphery disparity in Guangdong or the coastal–inland divide in Zhejiang is highly related to the triple processes of economic transition. For the case of Guangdong, while the functioning of these mechanisms has been strengthened in the periphery area, globalization forces are increasingly domesticated in the core region of the PRD and emerging new economic spaces have widened the gap between the core and the rest of the province. In contrast, the results of GWR modeling in Zhejiang indicates that fixed-asset investments and industrialization are factors that have been more influential in shaping uneven regional economic development in the process of economic transition. On par with the recent scaling-up of the Wenzhou model, the new coastal–inland divide has replaced the traditional north–south divide in Zhejiang.

8.2 Theoretical and policy implications

Our research has both theoretical and policy implications. From a theoretical perspective, we have affirmed the weakness of new convergence theory, which is argued to be devoid of time and space (Wei 2000; Wei and Ye 2004, 2009). Indeed, convergence or divergence trends are greatly confined to the initial levels and cycles of economic development (Petrakos, Rodríguez-Pose, and Rovolis 2005; Gorzelak 2019). In China, the evolution of regional inequality in different sub-periods does not follow either convergence or divergence schools of thoughts. Our analyses demonstrate more complicated patterns of regional inequality, which corroborates a more meso-scale perspective and grounded approach towards uneven regional development.

Moreover, we carefully analyze the effect of self-reinforcing spatial agglomeration and the dynamics of the core–periphery model. Although our results substantiate the debate over the new economic geography (NEG) model (Krugman 2011; Gardiner *et al.* 2013), the geographies of regional polarization have challenged the equilibrium or static viewpoint towards regional convergence or divergence. Specifically, spatial agglomeration is conditioned upon the geographical context and local scales (Storper 2018). With the aid of more recently developed ESTDA techniques, our findings confirm that when explaining the geographical concentration of economic activities and regional inequality, the major theoretical thoughts such as neoclassical, new trade, and new economic geography models, could be powerful but may not provide the most comprehensive account.

We argue that the integration of western theories and the ground-specific context in China is a better approach to analyzing China's regional development and disparities. Our results suggest that spatial inequality of economic development in China is mediated by varying geographical contexts, and the triple process of marketization, globalization, and decentralization. For example, in the case of Guangdong, the globalization force has strengthened the core–periphery divide between the PRD and the periphery, although, in some developed countries, globalization and investments from outside have reduced regional inequalities (Ezcurra and Rodríguez-Pose 2013).

Our findings also have policy implications for spatial development and planning in China. First, programs at the national level or the top–down approach alone might not be effective in reducing regional inequalities. We have found that national strategies or inequality-reduction policies that target the central and western provinces might contribute to increased intercity or inter-county inequalities. Policies from below or bottom–up strategies are also needed to more effectively reduce emerging "poverty traps" in the western and central regions as well as in specific poor regions within provinces (Li, Sato, and Sicular 2013).

Second, as China's economic transition continues and reform deepens, the triple process of globalization, decentralization, and marketization will certainly leave its footprints. For instance, we have identified that in the case of Guangdong, the development of "new" and "knowledge-based" economies in the PRD may reinforce the already evident core–periphery divide. How lagging regions could lure new investments with local resources is a challenging issue for policymakers, especially in the context of the knowledge economy (Cooke and Piccaluga 2009). In this regard, a more integrated development model, which relies on both the international market and booming domestic market, may better sustain economic growth and alleviate the regional uneven distribution of income.

Last, as China's economy becomes more reliant on new growth strategies (e.g., high-end service and high-tech sectors), new forms of regional inequality have been generated as indicated in our empirical analysis. Similarly, despite the positive impact of rural industrialization or grassroot-level enterprises on regional development, new economic spaces have emerged in provincial China, as evidenced in Zhejiang and Guangdong Provinces (Lu and Wei 2007; Wei, Lin, and Zhang 2019). Places with the advantage in technology and innovation are moving further ahead in development, intensifying the digital divide, which is even more difficult to overcome (Warf 2020). Policymakers have to think more proactively about the distributional impacts of new economic development strategies in favor of more developed regions (Chen and Groenewold 2011, 2015).

For instance, technological change does provide some opportunities for less developed regions, which the government should certainly pay special attention to (Liefner and Wei 2013).

8.3　Future studies

Restless transformations in the economic landscapes of China have provided the best laboratory for research on regional inequality and future scholarly endeavors. First, although recent down-scale analyses at the county level have been informative, as shown in our work and others (He, Bayrak, and Lin 2017), the interrelationship between spatial inequalities at multiple scales has by no means been thoroughly explored. In the era of big data, spatial inequality may be addressed using alternative data sources that are interpolated across different geographical scales (Lu *et al.* 2015; Zhou *et al.* 2015). Firm-level survey data becomes an alternative dataset as such data could be readily decomposed into different scales (e.g., regional, urban–rural, coastal–inland, and intra-provincial versus interprovincial). Rizov and Zhang (2014) studied the micro-level firm statistics to describe the sources of regional inequality in China and found clear evidence of regional convergence in terms of productivity level (Lemoine, Poncet, and Ünal 2015). However, most of the firm-level data is focused on manufacturing, and results can hardly be compared with studies using output data (Ge 2009; Rizov and Zhang 2014; He, Zhou, and Zhu 2017).

As China has experienced unprecedented urbanization, increasing attention has been paid to urban inequalities. The emergence of big data has also provided a new horizon for researchers to explore the spatiality of inequality even at neighborhood scales (Long, Shen, and Jin 2016). Scholars debate over inequalities in urban China, including emerging problems similar to those found in the United States, such as residential segregation, spatial mismatch, and the digital divide (Wang and Chai 2009; Lin and Gaubatz 2015; Wang, Liao, *et al.* 2016). Studies have found intensifying housing inequality in China, reflecting the structural forces that shape neighborhood-level inequalities, such as the financialization of the housing market and the gentrification of less developed neighborhoods (Wang 2012; Li, Wei, and Wu 2019). Spatial agglomeration of resources in cities has also led to the rising gap between urban and rural areas and resulted in a deterioration in some rural counties and small towns, with notions of shrinking cities and ghost towns (Fu and Ren 2010). Therefore, the book also calls for more studies dealing with the urban–rural divide and urban inequalities in China.

Scaling down to the individual level or interpersonal inequality (e.g., wage inequality) in China can also improve the work on regional inequality (e.g., economic output disparities) since both scales of inequality remain largely disconnected. Social scientists, especially sociologists, have produced a valuable body of literature on individual or interpersonal-level inequality in China using census or survey data (Brajer, Mead, and Xiao 2010; Xie and Zhou 2014). However, the spatial dimension of this level of inequality remains largely understudied, although the research on this topic has been found critical in recent studies in more developed economies (Moser and Schnetzer 2017; Rey 2018).

Second, although GDP per capita serves as the most commonly used indicator in the literature, recent studies have broadened our understanding of regional economic inequality by using alterative indicators and datasets. While this book focuses on regional income or economic inequality, the scope of regional inequality studies in China has been broadened to spatial inequality in social and public services, and regional disparities in other dimensions such as innovation (Li and Wei 2014; Wang, Cheng, *et al.* 2016; Wang, Liao, *et al.* 2016). Under the reform, the spatial distribution of public services has experienced dramatic changes. Public services developed hand-in-hand with economic growth, whereas the distribution of these services in China is highly uneven. Health care services, for instance, have been agglomerated in central cities, while rural areas and inland provinces have lagged further behind during the reform era. Financial exclusion has also been noted, and poor farmers are still spatially excluded from important financial services such as bank loans (Yeung, He, and Zhang 2017). Zhou *et al.* (2015) used satellite nighttime light images and population census data to analyze the degree of intraregional inequality. Other dimensions of social inequality such as the digital divide and inequality in happiness also create new opportunities for research (Lam and Liu 2014; Wang, Liao, *et al.* 2016), which echoes the increased interests in the interrelationship between interpersonal and spatial inequalities.

Third, regional inequality has also been shaped by the mobility of people and places, and the connections between different places over space and time. Recent research has drawn our attention to the problem of intergenerational mobility in developed countries (Rothwell and Massey 2015; Ewing *et al.* 2016), and our study has found the strong agglomeration effect in regional development and the lock-in of least developed places. The application of newly developed spatial or social network analysis techniques could help advance our understanding of the role of spatial networks in regional economic inequality in China. While this line of inquiry has resulted in recent publications addressing spatial inequality in developed countries, more studies focusing on internal flows and connections within China are intriguing (Wei 2017), especially those done using spatial linkages, input–output, and trade flow data (Liu, Dai, and Derudder 2017).

Lastly, China's development is, to some extent, at the expense of environmental pollution and degradation. Focusing on issues related to environmental inequalities, one of the most heated debates is the spatial convergence of carbon dioxide (CO_2) emissions (Huang and Meng 2013; Wu and Chen 2016), and air pollution (Cao *et al.* 2019). Future studies could further our understanding of the spatial inequalities in energy consumption, which could shed light on the broader concern about the relationship between development and environmental sustainability in China (Wang 2013; Sheng, Shi, and Zhang 2014). More broadly, spatial inequality is critical to reaching the UN's Sustainable Development Goals, and a comprehensive study of different dimensions and scales of inequality and their relationship with the natural environment should improve our understanding of sustainable development.

References

Brajer, V., R. W. Mead, and F. Xiao. 2010. Adjusting Chinese income inequality for environmental equity. *Environment and Development Economics* 15: 341–362.

Cao, K., W. Zhang, S. Liu, B. Huang, and W. Huang. 2019. Pareto law-based regional inequality analysis of PM2.5 air pollution and economic development in China. *Journal of Environmental Management* 252: 109635.

Chen, A. P., and N. Groenewold. 2011. Regional equality and national development in China: Is there a trade-off? *Growth and Change* 42 (4): 628–669.

Chen, A., and N. Groenewold. 2015. Emission reduction policy: A regional economic analysis for China. *Economic Modelling* 51: 136–152.

Cooke, P., and A. Piccaluga. 2009. *Regional development in the knowledge economy.* London: Routledge.

Ewing, R., S. Hamidi, J. B. Grace, and Y. D. Wei. 2016. Does urban sprawl hold down upward mobility? *Landscape and Urban Planning*, 148: 80–88.

Ezcurra, R., and A. Rodríguez-Pose. 2013. Does economic globalization affect regional inequality? A cross-country analysis. *World Development* 52: 92–103.

Fu, Q., and Q. Ren. 2010. Educational inequality under China's rural–urban divide: The *hukou* system and return to education. *Environment and Planning A: Economy and Space* 42 (3): 592–610.

Gardiner, B., R. Martin, P. Sunley, and P. Tyler. 2013. Spatially unbalanced growth in the British economy. *Journal of Economic Geography* 13 (6): 889–928.

Ge, Y. 2009. Globalization and industry agglomeration in China. *World Development* 37 (3): 550–559.

Gorzelak, G. ed. 2019. *Regional development in an age of structural economic change.* London: Routledge.

He, C., Y. Zhou, and S. Zhu. 2017. Firm dynamics, institutional context, and regional inequality of productivity in China. *Geographical Review* 107 (2): 296–316.

He, S., M. M. Bayrak, and H. Lin. 2017. A comparative analysis of multi-scalar regional inequality in China. *Geoforum* 78: 1–11.

Huang, B., and L. Meng. 2013. Convergence of per capita carbon dioxide emissions in urban China: A spatio-temporal perspective. *Applied Geography* 40: 21–29.

Kanbur, R., Y. Wang, and X. Zhang. 2017. *The great Chinese inequality turnaround.* Washington, DC: International Food Policy Research Institute.

Krugman, P. 2011. The new economic geography, now middle-aged. *Regional Studies* 45 (1): 1–7.

Lam, K.-C. J., and P.-W. Liu. 2014. Socio-economic inequalities in happiness in China and U.S. *Social Indicators Research* 116 (2): 509–533.

Lemoine, F., S. Poncet, and D. Ünal. 2015. Spatial rebalancing and industrial convergence in China. *China Economic Review* 34: 39–63.

Li, H., Y. D. Wei, and Y. Wu. 2019. Analyzing the private rental housing market in Shanghai with open data. *Land Use Policy* 85: 271–284.

Li, S., H. Sato, and T. Sicular. 2013. *Rising inequality in China: Challenges to a harmonious society.* Cambridge: Cambridge University Press.

Li, Y. R., and Y. D. Wei. 2014. Multidimensional inequalities in health care distribution in provincial China: A case study of Henan Province. *Tijdschrift voor economische en sociale geografie* 105 (1): 91–106.

Liefner, I., and Y. D. Wei. 2013. *Innovation and regional development in China.* London: Routledge.

Lin, S. N., and P. Gaubatz. 2015. New Wenzhou: Migration, metropolitan spatial development and modernity in a third-tier Chinese model city. *Habitat International* 50: 214–225.

Liu, X., L. Dai, and B. Derudder. 2017. Spatial inequality in the southeast Asian intercity transport network. *Geographical Review* 107 (2): 317–335.

Long, Y., Y. Shen, and X. Jin. 2016. Mapping block-level urban areas for all Chinese cities. *Annals of the American Association of Geographers* 106 (1): 96–113.

Lu, L., and Y. D. Wei. 2007. Domesticating globalisation, new economic spaces and regional polarisation in Guangdong Province, China. *Tijdschrift voor economische en sociale geografie* 98 (2): 225–244.

Lu, S., X. Guan, D. Yu, Y. Deng, and L. Zhou. 2015. Multi-scale analysis of regional inequality based on spatial field model: A case study of China from 2000 to 2012. *ISPRS International Journal of Geo-Information* 4 (4): 1982–2003.

Moser, M., and M. Schnetzer. 2017. The income–inequality nexus in a developed country: Small-scale regional evidence from Austria. *Regional Studies* 51 (3): 454–466.

Petrakos, G., A. Rodríguez-Pose, and A. Rovolis. 2005. Growth, integration, and regional disparities in the European Union. *Environment and Planning A* 37 (10): 1837–1855.

Rey, S. J. 2018. Bells in space: The spatial dynamics of US interpersonal and interregional income inequality. *International Regional Science Review* 41 (2): 152–182.

Rizov, M., and X. Zhang. 2014. Regional disparities and productivity in China: Evidence from manufacturing micro data. *Papers in Regional Science* 93 (2): 321–339.

Rothwell, J. T., and D. S. Massey. 2015. Geographic effects on intergenerational income mobility. *Economic Geography* 91 (1): 83–106.

Sheng, Y., X. Shi, and D. Zhang. 2014. Economic growth, regional disparities and energy demand in China. *Energy Policy* 71: 31–39.

Storper, M. 2018. Separate worlds? Explaining the current wave of regional economic polarization. *Journal of Economic Geography* 18 (2): 247–270.

Wang, C. 2013. Differential output growth across regions and carbon dioxide emissions: Evidence from U.S. and China. *Energy* 53: 230–236.

Wang, D., and Y. Chai. 2009. The jobs–housing relationship and commuting in Beijing, China: The legacy of Danwei. *Journal of Transport Geography* 17 (1): 30–38.

Wang, L. 2012. Social exclusion and education inequality: Towards an integrated analytical framework for the urban–rural divide in China. *British Journal of Sociology of Education* 33 (3): 409–430.

Wang, M., F. H. Liao, J. Lin, L. Huang, C. Gu, and Y. D. Wei. 2016. The making of a sustainable wireless city? Mapping public wi-fi access in Shanghai. *Sustainability* 8 (2): 111.

Wang, Z. Y., Y. Q. Cheng, X. Y. Ye, and Y. H. D. Wei. 2016. Analyzing the space–time dynamics of innovation in China: ESDA and spatial panel approaches. *Growth and Change* 47 (1): 111–129.

Warf, B. 2020. *Geographies of the internet.* London: Routledge.

Wei, Y. H. D. 2000. *Regional development in China: States, globalization and inequality.* London: Routledge.

Wei, Y. H. D. 2017. Geography of inequality in Asia. *Geographical Review* 107 (2): 263–275.

Wei, Y. H. D., J. Lin, and L. Zhang. 2019. E-commerce, taobao villages and regional development in China. *Geographical Review* Nov 23: 1–26.

Wei, Y. H. D., and X. Y. Ye. 2004. Regional inequality in China: A case study of Zhejiang Province. *Tijdschrift Voor Economische En Sociale Geografie* 95 (1): 44–60.

Wei, Y. H. D., and X. Ye. 2009. Beyond convergence: Space, scale, and regional inequality in China. *Tijdschrift voor economische en sociale geografie* 100 (1): 59–80.

Wu, M., and B. Chen. 2016. Assignment of provincial officials based on economic performance: Evidence from China. *China Economic Review* 38 (Supplement C): 60–75.

Xie, Y., and X. Zhou. 2014. Income inequality in today's China. *Proceedings of the National Academy of Sciences* 111 (19): 6928–6933.

Yeung, G., C. He, and P. Zhang. 2017. Rural banking in China: Geographically accessible but still financially excluded? *Regional Studies* 51 (2): 297–312.

Zhou, Y., T. Ma, C. Zhou, and T. Xu. 2015. Nighttime light derived assessment of regional inequality of socioeconomic development in China. *Remote Sensing* 7 (2): 1242–1262.

Index

Printed in the United States
By Bookmasters